us to join him on a journey of a lifetime: our lifetime. It is an invitation to turn our actions and our consciousness upside down, not by conforming to the system but subverting it. Noel understands *shalom* as a wholeness that is physical, ecological, political, and spiritual. With deep sympathy for the rich religious traditions of ancient faiths, and those of good faith, Noel's search for *shalom* goes beyond the individual yet is always personal. If you are suspect of institutional religion, but unimpressed by the self-referencing anaemia of western spirituality, you will be uplifted, engaged and challenged by Noel's invitational and generous exploration of practical, political spiritual life. This is a radical spirituality rooted in a practical ethic and a broad spiritual conversation.' **Keith Hebden** – *priest, activist and writer who facilitates workshops and events on political Christianity but is mostly committed to speaking truth to power at the local-community level. He edits* A Pinch of Salt, *an occasional Christian anarchist magazine in the UK*

'Noel Moules writes that his book is for, amongst others, "Those who are simply looking for common ground between faiths and beliefs so we can work together to change the world"; this is something that many humanists do indeed look for. While his worldview and language are not ours, his book offers much of interest to those who are curious about the inner, less dogmatic, less traditional aspects of contemporary Christianity, the "authentic spirituality" and shared values that drive us to "work to put right what is wrong in the world". It is important for atheists to pay attention occasionally to what other people really believe, as opposed to what we assume they believe or what we learnt in school (sometimes a long time ago) about religion, and Noel Moules' book could help in that process.' **Marilyn Mason** – *has been a teacher and previously the Education Officer for the British Humanist Association*

Acclaim for *Fingerprints of Fire ... Footprints of Peace*

'In *Footprints of Fire* Noel Moules offers us an inspirational vision of a spiritual path which is passionately Jesus-centred but at the same time deeply respectful of other faiths and insights. For groups like Liberal Quakers, who tend to love Jesus but mistrust the institutional church, I predict that this book will become an essential handbook for spiritual renewal and transformative action. This is a manifesto of faithful discipleship that knows the power required to overcome war, injustice and environmental destruction with the love of God's *shalom*. Noel gives us hope just when we need it most.' **Stuart Masters** – *senior programme leader at Woodbrooke Quaker Study Centre, UK*

'Many people today find the Christian faith irrelevant, meaningless and lacking any kind of radical edge. Those outside it are not attracted to what they see represented by the church, and those who have been part of the Christian community are often bored and disillusioned. Noel Moules responds to this dissonance with a number of concepts that point us to a more open-ended, inclusive and life-giving faith paradigm. He asks questions about existence, meaning and identity and brings fresh perspectives and interpretation that could re-energise the church. His introduction to the concept of *shalom* and the four key relationships that form it – our relationship with God, with and within ourselves, with other people and with nature, for me, was one of the excitements of the book. To live under the umbrella of *shalom* has to be transformative and lead to action for a better world. Faith is not about believing a set of abstract propositions; rather it is an integrated way of living out of what we believe.' **Jenny McIntosh** – *founder of Spirited Exchanges, an umbrella initiative for a variety of responses offering support, resources and accompaniment to those on their faith journey outside of the church*

'I loved reading this book, because I share with Noel a common affection for a life lived in India and a common appreciation for the forests in the foothills of the Himalayas. But also because I resonated so deeply with so many of the truths of which Noel speaks that at times reading *Fingerprints of Fire ... Footprints of Peace* felt like reading a fifth Gospel, one that many post-modern, New-Age searchers, seeking the Way of Jesus, would find invaluable – because it is totally approachable, immediately accessible and easily comprehensible. I think this book is Noel's special gift to us as his fellow-travellers. It is a very beautiful book

– a "beauty-filled" book – a book filled with the beauty of wise ideas, perceptive insights and helpful suggestions to guide us on our journey towards integrity, inclusivity, community, peace and justice.' **Dave Andrews** – *activist, teacher and author of many books. He is an elder for Servants to Asia's Urban Poor. Dave has lived in communities with marginalised groups in India, Afghanistan, Nepal and Australia over forty years*

'This is a really important book. I would recommend it to both contemplatives and activists. Noel has an integrated approach with a language that really resonates. He carefully unpacks the meanings to give us new lenses with which to see things, and helps us to shed our preconceptions. This book gives us a sense of where we are going and a truly holistic vision of *shalom*. It makes an inspiring contribution, providing a much-needed shift in our cultural landscape at the kairos moment of opportunity in which we find ourselves. *Shal-OM*.' **Louise Donkin** – *founder and director of SPEAK, the international student and young adults' Christian peace and justice network*

'This book offers a "Jesus perspective" on a rich tapestry of social and philosophical issues, while studiously avoiding in-house Christian jargon (a helpful glossary is provided at the end). This project is biblically informed, interreligiously literate, and thoughtfully inclusive, endeavoring to connect with both Christians and non-Christians alike. Each of the chapters takes on different aspects of engaged discipleship, a holistic mix of the socio-political (such as peace, anarchism, creation) and the personal-spiritual (such as mysticism, wisdom, values). Noel likes to make bold assertions – "You are not going to heaven, or to hell" (he is unashamedly universalist) – which invite conversation, reflection and challenge. The book is framed by poignant reflections on its title: an appeal to engage the world with "fingerprints of fire" and leave behind "footprints of peace". I consider this book a "catechism for the non-dogmatic" and recommend it warmly.' **Ched Myers** – *biblical scholar, teacher and author around the themes of social justice, political theology and ecological discipleship, works with Bartimaeus Cooperative Ministries, USA*

'Through his book, *Fingerprints of Fire … Footprints of Peace*, the very caring, well-grounded yet deeply spiritual character of Noel Moules shines out. For anyone who fears Noel might be a loud bible-thumping Christian extremist, nothing could be further from the truth, as the reader will discover. Noel's book speaks to

Christians, giving them a wonderful illustration of how to live a deeply Christian life whilst entering into peaceful and respectful dialogue with non-Christians. It also speaks to non-Christians in providing a re-framing of Christianity that demonstrates a Christian love that is, sadly, absent from the character of some of the more vociferous Christians. Indeed, much of Noel's writing speaks to a spirituality that transcends faith descriptors.' **Mike Stygal** – *teacher,* shaman, *founder and facilitator of the on-line dialogue forum, Pagan-Christian Moot, and district manager of the Pagan Federation UK*

'This book engages us with many short stories. It is a gift of the writer, Noel Moules, to listen to others, enter conversation with them and then reflect on the experience in order to explore his own understanding of God, community, Eucharist, peace and justice. Work for peace, he tells us, is about getting our hands dirty, paying a price, changing the world in the here and now. Such activism must be grounded in self-knowledge, draw sustenance in the community of the Peacemeal (eucharistic community) and follow the life and words of Jesus. As a cradle Catholic and peace activist it has both opened my eyes to fresh ways of thinking and encouraged me to "hang on in there" for the long haul.' **Pat Gaffney** – *General Secretary of Pax Christi, the international Catholic movement for peace. In 2005 she was a Nobel Peace Prize nominee*

'In this luminous book, Noel Moules passionately communicates wisdom in conversation with the life questions and lifestyles of people today. Noel's vision is huge: he believes that *shalom* is the heart of God, the character of Jesus, the way to live, and the destination of creation. His intended audience also is huge: he dialogues sympathetically with people of many religious traditions, and with Christians who have opted out of churches that they found oppressive, while being true to his convictions – that the God revealed in Jesus is the God of *shalom*, and that people who follow in Jesus' steps will be "*shalom* activists". Noel's style is attractive: personal, glittering with memorable images, and "assertively gentle" – inviting his readers to look anew at controversial issues, such as our relationship to wild creation. All who read this book – those who follow Jesus and those who don't – will find Noel to be a wise guide, a bringer of new insights and a joyful bearer of hope.' **Alan Kreider** – *Professor of Church History and Mission, Associated Mennonite Biblical Seminary, Elkhart, IN,*

USA (retired); author (with Eleanor Kreider) of Worship and Mission After Christendom

'The striking thing about this book is its openness – deeply rooted in the Christian tradition and the person of Jesus but opening up questions on all sides, and always open to inspiration from and dialogue with other religious traditions and non-religious beliefs, including atheism and humanism. Working with a series of images rather than a set of doctrines, it invites us to join the journey of exploration, whatever our starting-point. I hope that my fellow-humanists will take up the challenge.' **Richard Norman** – *teacher, author, a vice president of the British Humanist Association*

'This is a book about Jesus – but a Jesus that you may not immediately recognise. Noel Moules looks beyond the familiar images of stained-glass saints and moralistic mantras to offer a new perspective on the sort of spiritual connections that might sustain us through the seismic upheavals that characterise today's world. Combining ancient wisdom with contemporary insights, he invites readers to re-imagine their own humanity as well as offering a distinctive portrait of the life and teachings of Jesus.' **John Drane** *–author and theologian who teaches practical theology in universities and colleges around the world, with a particular expertise in relating faith to contemporary culture*

'A personal manifesto, an extended reflection on the implications of the dynamic concept of *shalom*, a fresh perspective on familiar biblical texts, a provocative and unsettling critique of standard assumptions, a passionate presentation of values and convictions forged during decades of study, teaching and interaction with people from many backgrounds, a multi-faceted exploration of faith and identity, which draws on the wisdom of many different traditions but is profoundly Jesus-centred – Noel Moules sums up the integrating themes of his life and teaching, sharing stories, posing questions, challenging conformity, encouraging creativity and inviting readers to journey with him into new understandings and ways of living.' **Stuart Murray Williams** – *author, teacher, founder of Urban Expression, which pioneers urban church planting, and the chair and co-founder of the Anabaptist Network UK*

'When I first met Noel Moules he enthusiastically described himself as a "*Shalom* Activist"; this exciting read unpacks that powerful description. Teacher, storyteller, messianic anarchist, Noel invites

Fingerprints of Fire ... Footprints of Peace

a spiritual manifesto from a Jesus perspective

Fingerprints of Fire ... Footprints of Peace

a spiritual manifesto from a Jesus perspective

Noel Moules

Winchester, UK
Washington, USA

First published by Circle Books, 2012
Circle Books is an imprint of John Hunt Publishing Ltd., Laurel House, Station Approach,
Alresford, Hants, SO24 9JH, UK
office1@jhpbooks.net
www.johnhuntpublishing.com
www.circle-books.com

For distributor details and how to order please visit the 'Ordering' section on our website.

Text copyright: Noel Moules 2011

ISBN: 978 1 84694 612 7

A CIP catalogue record for this book is available from the British Library.

Cover design: Andy Stonehouse (enquiries@s2design.co.uk)

Page 18
Robert van de Weyer, *Guru Jesus*, SPCK, 1975

Page 163
Sara Miles, *Take This Bread*, Ballantine Books, 2008, pp. 57-59

Printed in the USA by Edwards Brothers Malloy

We operate a distinctive and ethical publishing philosophy in all
areas of our business, from our global network of authors to
production and worldwide distribution.

for
Rowena

Contents

Reading this book

The Journey   1

Reading This Book

Reading options: I want to encourage you to feel free to read this book in a way that suits your interest and personality best:

- You may of course wish to read the book from beginning to end as an unfolding pattern of thought;
- You may prefer to read randomly, dipping in and out of chapters that catch your eye, or exploring themes that particularly interest you;
- You may wish to take your time thinking through the ideas being suggested, even reading and discussing a chapter with a group of friends before choosing to move on to read another one.

Glossary: At the back of the book there is a glossary of different words from across the cultures and faiths mentioned in the text. If you are reading the book randomly, you may come across a word or an idea that is new to you – though it might have been explained previously – or if you simply want to remind yourself of the meaning of a word or phrase, you can find it there. I hope this is helpful.

Endnotes: You will notice that each chapter has many 'endnotes'. I use them for three reasons:

- To prevent the pages being cluttered with numerous texts and references;
- To help you identify the sources of ideas that are not my own, or to show you where you can find more information on a subject, should you wish to;
- To add more information to the discussion – imagine them as someone making an aside during an animated conversation. I hope you will find this acceptable, a help and not an obstacle.

Biblical quotations: Throughout the book I quote many biblical texts. For those to whom this matters I hope you will see my thinking is firmly rooted in the scriptural tradition, however radical it may appear at times. For those to whom it does not matter I hope you will nevertheless notice the beauty of the words and ideas from a book about which there is often understandable scepticism. I do not use a set translation, but all the biblical references are stated so if you wish you can follow them up in your own translation.

Taking things further: Once you have read this book some of you may wish to pursue some of the ideas in more detail. Here are three possibilities:

- Contact me personally with questions or comments about the issues raised by this book by emailing me at: fingerprints@anvil.org.uk

- Visit the on-line 'Interactive Guide' for videos, resources, study-questions and further reading related to the subjects covered in this book at: <www.workshop.org.uk/fingerprints>

- For more information about the 'Workshop: because faith is a journey' learning programme, visit: <www.workshop.org.uk>

The Journey

It was the late train home. I couldn't believe it – the compartment was empty, I could work undisturbed for the next two hours. What a relief! Settling happily in my corner seat I got out some books and papers. Suddenly, to my horror, moments before leaving the station, the carriage door flew open to an invasion of rowdy young adults, about twenty in all. Football fans in high spirits, well lubricated with alcohol, two of them seriously drunk. They filled up the space around me, not a single seat unoccupied. I shrank into my corner wanting to disappear; trying to zone out the noise I focused on my papers, avoiding all eye contact.

Scarcely ten minutes after departure, amid the laughter and the shouting, I became aware of a voice speaking to me. 'Excuse me.' I glanced up at the young man opposite, who was looking at me enquiringly. 'I can't help noticing your papers, are you a religious teacher or something? Are you a Christian? I don't believe in God myself, but the questions and ideas are fascinating.' I was taken aback. Had I actually heard him correctly? So began one of the most remarkable conversations about faith and spirituality I have ever experienced. For the rest of the journey we talked about everything! Prayer, pain, suffering and evil, spiritual experiences, death and dying, other faiths and great spiritual teachers. We spoke a lot about Jesus, but also about poverty and injustice, peace and war and how could we really understand God. We moved from topic to topic seriously and thoughtfully.

Others in the group soon picked up on our conversation. My companion gave it focus, but his friends all became involved, listening, commenting, and giving their opinions. On several occasions the whole carriage seemed to be loudly debating some detailed theological point! It all took place amid the friendly exchange of beer cans and the occasional interruption as they struggled to separate the drunken lads from fighting each other.

A few minutes from our destination my friend fixed me with his gaze and said, 'You have got to find a way of speaking to people like us. Your ideas really make sense. We want to hear more of what you are saying.' I was stunned. Moments later the train stopped, there were handshakes all round and they were gone, much as they had arrived laughing and shouting into the night.

There are whole fresh ways of looking at faith from a Jesus perspective that are liberating, healing, holistic and empowering. Ways of connecting with spirituality in this complex world of today that are breathtaking.

This book is for ...

- Those in the Christian community with whom I want to explore fresh possibilities;
- Those on the outside looking in, asking 'Could there really be anything here for me?'
- Those who come to me every year declaring they are giving God one last chance;
- Those who are simply looking for common ground between faiths and beliefs so we can work together to change the world.

This book is for those who want more. I hope you find these pages a welcoming place to reflect.

This is a passionate book filled with conviction but also many questions.

Its focus is on the person of Jesus, but at the centre of an open space. I hope it will feel spacious – a place for questioning and doubt, for argument, disagreement and discussion as well as encouragement, affirmation and conviction.

I am committed to a 'listening spirituality' that is sensitive and always learning.[1]

I use the phrase 'from a Jesus perspective' throughout my writing. This is not an attempt to avoid using the term 'Christian' and the negative connotations many associate with that word. Rather it is asking the reader to look at things with fresh eyes, focused through a liberated understanding of the person of Jesus.

How easily our vision and thinking get narrowed. This is an invitation to stand at the centre of a circle and imagine being surrounded by a limitless horizon interpreting what you see from the outlook of the person of Jesus, in terms of how he lived and taught and what that might mean for us today.

Finally, this is a very personal book, shaped by my own spiritual journey, asking the question, 'How should I understand myself as someone seeking to live from a Jesus perspective?'

The different chapters of this book start to answer this question. They express who I aspire to be. They are not a 'pick-and-mix' list, but an integrated whole: like different facets of a single diamond.

Having picked up the book and read this far, I hope you will continue to read. Let's journey together and join in a shared conversation …

Endnote

1   This phrase, 'a listening spirituality', was coined by an American Quaker, Patricia Loring, and quoted in *Rooted in Christianity, Open to New Light: Quaker Spiritual Diversity*, Pronoun Press, 2009, p. 75.

Fingerprints of Fire … Footprints of Peace

1 Fingerprints of Fire
– touching our identity

My fingerprint is a symbol of who I am, an icon of my identity. Fingerprints are common to every human being, yet unique to each individual. I rarely think of my fingertips and the marks they make, yet each time I touch something they leave their impression. Not only do they imprint the surface with microscopic contours as distinct as a personal signature, but also they leave behind molecular DNA that can trace every touch I make directly back to me.

Fingerprints remind me of the physical power of touch; whether an intimate expression of love, or a kind and compassionate gesture that reaches out to draw someone to a place of safety. Without physical touch, neither animals nor humans will thrive. A fist leaves no fingerprints, only bruises. Touching should always be life-giving.

* * * * *

I was at a conference for young activists, invited to speak about the way different faiths understand the concept of peace. The session went well, provoking animated discussion during our mealtime conversation. There was much talk about spiritual influences and choices. Around the table phrases such as 'I am a Christian' and 'Are you a Buddhist?' began to be used. Across from me sat a young woman, thoughtfully listening to everything being said. She took her time; I could see she was reflecting. Then in a clear, gentle voice she asked, 'I am Fran, why do I have to be anything else?' This question, simple yet so profound, hit me like a thunderbolt, like a *koan* – that disturbing statement given by a Zen Buddhist master to aid enlightenment; it lives with me to this day.

Her question is about identity; how do I understand it? It is about me: who am I and how do I understand myself? What is *my* unique fingerprint?

The brilliance of Fran's question is the way it reveals how culture and religion each tend to deal with personal identity by wrapping us in 'garments' designed and sewn together by other people for us to wear. We take them without thinking and dress in them with gratitude, because we want to belong. This almost always leads to a self-understanding that is conformist and creates attitudes that easily become doctrinaire, leaving personal individuality and true identity as secondary, and in extreme circumstances virtually erased.

Clothing is a very powerful symbol of identity; it is intriguing the way it both covers and reveals us at one and the same time. If we choose to use the metaphor of 'garments' when thinking about identity, we need to see ourselves as 'bespoke people', with an identity that is tailored to communicate who we really are, and not one that is like a uniform or an 'off-the-peg' fashion item.[1]

It is the statement, 'I am Fran' that cuts to the heart of the issue. Authentic identity always begins with who and what we are deep within ourselves. As Jesus says: 'Out of your innermost being will flow rivers of living water.'[2]

As I reflect on Fran's question, my imagination sweeps me far back in time to a biblical story. I am standing in the searing heat of the Sinai wilderness where a shepherd called Moses pauses in the shadow of a dark brooding peak, known by the locals as 'the mountain of God'.[3] In front of him a desert scrub-bush burns with fire but is not consumed. He is standing in the divine presence.

The moment is tantalising. Moses asks for God's identity.

In reply he is given four Hebrew consonants – YHWH – probably pronounced *Yahweh*.[4] A name so simple yet so profound, a form of the verb 'to be', and usually translated, 'I am who I am' or 'The One who is'.[5]

'God is who God is.' This means God's identity is only found within itself. It doesn't depend on any other source. It is also only revealed in divine action and God's moral and spiritual qualities.

For ancient and indigenous peoples your name reveals your character. That is why God's name is so significant.[6]

The focus of God's identity is found in the word 'holy'. The Hebrew word is *qadosh*. It has an intriguing double meaning – 'belonging to' and 'separate from'. The best English word to translate *qadosh* is 'unique'. God invites everyone to 'Be unique as I am unique'.[7]

God is the unique one, the 'I am'; the one whose identity and character flows from the depths of divine being and nowhere else.

God refuses to be defined.

Why should I be any different?

* * * * *

Jesus is a Palestinian *rabbi* in whom the life of the Spirit is complete, someone who fully integrates the human and divine, the physical and spiritual. On at least ten occasions he refers to himself as, 'I am ...' confidently connecting to the YHWH title.[8]

Jesus' identity is centred deep within himself; external factors and forces are there, but they are secondary. He also frequently refers to a source beyond himself, speaking about things 'from above' and 'the one who sent me'.[9]

Like God, Jesus refuses to be defined. People constantly try to label him with titles like 'Messiah'. He rejects them, using instead the Aramaic phrase, *bar nasha* – 'son of man', literally 'a human being'. He says clearly, 'I am just a person.'

Jesus' sense of identity is striking. He has personal confidence, strength and security – as comfortable in urban Jerusalem as in rural Galilee. He can talk to the religious leaders of the Sanhedrin as easily as to a leper or roadside beggar. He can creatively defuse hostile theological questions set to trap him by Scribes and Pharisees, and with equal skill calm the traumatised. Jesus is as relaxed at the meal table with tax collectors and prostitutes as he is at a banquet laid on by a local dignitary. When a woman of ill repute publicly kisses his feet, her actions cause him no embarrassment whatever, though everyone around is scandalised. He breaks the traditions of Sabbath-keeping when he considers it necessary, but is quite happy to comply with social expectations when matters of justice or integrity are not at stake.

This confident identity would have been hard-won. Emerging during Jesus' childhood, it was forged through grappling with temptation, grief, frustration and anger, by learning obedience and making creative personal choices with the empowering of the Spirit.[10] This should encourage and inspire each of us in our spiritual journey.

One of the most powerful reflections on Jesus' sense of identity comes from an account of his final meal with those closest to him:

Jesus, knowing the Father had given all things into his hands,
and that he came from God and was going to God,
rose from supper, laid aside his garments, and girded himself with a towel.
Then he poured water into a basin,
and began to wash the disciples' feet,
and to wipe them with the towel with which he was girded.[11]

Everything is here. Jesus is at the centre of powerful political events that are focused on destroying him, but he is serenely confident. He is at peace within himself, and completely free and therefore he can wait on his followers like a servant. He is both the master and the slave in the same moment; such is the power of his sense of identity! He knows who he is and other people's perceptions about him are irrelevant.

★ ★ ★ ★ ★

So who am I?

The argument that I am a sophisticated collection of cells, the consequence of chance and a selfish gene, hard-wired for survival, my behaviour determined by genetics and culture and my spirituality explained by complex neuropsychology, is compelling.

The question remains: 'Is that all?'

The science may well be correct, but is the reductionist interpretation true? Why, when presented with all these incredible facts, do I still feel everything has not been said? Where does this primal sense of something more, beyond myself, come from?

I don't *have* a body; I *am* a body. Yet as a body I am more than just physical. Is there a depth to what it really means to be physical that is beyond the ability of science to measure? While we may each draw contrasting conclusions, most people of faith share the basic conviction that there is more.

When I ask, 'Who am I?' from the perspective of Jesus, I am told, 'You are made in the "image and likeness of God," in fact you are "little less than God".' We have been shaped from the earth, yet brought alive by the very Spirit-breath of God; quite literally a mixture of heaven and earth – completely one with wild nature, yet sharing personhood with God.[12] This is something dynamic, not static; calling each of us to image God in the way we live. Jesus is our reference point. In him we see the image and likeness of God most clearly revealed. Jesus says what is true for him can be true for us also.[13]

This is my fingerprint.

What is true for me is true for everyone. God's image and likeness is seen most fully in the diversity of humanity together. This reality has revolutionised my life. Previously most people were peripheral to my vision as I concentrated on the few at the centre of my gaze. Then suddenly everyone I met began to look different. Whether they were youthful or mature, touched by beauty or marked with pain and even disfigurement, the image of God in them began to appear before my eyes.

Nothing can erase this image from a person. Nothing can prevent them from finding the true fulfilment of everything they are as divine destiny unfolds. When I am out walking in the street I try to focus a meditation on the faces of the people I see around me. Sometimes the impact is almost overwhelming.

In India – the land of my birth and early childhood – and across southeast Asia, the most common greeting is the word-gesture *namaste*[14] – the palms of the hand held together near the heart, the head gently bowed and whispering *'Namaste'* – which implies 'I honour the divine in you'.

I have found it liberating to incorporate this concept into my normal people-responses as a reminder, 'I honour the image and likeness of God in you.' The more I acknowledge the image of God in others the more I identify it in myself and respond accordingly. It is a simple practical action that nurtures my spirit and opens me up to fulfil the instruction of Jesus, 'Love your neighbour as yourself'.[15]

* * * * *

A story about the Desert Father, *Abba* Joseph of Panephysis:

> *Abba* Lot went to see *Abba* Joseph and said to him,
> '*Abba*, as far as I can I say my daily liturgy, I fast a
> little, I pray and meditate, I live in peace and as far
> as I can, I purify my thoughts. What else can I do?'
> Then the old man stood up and stretched his hands
> towards heaven. His fingers became like ten lamps
> of fire and he said to him, 'If you will, you can
> become all flame.'[16]

What does this really mean?
How can I become all flame?
How does this touch my identity?

Fire is a powerful global spiritual symbol. In Zoroastrianism, *Ahura Mazda*, the God of goodness, is seen as a fire of uncreated light, filled with wisdom, truth, righteousness and purity.

Terrifying in its ability to consume and destroy and yet comforting in its gift of heat and light, fire speaks of God. Fire purifies, illuminates, brings warmth and healing; it stimulates fertility. In the Orthodox Christian tradition the symbol of fire is always understood as an expression of the love of God in its very purest form on every occasion it is used, including judgement.[17]

Becoming 'all flame', being 'ablaze with the Spirit', is at the heart of discovering identity from a Jesus perspective.[18] It begins deep within the core of our being, a spark of light igniting a flame that starts a process of gentle transfiguration into godliness. In each person the nature of this change is unique. It involves the whole of us and its outcome is primarily practical, revealed in the way we live our daily lives.[19]

Like Fran, I choose to stand boldly and declare, 'I am Noel, why do I have to be anything else?' This is liberating, affirming and true. And yet beyond this, further exciting questions remain. 'What does it *actually* mean to be Noel?' or for you to be *you*?

Standing confident in my growing sense of identity, I can look out towards others, touching people and wild nature with fingerprints of fire – fingerprints that leave life-giving DNA on everything they touch. The fire burns up injustice, heals, brings warmth to relationships and illuminates the way ahead.

Endnotes

1 Interestingly, the strongest sense of personal identity may actually be seen in nakedness rather than clothing. There is an intriguing statement in the second Genesis creation story, 'They were both naked and unashamed' (Gen 2:25); here is vulnerability with dignity, freedom with respect and innocence with honour.

2 Jn 7:38; cf. Exod 17:1–6; Ps 78:15–16; 105:40–41; Ezk 47:1–11.

3 See Exod 3:1–22, especially vv. 13–15.

4 See Exod 3:13. The YHWH is technically known as the *tetragrammaton* – literally 'the four letters'! Many faiths have many names for God – the biblical text is no exception – but they are all essentially titles rather than names, here in this story we get closest to the very name of God itself.

5 While much is uncertain, the name emphasises God in personal terms. Nevertheless, we are left with the difficulty of how to translate this powerful, abstract and liquid phrase. There are a number of possibilities:
 - There are those that emphasise God's 'being': 'The One who is'; 'The One who will be', or 'The Eternal One';
 - There are those that emphasise God's 'activity': 'The One who causes to be', 'I will be what I will be', 'He who causes to come into existence'.
 Probably there is no satisfactory translation; which only emphasises the profound nature of God and the importance of this moment of revelation.

6 In the ancient world and some indigenous societies a newborn child is usually given a 'birth' or 'child' name; then at puberty, when the whole community has had the opportunity to determine their character and personality, they are given their true name. This is graphically illustrated in the biblical story of Jacob (Gen 25:26, 29–34; see also 32:22–32), whose name meant 'supplanter', implying 'cheat', 'twister', 'cannot be trusted' – imagine introducing yourself to polite society with a name like that!

7 Lev 11:44; see 1Pt 1:16.

8 See Jn 6:35; 8:12, 58; 10:9, 11; 11:25; 14:6; 15:1; 18: 4–7; Mk 14:62.

9 See Jn 3:31 and Lk 10:16; Jn 12:45 *et al.*

10 Temptations (Lk 4:1–4; Mk 1:13; Mt 4:1–11 and throughout Jesus' ministry), grief (Jn 11:3–36; Mt 23:37–38); frustration (Mt 23:1–38); anger (Mk 3:1–6); learning obedience (Heb 5:8–11); making creative personal choices (Lk 9:51–53; Mt 26:38–39, 42) and the empowering of the Spirit (Mk 1:12; Jn 3:34).

11 Jn 13:3–5.

12 See Gen 1:26–27; Ps 8:4–5. Gen 2:7 is an astonishing text, which pictures God moulding the human form (Hebrew *adam*) from the red clay (Hebrew *adamah*), then breathing the divine Spirit (Hebrew *ruach*) into it and the clay shape of the human person becoming a living being (Hebrew *nephesh*) – often translated 'soul'. We don't 'have a soul', we 'are a soul'!. This is a mystery we share with the rest of wild nature. 'Imaging God' describes our role rather than our status. We shall discuss all of this in more detail in our chapter about being a *Creation Companion*.

13 An early Christian reflection (Col 1:15) speaks of Jesus as 'the image of the invisible God'; see also 2Cor 4:4; Heb 1:3; Mt 10:25; cf. Lk 6:40.

14 The word *namaste* comes from two Sanskrit words: *namas* – meaning 'to bow' and 'to honour', and *te* – meaning 'to you'. The gesture of the two palms of the hand pressed together symbolises the uniting and harmonising of all aspects of a diverse universe. The western handshake emphasises the equality between two parties; the *namaste* points beyond to the source of our relationship in God.

15 Mt 19:19; 22:39; Mk 12:31, 33; Lk 10:27.

16 I have adapted the text of this story, but it can be found in Benedicta Ward

(trans.), *The Sayings of the Desert Fathers: The Alphabetical Collection*, Cistercian Studies Series (No. 59), 2005, p. 103; and Richard Foster, *Prayer: Finding the Heart's True Home*, Hodder, 1992, p. 5. I am grateful to my friend Keith Judson for drawing my attention to this story.

17 See <http://www.stnectariospress.com/parish/river_of_fire.htm> section XV11. We shall deal with the significance of fire in the biblical tradition in much more detail in a number of other places in the book.

18 See Rom 12:11.

19 We shall discuss this further when we talk about being a *New Age Traveller* and *Radical Mystic*. Suffice it to say that the biblical image sees us brought to life by the in-breathing of the Spirit of God (Gen 2:7); there is the promise to pour out the Spirit onto all flesh (Joel 2:28–29) and of a new covenant of the Spirit (Ezk 36:26–27). Jesus will baptise in Spirit and fire (Mt 3:11) and that is the exact imagery used to describe the Pentecost-experience of the earliest Jesus-community in Jerusalem (Acts 2:1–3).

2 New Age Traveller
– journeying at the edge of time

'You are standing at the very frontiers of existence. In the whole history of time no one and nothing has ever lived or experienced this moment before.' This thought seemed to come from nowhere – it changed my life.

Live each moment like a child on a winter morning, gleefully jumping into deep untrodden snow, delighting to make your very own mark on the pristine white canvas spread out in front of you.

Connect with the feeling of walking on a tide-washed beach at dawn, your bare feet making solitary footprints in the damp sand, and then pausing to look back with that sense of excitement that you are treading somewhere completely new.

You are, right now, living at the very cutting edge of time, like a surfer riding the rip-curl of a great wave as it breaks towards the shore.

This is something deeply personal, yet universal. It is 'living in the moment', but at the same time being aware of cosmic history and destiny as we make our choices.

Life is given to us – one breath, one heartbeat, one blink of the eye, at a time – to be embraced, savoured, enjoyed, explored and then left as a treasure and a memory as we move forward to the next.

Life is also hard. It is too often marked with pain, anguish and cruelty. Yet this stark reality does not take away the truth that we have the opportunity to grasp it moment by moment as a divine gift. However traumatic our personal experience might be we have the opportunity to discover God within it – not as someone who dulls our senses like a religious drug, but rather as a companion who actually shares the journey and the struggle with us. Time and again people have proved this to be a tough but trustworthy path towards wholeness. This is important to understand as we look for the path towards identity.

* * * * *

I spent my early childhood in the foothills of the Himalaya, the greatest mountains on earth. I remember the dark forests and the vast blue skies; rugged rocks, brilliant flowers, tall pine trees that sang with the breeze and of course the ever-changing colour of the snows that towered above every horizon.

I have a vivid memory of lying on my back in front of a tent in a forest clearing, looking up into a vast crystal-clear night sky. We were on the road travelling; our campsite was surrounded by dense forest. Everything was silent, except for the eerie sound of a leopard calling from across the valley. The heavens were literally ablaze with countless stars. All these decades later I vividly recall being spellbound. It seemed to me that I was looking out into the future with the promise of a limitless journey forward, too vast for me to truly comprehend. I still remember the shudder of awe that swept over me.

Of course I was mistaken. The starlight I was seeing had taken thousands, probably millions, of years to reach my eyes. This was ancient radiance, fragments of the past breaking into my present, not beacons from the future beckoning me forward as I fancifully imagined.

Yet I was *not* wrong. Everything is going somewhere, like a great river flowing forward or some undulating path that stretches out into the unknown. Life is a journey, to be embraced one moment at a time, one step at a time, at the leading edge of time.

I believe we are all wayfarers at heart.

So it should be no surprise that a unifying metaphor found among people of faith and belief down through the ages is a 'spiritual journey'. Sidhartha, the Buddha, taught that it was 'the noble eight-fold path' that leads the devotee to awakening and ultimately *nirvana*. The written teachings of LaoTse, the Chinese founder of Taoism, are called 'The Way and its Power'. Judaism sees obedience to the 613 commandments of the *torah* as walking a pathway that ultimately leads to life. In Islam *sharia* sets out the way to live; the Arabic word literally means 'the path that leads to the water of life'. Searching the internet quickly shows that almost every faith and belief speaks of itself in terms of being 'a way' – 'the Sikh Way', 'the Baha'i Way', 'the Pagan Way', 'the Humanist Way' and many more.

Jesus describes himself as 'the Way' that leads to truth and life; he calls people to follow him.[1] He describes himself as both the pathfinder and the path itself. He warns us to avoid the 'broad way' that is easy to travel but destructive in its destination, rather to put in the single-minded effort to find the life-giving 'narrow way'.[2] Jesus speaks of people as 'lost' and disorientated, struggling to journey morally and spiritually.[3]

The earliest Jesus-community identified themselves as people of 'the Way'.[4] This defined how they lived; *the* Way of Life becoming *their* way of life as they followed in his steps; a path of light in the darkness, offering guidance, forgiveness and companionship.

✶ ✶ ✶ ✶ ✶

Today, within our wide community of people spiritually journeying, you will find some who are spoken of as 'New Age Travellers'. The name, coined in the 1970s, describes groups who travel between music festivals and fairs and follow an alternative lifestyle. A variety of spiritual sources motivate them, from eastern mysticism, mythology, philosophy, psychology, science, science-fiction, indigenous faiths and much more; each drawing upon the other.[5] At its heart the New Age movement is engaging with profound questions.[6] Two characteristics are especially important: it is *counter conscious*, thinking differently, and it is *counter culture*, living differently; both are vital to our theme.

The phrase 'New Age' is astrological; the zodiac calendar suggests the current 'Age of Pisces' is dying (symbolised by a fish – *ichthus*[7] – seen by many as the age of the church), giving way to the 'Age of Aquarius', the time of 'the mind's true liberation'. The idea of the 'traveller' connects with nomadic peoples who move from place to place, living in harmony with the natural environment. There is also empathy with the Roma people, 'Gypsies', with their clear identity and alternative values enabling them to live with simplicity and freedom, counter to the surrounding culture, often in the face of severe persecution.

The seeds of contemporary 'New Age' ideas go back to ancient India, with strong Hindu and Buddhist influences.[8] However, there is also a contrasting strand of 'new age' thinking within the Hebrew biblical tradition. Prophets spoke of a 'renewed heaven and earth'[9] (something we will discuss in more detail in the next chapter), and by the time of Jesus the Jews were talking about 'this age' and 'the age to come'[10] while also discussing 'the kingdom of God'.[11] In Jesus this thinking is dramatically focused and radicalised.

It begins at his baptism.

Jesus' baptism is not just some personal spiritual experience for him; it is the very moment at which the new age and the new creation begin to be born.

A prophet and baptiser called John was capturing the popular imagination with a powerful message that the longed-for rule of God was coming, in fact it was so close you could reach out and touch it. John urged people to prepare by being baptised in water – asking forgiveness and promising to live a future life of godliness. John was adamant he was only a herald preparing the path for a truly important person soon to come, 'Who will baptise you in holy Spirit and fire!'[12]

Jesus joins the crowd listening to John. He then joins the queue to be baptised. As he steps into the water, John instantly recognises him. After some initial hesitation the rugged ascetic baptises Jesus.

When Jesus steps out of the water, something breathtaking happens. The sky is ripped apart (literally 'shredded'), the Spirit descends as a dove, and God's voice affirms Jesus' uniqueness. Everything about this account tells us this is an event impossible to describe. The writers are forced to employ symbolism from the original biblical creation stories to draw out its significance.[13]

Trying to grasp the power and importance of this moment, my imagination pictures a sweeping horizon line in silhouette under a vast open sky, with the figure of Jesus walking slowly across it. Suddenly a huge tsunami-wave of Spirit and fire rises to fill the high-arched sky behind, the rip-curl breaking to engulf the whole cosmos in life-giving liberating power; setting it free from evil and injustice, overwhelming it with love, extravagant goodness and peace.

＊ ＊ ＊ ＊ ＊

Following this momentous River Jordan moment, which few at the time would have understood, Jesus begins the life of a travelling *rabbi*; a very public journey through the towns and villages of Judea and Galilee, which will come to an astonishing climax in Jerusalem and change the world in the process.

As we watch him walking the roads, teaching the crowds and healing the sick, we notice how from time to time he will stop, look deeply into the eyes of an individual and quietly say, 'Follow me.'[14]

Jesus is drawing together a community of 'disciples'.[15] They are truly New Age Travellers, beginning to learn what it means to be part of this new creation Jesus is ushering in. We continue in that path.

As a company of itinerants on the road with their teacher they were not unusual. Many a Jewish *rabbi* had their *talmidim* – followers living full-time with them, learning their wisdom and the practical implications of their teachings.

It is in the culture of India that this tradition is most deeply developed. Here the *guru–shishya* relationship is the model of life-learning and spiritual development. A Hindu seeking enlightenment will search out a *guru* they believe can enable this to happen and then commit themselves in total obedience to this spiritual master, becoming a *shishya* ('one who learns') – in the Buddhist tradition they become *savaka* ('one who listens').

Both 'listening and 'learning' are vital in spiritual formation.

The disciple then begins to follow a *yoga*, 'a pattern of daily living' shaped perhaps by 'meditation' (*raja*),[16] 'action' (*karma*), 'knowledge' (*jnana*), or 'devotion' (*bhakti*) or 'physical exercise' (*hatha*), given by the *guru* to support their spiritual development and journey.

There is a moving Christian example of the power of single-minded commitment and obedience on the part of the *shishya* to the *guru*. In February 1969 Robert van de Weyer took a 'year out' before going to university and joined the 'hippy trail' to India. He was a confessed agnostic, but while in the sub-continent he became fascinated by the concept of the *guru*. He met many, but none inspired sufficient confidence for him to give them total obedience. Reflecting back on his school days he remembered stories about Jesus, who at the time struck him as probably being the happiest man in the world. While he had problems with most traditional Christian doctrines he nevertheless decided that on Christmas Day 1970 he would make Jesus his *guru* and live the next six months in total obedience to his commands and teachings whether or not he understood them or agreed with them. These are some of the comments from his diary:

> *9th Feb 1971* – My agnosticism is beginning to waver ... I also have a strong impression of an outside force working within me. It seems to have demanded my submission and I have submitted to it. I feel I have no control over it ... I say, 'Thy will be done.'
> *27th Feb 1971* – As a disciple of Jesus I am now bound in love to people I loathe!
> *3rd April 1971* – I hardly think I need wait the full six months. I am already firmly nailed to the cross of Jesus and am enjoying it enormously. I feel at the moment I am falling in love with Jesus.[17]

He would later write:

> June 25th passed without my even noticing it, for I now firmly think of myself as a Christian ... But I am still a novice, and in dark apathetic moments find myself doubting my faith ... I want to be happy. Therefore I had best follow the example of someone who is himself happy. I need only read a few chapters of the Gospels to remind myself how profoundly happy Jesus was.*

* * * * *

The word *guru* is a fascinating one; it is much more than just 'teacher'. It is formed out of two Sanskrit words, *gu* ('darkness') and *ru* ('to push away forcibly' or 'to scatter'). A *guru* is someone whose presence and teaching 'pushes away darkness' and by implication radiates light (*prakasha*). The parallels between Jesus and the concept of the *guru* are intriguing.

Jesus says, 'I am the light of the world, whoever follows me will never walk in darkness but will have the light of life.'[18] He also says, 'You are the light of the world ... let your light so shine before others ...'[19] and again, 'A disciple ... will be like their teacher.'[20] Jesus invites people to follow him as a learner-disciple for the purpose of becoming like himself – Christlike.

The disciple is an apprentice, learning all the skills of the master craftsman. A moving Indian tradition speaks of the *guru* being like a mother cradling her child and pointing out to them who their father is.[21] Jesus says, 'Whoever sees me, sees the one who sent me.'[22] Both Jesus and the *guru* have as their prime concern to point the disciple to the spiritual source of all things and enable that power to shape their life.

Spiritual encounter is central to being a disciple of Jesus – the 'water, Spirit and fire' imagery of baptism stresses presence, impact and change. Jesus speaks of 'being born of the Spirit';[23] the very breath of God (an image from the creation story) beginning the process of transfiguration. It is a living relationship in which there is learning and discovery. Jesus uses a powerful image to illustrate this when he says:

> Take my yoke upon you, and learn from me;
> for I am gentle and humble in heart,
> and you will find rest for your souls.
> For my yoke is easy, my burden is light.[24]

A yoke sounds restricting but, as someone said, 'It is the only thing you can add to a burden to make it lighter.' A yoke speaks of partnership; a pair of oxen yoked together to share the load, hauling carts along roads or pulling a plough across a field. Jesus and the disciple are pulling together and learning together.[25] The idea of a yoke as a symbol of spiritual formation is used across world faiths. A Jewish *rabbi* would speak of proselytes 'putting on the yoke of the *torah*'. The Sanskrit word *yoga* means a 'yoke', a 'pattern of daily living' with focus and purpose. I love the idea of 'the *yoga* of Jesus'; what we know for certain is that, paradoxically, it is both gentle and liberating.

Authentic Jesus-discipleship is searching, challenging yet exhilarating, walking the path as travellers into the new age he inaugurated.

We are to be '*counter conscious*'. We are to *think* differently. The Greek word *metanoia* is the key. It means, 'to change your mind and think in an alternative way', also 'to bring about a complete reorientation of our personality'.[26]

We are to view the world from a completely different perspective, engaging life from a divergent and challenging trajectory. Ours is to be 'the mind of the *Messiah*'; constantly renewed by the Spirit, while at the same time shrewd and practical.[27]

'Right Mindfulness' is the seventh step on the 'Noble Eightfold Path' of Buddhism; it is also essential when walking the 'Way of Jesus'. We are to live each moment 'mindfully'; in thoughtful watchful awareness of everything we do and say, constantly challenging our own attitudes and popular expectations.[28]

We are to be '*counter culture*'. We are to *live* differently, moving to a different rhythm with an alternative understanding of values. We are to rediscover ancient paths while at the same time living each moment at the leading edge of existence.

We celebrate the glorious complexity and diversity of human culture, but at the same time we challenge those concentrations of power in societies that stifle spirituality and humanity. We work tirelessly to overthrow them.

Personal growth and development are central. We have the responsibility to 'work out our own salvation' in harmony with the enabling Spirit of God already at work within us. Our attitude should be like that of an athlete in training. Our goal is maturity:[29] 'We shall become mature people, reaching the very height of Christ's full stature.'[30]

It is about transfiguration:

> And we, with unveiled faces reflecting like mirrors the glory
> of the Lord,
> are being transformed into the same image from glory to glory,
> this is the work of the Lord who is Spirit.[31]

Finally, Jesus-discipleship is also about enabling others to experience things that may not have been possible had they not met us, bringing reciprocal joy:

Edward Whymper, the British mountaineer – who in 1865 was the first to successfully reach the summit of the Matterhorn – was in the Alps for what he decided would be his last season of climbing. For years a man with severe physical disabilities had worked in his equipment room, at his climbing base in the town of Zermatt, faithfully keeping the ropes dry, the boots cleaned and the ice axes in order. Watching him at work Whymper thought, 'This man has enabled hundreds of climbers to reach the top of the highest peaks and experience the thrill of the achievement, but he has never known that joy himself.' Summoning several of his finest guides they planned to put this right. On a clear day they began their climb with the man carefully roped between them. For hours he scrambled, being pushed and dragged up the face of the mountain. Then within a few yards of the summit they encouraged him to crawl the final distance alone. A short while later Whymper joined him. The man was kneeling in the snow, tears pouring down his cheeks, repeating the words, 'It is beautiful, it is *so* beautiful!' Whymper said that of all his moments on the summit of mountains, this was the most wonderful.[32]

* * * * *

Authentic 'church' is a community of disciple-learners mutually committed to nurture spiritual growth and work together with God to establish the new creation – a company of New Age Travellers journeying at the edge of time, leaving behind them footprints of peace.

What inspires my spiritual journey?
Why is being 'counter conscious' and 'counter culture' important?
What does this 'new age' or 'new creation' actually imply, how does it shape my identity?

Endnotes

1 Jn 14:6; cf. Heb 10:20 – see also endnote 14 below.
2 Mt 7:13–14; cf. Lk 13:24. In the ancient world 'broad roads' were always built by armies, and their destination led, without question, to the 'destruction' of war and violence. Because journeying these roads was 'easy' merchants and traders, happy to take advantage of the benefits of militarism, soon used them, followed by every other traveller looking for an 'easy' path and wanting to 'feel safe'. Here is militarism and commercialism hand-in-glove, supported by a population indifferent to the destruction left in their wake.
3 See Mt 18:11 (in footnote or margins in many translations); Lk 15 where 'sheep'

(vv. 3–7), shekels (vv. 8–10) and 'sons' (vv. 11–32) are 'lost'.

4   See Acts 9:2; 19:9, 23; 22:4; 24:14, 22. The idea of 'the Way' is based on Jesus' declaration, 'I am the Way, the Truth and the Life' (Jn 14:6) and also a messianic interpretation of the 'highway of *Yahweh*' in the Hebrew scriptures (see Isa 40:3).

5   Literature on the New Age movement is immense; two excellent books from a Christian perspective are Russell Chandler, *Understanding the New Age*, Zondervan (rev. edn), 1993; and John Drane, *What is The New Age Still Saying to the Church?*, Zondervan (rev edn), 1999. More mainstream, the 'scripture' of the early New Age movement, is Marilyn Ferguson, *The Aquarian Conspiracy*, Paladin, 1980.

6   The spiritual awakening and hunger expressed in the New Age movement should excite Christians. Areas in which there is significant common ground between them are:
- *Cooperation:* personal support and shared lifestyles
- *Networking:* building community and links with others
- *Peace:* nonviolence and promoting reconciliation
- *Globalism:* having an international perspective
- *Ecology:* conservation of bio-systems and resources
- *Environment:* the development of gentle, sustainable lifestyles
- *Health:* good diet and physical well-being
- *Creativity:* quality, spontaneity and innovation
- *Potential:* encouraging positive attitudes and fulfilment
- *Transformation:* a total change of mind and thought.

7   The sign of the fish – *ichthus* in Greek – was a very early Christian symbol, each letter representing a word in the declaration 'Jesus Christ Son of God Saviour' (*Iesous Christos theou uios soter*).

8   The phrase 'New Age' originally found popularity in the West with the founder of the Theosophical Society, Helena Blavatsky (1831–91) who, strongly influenced by Indian philosophy, spoke of 'a coming new age'. Another theosophist, Alice Bailey (1880–1949), spoke of her messianic vision of a coming New Age with a new world teacher, which found increasing resonance with people.

9   See Isa 65:17; 66:22.

10 See Mt 12:32; Mk 10:30; Lk 18:30.

11 The phrase 'kingdom of God/heaven' is used eighty-four times in Matthew, Mark and Luke, with numerous other references to 'kingdom' and 'king'. 'Kingdom of heaven' is identical to 'kingdom of God'; it is just the more natural Jewish turn of phrase with their reluctance to speak the name of God. While Jesus' use of the term has powerful socio-political implications it begins by calling individuals to live under the rule of God or in harmony with the character of God. See Mt 4:17; 19:23; Mk 10:15; Lk 6:20 *et al.*

12 Extended accounts of Jesus' baptism are found in Mt 3:1–17; Lk 3:1–18, see also Mk 1:9–11; notice the important imagery of 'Spirit and fire' once again, following our discussion of it in the previous chapter.

13 They use images from the creation stories in Genesis. The waters evoke 'the primal deep' with the Spirit hovering over the surface. God's creative voice speaks. The central focus is on Jesus who, like the original Adam, images the likeness of God. In this instant, in the aftermath of Jesus' baptism, the writers believe that what is happening is the long-promised new age of the new creation beginning to come into reality now. Rather than remaining as an event yet to come sometime in the distant future, it is breaking into the world of time and space ahead of time, here and now because of the person of Jesus!

14 See Mt 8:22; 9:9; 19:21; Mk 1:17–18 – the Greek word *akolouthein* ('to follow')

has a very strong sense of relationship associated with it
15 'Disciple' comes from the Latin: *discipulus* – 'one who learns'.
16 Of course in Sanskrit *raja* means 'king' or 'royal', but in Indian tradition *raja yoga* is understood as 'meditation'.
17 See Robert van de Weyer, *Guru Jesus*, SPCK, 1975 – my brief reference to this story does not do justice to the very moving account portrayed in the book.
18 Jn 8:12.
19 Mt 5:14, 16.
20 Lk 6:40.
21 1 Try not to let the 'patriarchal tinge' of this image detract from the principle it is trying to communicate.
22 Jn 12:45.
23 Jn 3:6, 8.
24 Mt 11:29–30.
25 There is a beautiful Coptic icon, called 'Christ and St Menas', where Jesus is pictured sitting side-by-side with the saint with his arm around his shoulder (a copy hangs by my desk as I write). To me it communicates exactly the emotion I feel when I think of the shared yoke.
26 See further Alan Richardson, *A Theological Word Book of the Bible*, SCM, 1957, p. 192.
27 See 1Cor 2:16, also Eph 4:23; Rom 12:2, and the parable of the 'Dishonest Steward' in Lk 16:1–13, esp. v. 8.
28 The concept of 'mindfulness' is particularly associated in recent times with the teaching of the Vietnamese *Zen* master, Thich Nhat Hanh, in writings such as *The Miracle of Mindfulness*, Rider & Co., 1991.
29 See Phil 2:12–13; Heb 6:1. I recognise that the idea of 'salvation', while central to biblical faith, has been contaminated in popular thinking by inept evangelism and church teaching, and provokes a negative reaction in many people. It is an English word used to translate a range of Hebrew and Greek ideas. It has the sense of 'bringing people into a wide space where they can develop without hindrance and reach their full potential'. It can also imply 'rescuing someone from threat and harm' and 'victory in battle'. While 'salvation' begins to be experienced in the present it becomes a full reality within the renewed creation
30 Eph 4:13.
31 2Cor 3:18.
32 This story used to be told by my father, Len Moules, a missionary–mountaineer, and was an inspiration to me in my childhood. More information about my parents and their work on the Tibetan border in north India can be found in: Leonard Moules, *Three Miles High: Northward to Tibet*, London, CLC, 1948; Leonard Moules, *Some Want It Tough*, London, CLC, 1961; Pat Wraight, *On to the Summit: The Len Moules story*, Waynesboro OM Literature, 1981.

Fingerprints of Fire . . . Footprints of Peace

3 Cosmic Visionary
– embracing horizons of hope

The truth seems simple. It's a challenging choice; either the world has no meaning whatever and is essentially absurd, or it is filled with purpose and moves towards a goal in which all things find total fulfilment.

Ultimate reality seems to offer only one of two possibilities – nihilism or universalism – everything else appears to be a conversation between these two points of reference.[1]

Nihilism is compelling.[2] It believes everything that exists is simply the result of chance, and the whole of life is futile and meaningless. Life has only the meaning we impose upon it. We are like ancient stargazers looking up at the night sky, visualising pictures by joining the twinkling specks of light with imaginary lines; they bear no relationship to reality, they are simply make-believe. Graphically stated: 'Existence has no pattern save what we imagine after staring at it for too long.'[3] Any apparent meaning will ultimately evaporate into original nothingness as though it had never existed.

The seeds of these ideas are found in the earliest human thinking. Ancient Babylonians believed the cosmos was created from the dismembered body of Tiamat, the goddess of chaos.[4]

Nihilism forms the backdrop to the teaching of Qoheleth, the author of the book of Ecclesiastes in the Hebrew scriptures:

> 'Meaningless! Meaningless!' says the Teacher,
> 'Utterly meaningless! Everything is meaningless.
> What do people gain from their toil at which they toil
> under the sun?'[5]

These ideas are also found scratched on ancient tombstones around the Mediterranean world: 'I was not, I was, I am not, I do not care.' There is of course no God, no such thing as right or wrong, no beauty or value to anything. Such ideas are fantasies, a projection of our perverse mind, which insists on giving meaning and purpose to everything.

Even a non-theist approach to life like Humanism can be no more than a crust of culture that has formed on the surface of an essentially pointless existence, giving the illusion of something substantial while the magma of meaninglessness upon which it floats pours into the abyss.

Nihilism is fast becoming the casual everyday assumption in our society. With a shrug of the shoulder we are told, 'God does not exist, nothing has meaning, enjoy yourself, when you are dead you are dead, so what?' This is more than just atheism; the shards of Christendom and modernism may cling to it, but at its core there is the absence of anything.

I respect the integrity of popular nihilism. For many it is the only truthful position to take, but its implications are profoundly disturbing.[6]

It is vital that each one of us takes the time to sit quietly on the edge of the chasm of nothingness, to stare down into its bottomless depths and allow the vertigo to overwhelm us. Let it sink in, because in truth I believe this is one of only two possibilities about the world.

＊ ＊ ＊ ＊ ＊

I gaze into the abyss. The darkness of the void takes on the form of a storm that threatens to engulf me. Winds scream and tear at my body, waves thunder around me. My balance slips and I lose any sense of direction. Black clouds tower and engulf every horizon, and even seem to fill the deepest recesses of my mind. I am overwhelmed. It takes all my courage and self-control to keep any focus. I feel I am standing on the brink of utter oblivion. And then I hear it. At first it is no more than the faintest whisper, but there is no mistaking it is there. It seems to hang in the wind, very slowly gaining intensity and clarity. A sound so faint and fragile, a whisper of such astonishing beauty it immediately captivates me. It has simplicity, but at the same time it resonates like a complex chord of exquisite harmony, delicate, yet now with the disturbing impact of a thunderclap. It is just a single word – '*Shalom*'. I am hit by its power and velocity, out of all proportion to its subtle beginnings. Its presence changes all my perspectives, the storm becomes irrelevant, the horizons become vast, and my overwhelming feeling is one of hope.

There is a similar story, where Jesus is asleep in a boat when a storm suddenly breaks. It is so terrifying even the hardened fishermen on board are panic-stricken. Crashing waves threaten to swamp the fragile craft and razor winds rip at the sails in an attempt to tear them from the mast. Aware of the fear in the boat Jesus rouses himself, stands at the prow and with a single word shouts into the tumult – *'Shalom!'* In the next moment, almost as though it was being exorcised, the storm writhes and then collapses, the churning waters convulse and then become calm. The astonished disciples, regaining some of their composure, can only keep muttering to each other, 'Who is this person? Even the wind and the waves obey him!'[7]

Years later, the early Christian community told this story to make a profound point. To the Jew the sea was a symbol of the universe chaotic and out of control, 'the hills' were where they felt safe and secure. Jesus' calming the storm with the word 'Shalom' was not simply seen as rescuing a group of frightened disciples from drowning, but as a powerful sign declaring that his work and message would find its ultimate fulfilment by drawing the whole universe to a place of peace.

∗ ∗ ∗ ∗ ∗

Hope is that ability to sense outcomes that are good and inspire us to live towards them. We are told it 'springs eternal';[8] yet were every fragment of hope extinguished it is unlikely we could thrive or even function.[9] However, human stories from across the world and throughout history show people's capacity for hope is astonishing.

People hope in different ways. Some look for a reoccurring 'golden age', others for a just and classless 'Utopia' established by revolution. Many hope to break free from the illusion of this world into a reality elsewhere.[10]

Popular hope focuses on acquiring wealth, the cult of celebrity, scientific ingenuity, political shrewdness and international peace treaties.

The Greek myth of Pandora is haunting. The god Zeus gives the first woman a grain-jar filled with evils, which she unwittingly allows to escape into the world, with only 'hope' remaining secure in the container.[11] Zeus did not want people to throw their lives away; rather he wanted them to live in continual torment. So he gives humanity hope, the most evil of evils, because it infinitely prolongs their torment.[12]

For Jesus hope is quite different. It is a 'living hope',[13] directly linked to his relationship with God. Early Christians confidently declared, 'Christ is our hope.'[14] It embraces today, yet has a dynamic forward look. It affirms the present but sees the real climax of history lying in the future. However good this moment, 'the best is yet to come'.[15] This is not 'pie in the sky when you die' but a call to sustained hard work to bring it about. We 'work together with God' today to 'hasten the day of God'.[16]

Such hope is no opium-dream. It is a unique gift from God and can be counted on whether in crisis or calm. A person with this experience of hope creates an aura about them that increases other people's confidence that God exists and that there is a reason to believe in an ultimate destiny that is good.

Such a person is a 'Cosmic Visionary', displaying three essential qualities of hope:

- They stand tall at the centre of this unpredictable world expressing trust, confidence and faith, as if an anchor was embedded at the core of their personality holding them firm;[17]
- They are filled with a deep visceral yearning for the future. Strong biblical phrases like 'eager expectation', 'anxious longing' and 'inner groaning' are used.[18] It is as though the whole body is stretched forward in anticipation, craning the neck to see what is coming;
- They have a steadfast dynamic patience.[19] The Greek word is *hupomone*, suggesting hope as tenacity. It was used to describe the inhabitants of a city under siege refusing to leave any stone unturned in their single-minded resistance against their oppressors.

Such hope is hard-won, forged in the furnace of real life with its share of failure and disappointment. It refuses to slacken its grip on the conviction that reality is rooted in God and this cosmos has a divine destiny. Like the biblical figure of Abraham, who for all his flaws and failures, 'hoped against hope';[20] or as Martin Luther King Jr said, 'We must accept finite disappointment, but never lose infinite hope.'[21]

Here hope and faith fuse together. They reach forward towards a vision not yet realised, all the time working hard to make it a physical and tangible reality.

This attitude will mature our character into something provocative, a life so uncommon will provoke people to ask, 'What is this hope you have?'

* * * * *

At the centre of a Jesus-focused hope is *shalom*. It burns at its core like nuclear fusion burns at the heart of the sun. *Shalom* is the vision of the 'Cosmic Visionary'. It is a popular Hebrew greeting whose four consonants have hidden within them the cipher to the secret of the universe.[22]

שלום

Shalom is usually translated 'peace',[23] but a better word would be 'wholeness'. The noun is created from the verb *shalem* – 'to make something complete'. It communicates the idea of 'intactness', 'integratedness', 'harmony'; it is 'everything fitting perfectly together', like an orchestra with its array of strings, woodwind, brass and percussion, each instrument distinctive yet together creating true symphony. *Shalom* is holistic in the fullest sense of that word.

Shalom is God's single most important gift to humanity and creation; there is nothing God has to give that is not found within it. It is God's goal; the direction in which everything within the cosmos is heading:[24]

> Of God's all embracing kingdom
> and of God's *shalom* there shall be no end.[25]

Jesus' goal was to inaugurate the 'kingdom of God';[26] God's purpose is to establish *shalom* – they are identical.

First and foremost *shalom* is about relationships. The four core relationships that form *shalom* are: our relationship *with* God, *with* and *within* ourselves, *with* other people and *with* wild nature (living and inert).

When *shalom* is truly present, each of these is held in perfect balance, like a spiritual gyroscope, or the points of a compass to guide us.

For *shalom* to be fully present, three essential qualities must also be in place. They are:

- Physical and material well-being and dignity for all things;
- Justice in every relationship;
- Spiritual integrity and uprightness within each individual.[27]

Shalom is quite simply salvation[28] in the most complete and positive sense it is possible to imagine.[29] This indeed is hope. It declares how things should be and proclaims how things shall be. It challenges the status quo; it is the all-embracing promise for the future.

Be assured: we shall have a great deal more to say about *shalom* in the rest of this book.

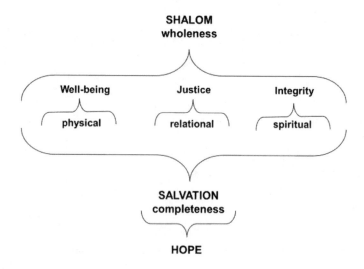

* * * * *

We look out into the vastness of deep space and ponder the question, 'What will be the ultimate fate of the universe?'

Will the 'big bang' reverse into a 'big crunch' with a return to dimensionless singularity?
Will the universe keep expanding, resulting in either a 'big freeze' or 'heat death'?
Will there be some final 'steady state' cosmos?
Will entropy finally win or might there be whole new dimensions of reality still to unfold?

An eminent astrophysicist speaks intriguingly of the current state of cosmological science being like 'the deep silence after a heavy snowfall'. 'We are waiting, and sensing something remarkable is about to happen in our understanding.'[30]

Jesus looks out into the future and speaks about 'the renewal of all things'. The early Christian community referred to 'the time of universal restoration'.[31] We have already mentioned, in the context of Jesus' baptism, Hebrew prophets proclaiming a 'renewed heaven and earth'.[32] Another early Christian voice says:

> But in accordance with God's promise,
> we wait for new heavens and a new earth,
> where righteousness is at home.[33]

For the nihilist a 'big crunch' or 'big freeze' is inevitable. The end is death and death is the end. For numerous religious people, existence beyond death is 'spiritual', whether it is *nirvana* or a paradise. For multitudes of Christians the goal is 'heaven', the destiny of the physical universe being irrelevant, even quoting, 'the heavens will be set ablaze and the elements will melt with fire'.[34]

Jesus challenges all these views head-on. The whole cosmos existing today has a destiny in God. This earth – this universe – will *not* be destroyed, but will experience complete re-creation. It will be renewed, not replaced; creation and humanity completely fulfilled and transformed.

You are not going to heaven. The biblical vision is that you will be part of a liberated community of humanity and wild nature integrating the heavenly and the earthly in a total holistic unity.

This is the 'New Age' that the tsunami wave of fire and Spirit, which we have already spoken about, is bringing in.

The key to this astonishing vision is found in the events surrounding the death of Jesus. The facts are tragic but straightforward. Jesus' liberated lifestyle and disturbing teaching were seen to threaten the authority of the *torah* and Temple upon which the fragile Jewish community depended for its identity and survival. The religious authorities saw only one solution: 'It is better to have one person die for the people than to have the whole nation destroyed.'[35] Jesus died, his body spread-eagled on a stake driven into the ground. However, the first Christians soon began to understand that the significance of these events went far beyond the unjust execution of a troublesome *rabbi*. They reflect:

> For in him all the fullness of God was pleased to dwell,
> and through him God was pleased to reconcile all things,
> whether on earth or in heaven,
> by making *shalom* through the blood of his cross.[36]

The early Christian community sees the cross on which Jesus is killed as the 'Tree of Life', an image that is central to both the primeval garden in Eden and the 'New Jerusalem' of the future.[37] Feeding on its fruit gives us immortality and we become like God, its leaves 'are for the healing of the nations'.[38] This is atonement in the truest sense of the word – 'at-one-ment' – the process by which enemies become friends.[39]

Jesus' death takes on cosmic implications. Three days after his burial the tomb in which his body had been placed was found empty – confronting us with the astonishing enigma of the resurrection.

However one seeks to understand the resurrection, this event is pivotal in the Jesus story and in our understanding of destiny.[40] The destructive power that we call evil, which tried to destroy Jesus and would potentially destroy the universe was forever broken by the power of the Spirit that raised Jesus from the dead.[41] This same Spirit, active in the original creation, is in the process of bringing about the re-creation of the cosmos:[42]

> God who raised Jesus from the dead
> will give life to your physical bodies as well,
> through the Spirit that lives in you.[43]

Jesus does not just die for people but for the whole creation. What is true for humanity is equally true for wild nature and the whole cosmos – our destinies are completely intertwined:

> For the creation waits with eager longing
> for the revealing of the children of God ...
> the creation itself will be set free from its bondage to decay
> and will obtain the freedom of the glory of the children of God.[44]

* * * * *

This cosmic vision of *shalom* climaxing in a renewed creation is awesome. However, our harsh experience of living each day with hatred, violence, suffering and death will lead many to believe it is just a fantasy.

Incredibly, *shalom* itself again provides the answer. We have seen that 'justice' is at its heart – this is the key. Justice is about what is 'fair' and 'right'. The Hebrew word it translates is *mishpat*, a powerful idea that means 'to put everything right'. This is also exactly the same word that is translated 'judgement'.

Judgement is the hinge upon which the door of hope swings.

Judgement creates the space for *shalom* to find fulfilment.

Both words – justice and judgement – disturb people because they link them to punishment and retribution. No, they are about the *process* of putting absolutely everything right. This *mishpat* process is already at work in the world, and God calls us to become involved in it (we will discuss this at greater length in our next chapter). However, *mishpat* comes to its climax in the events leading to the full transformation of the universe into the renewed heaven and earth.

The biblical language used to describe this cosmic transfiguration is disturbingly powerful; popular evangelists and many theologians have unscrupulously exploited it over the centuries, using it to generate fear rather than reflection. The purpose of the imagery is to communicate the thoroughgoing nature of God acting to put everything right. There are two primary pictures. The first is of seismic shaking, for example God says: 'I am about to shake the heavens and the earth, and to overthrow the throne of kingdoms.'[45] A time is imagined when God will take hold of the whole universe with both hands and shake the hell out of it.

The second image is of fire, as in these words:

> Then the heavens will pass away with a loud noise,
> and the elements will be dissolved with fire,
> the earth and everything that is done on it will be disclosed.[46]

This language is not to be taken literally; it is describing a reality impossible to put into words. This is not the destruction of the present universe but rather its total purification from evil, with every aspect of society being revealed for what it is. Then, along with the cosmos and wild nature, they are liberated, integrated and healed.

We work hard today to put things right, but this will finally be completed on what is symbolically called the 'Day of Judgement'.[47] Everyone who has ever lived will be part of this process. All those who have died will share in the resurrection experience pioneered by Jesus.

Remember *shalom* is first and foremost about relationships and *mishpat* about putting everything right.

The process of judgement is disturbing because when relationships are bitter, broken and hostile, reconciliation will be traumatic, deeply painful and full of anguish. Phrases like 'weeping and gnashing of teeth' with images of darkness and a lake of fire are not about destruction or annihilation as has been traditionally taught by some, but rather descriptions of the distress and agony of accepting responsibility for failure and harm, and the struggle towards authentic healing.

In our first chapter we argued that the biblical image of fire is always an expression of the love of God in its very purest form on every occasion it is used.

It is a consuming fire in terms of evil, a purifying fire in terms of relationships.

It is a fire of overwhelming, all-embracing love above all else.

To experience judgement is to be touched by God's fingerprint of fire.

You are not going to hell. The biblical imagery of 'hell' is about the total destruction of evil, not the eternal punishment of sinners.[48]

Universalism – which I believe to be our destiny from a Jesus perspective – is the conviction that God's grace, love and power will ultimately accomplish the full, complete and total salvation of all things in every dimension of creation. This is a huge topic for which we can only outline three basic principles here.[49]

First, Jesus speaks clearly about 'the renewal of all things'.[50] *Panta* is Greek for 'all things'; it means 'the totality of absolutely everything without exception'.

Second, if God exists the one thing we know is that God is love.[51] *Agape* is the Greek word for 'unconditional love' that was used by *rabbis* and early Christians. It speaks of a robust love, an overwhelming and all-embracing love, a love that is all-powerful yet never coercive, freely and sensitively winning every heart just as a lover does.[52] The principle is clear:

God will not take away a life; but will devise plans
so as not to keep an outcast banished forever
from God's presence.[53]

Here we see the passion of Jesus' life, death and resurrection, the work of the Spirit and our mission motivating God's universal salvation.

Finally, the centrepiece of universalism is judgement.

Mishpat is the moral *process* of putting everything right, not a legal *statement* about who is right and wrong. It is a spiritual and practical process to make relationships right, not a legal mechanism to punish wrongdoers.

This process involves bringing together all aggrieved parties into the presence of God, where the Spirit of truth discloses everything and nothing is hidden. The voice of the offended is clearly heard; those who have committed injustice are confronted with the harm they have inflicted. Everyone and everything that has suffered wrongdoing will be satisfied. Nothing whatever can or will be left unresolved.

This is no purgatory with its emphasis on individual purification, but rather the full restoration of relationships with all the vulnerability that involves, and the resulting anguish that needs to be assuaged. Today we see just a glimmer of the power of this process in the 'truth and reconciliation' movement and the work of 'restorative justice'.[54]

We have recognised the high levels of emotion and trauma such an experience of judgement will most certainly involve but, as the psalmist says: 'Weeping may endure for a night, but joy comes in the morning.'[55] When the process of judgement is complete, every person without exception will experience *shalom*.[56] True *mishpat* always means that after judgement: 'everyone will return to their home in *shalom*'.[57]

Universalism is popularly dismissed by mainstream Christians as a soft option in the light of the traditional view of judgement and punishment. However, properly understood it is by far the toughest option. It takes evil and its consequences seriously and does not cease working until every broken relationship is put right. It uniquely sees the extravagant goodness of God embrace every person and particle of the universe as part of the renewed heaven and earth.

The renewed universe shaped by this cosmic judgement will be in complete continuity with every good thing that already exists. There will be the total integration of the spiritual and divine with all that is material and physical.

Everything that is good from among the multitude of human cultures across the globe and throughout history will find its place within this new creation, every beautiful and enriching form of creativity included in this glorious life-giving festival of diversity:

> a great multitude that no one could count, from every nation, from all tribes and peoples and languages …[58]

Every aspect of wild nature – animal, plant and mineral, will be part of this creation reborn:

> Then I heard every creature in heaven and on earth and under the earth and in the sea, and all that is in them, singing …[59]

✶ ✶ ✶ ✶ ✶

I love walking in open countryside just before daybreak when the blue-black night sky reveals the faintest tinge of dawn. On a cloudless morning you will often see the spectacular light of the morning star, hanging like a jewel above the horizon, welcoming the new day. Its solitary beauty is stunning and you can see why it has captivated people for millennia. The early Christians used it as one of the images to describe Jesus as the focus of their hope, which they saw as:

a lamp shining in a dark place,
until the day dawns and the morning star rises in your hearts.[60]

To a 'Cosmic Visionary' this deep living hope is like the rim of dawn breaking over the curvature of the earth bringing in a new day beyond the darkness of the night. I am a child of the 'Morning Star', drawn towards this horizon of hope, inspired and energised to roll up my sleeves and work with God and all others of good will, in the power of the Spirit, to make this hope a reality. This is my calling and why I understand myself to be a '*Shalom* Activist'.

Endnotes

1 Of course this statement is both provocative and simplistic, but that does nothing to destroy its truth. I recognise that many indigenous cultures see existence as static, or better cyclical, where the current state of things is essentially permanent. However, science sees perpetual movement as a consequence of a 'big bang' with no place for a 'steady state' theory, to which even indigenous cultures are slowly having to accommodate themselves. Faiths such as Hinduism, Jainism and Buddhism with their belief that this world is *samsara* (a place of suffering, decay and death) and their goal being *nirvana* (lit. 'blowing out') seem to flow in a nihilist direction.

2 The word 'nihilism' comes from the Latin: *nihil*, which means 'nothing'. It appears to have been first used by Friedrich Jacobi (1743–1819) to characterise the Enlightenment negatively. It became popular when the Russian author Ivan Turgenev (1818–83) used it in his novel, *Fathers and Sons*, where one of the characters saw no meaning in anything. However, the ideas of *nihilism* predate the name by centuries.

3 Alan Moore says this through the character Rorschach in the graphic novel, *Watchman*, written by Alan Moore and Dave Gibbons, Titan Books, 1987.

4 The story is told in the Babylonian creation myth, the *Enuma Elish*. It continues to have a profoundly negative impact even in contemporary cultures. It not only provides a basis for nihilism, but it also supports the 'myth of redemptive violence'. Here a society justifies using organised violence against others on the assumption that unless they use violence to withstand an external threat they will in turn be overwhelmed by violence. The myth also hideously supports the idea that violence against women is acceptable.

5 Eccl 1:2–3; Qoheleth is the Hebrew name for the book and is best translated 'teacher' or 'philosopher'.

6 I recognise that this is a huge and important topic. However, it is not the purpose of this chapter or this book to develop it any further, but I would encourage the reader to give time to observe and think around the opinions I have expressed and draw considered conclusions about them.

7 Mk 4:35–41; Mt 8:23–27; Lk 8:22–25.

8   Quoted by Alexander Pope, 'Hope springs eternal in the human breast' in *An Essay on Man* in Epistle 1 in 1733, but he is believed to be quoting a much older and well-established English proverb.
9   Tragically we see this in suicide, in some cases of mental illness or certain types of brain injury, and for some it is a consequence of aging.
10 Whether *nirvana*, a paradise or heaven.
11 According to Hesiod, the Greek poet; yet another Greek poet, Theognis, gives an alternative version of the story in which the contents of the jar are blessings (probably based on an earlier version than Hesiod), and therefore 'hope' is good. This has become the most popular understanding of the story.
12 For this interpretation see Friedrich Nietzsche, *Human, All Too Human*, Penguin Classics, 1994,
13 See 1Pt 1:3.
14 See Col 1:27; 1Tim 1:1; Mt 12:21 (quoting Isa 42:1–6).
15 Biblical words most usually translated hope are: *betach* (Hebrew) and *elpis* (Greek). This hope is 'confidence in God whose goodness and mercy are to be relied on and whose promises cannot fail' (see Allan Barr, 'Hope in the New Testament', *Scottish Journal of Theology*, 3, 1950, p. 72.)
16 See 2Cor 6:1 (also Jn 5:17; 1Cor 3:6) and 2Pt 3:12.
17 See Heb 6:19.
18 See Prov 23:18; Rom 8:19, 23.
19 See Ps 130:5, 7; Rom 8:25.
20 See Rom 4:18; Abraham 'hoped against hope' and hoped when everything had turned to dust.
21 See John Cook, *The Book of Positive Quotations*, Fairview Press, 1997.
22 In using the word *shalom*, I wish to stress that I am very aware of the words of Rabbi Steven Schwarzschild and the cultural reality behind them when he says, 'I, for one, avoid the use of *shalom* as a Hebrew greeting these days. Among some Jews it seems to have become the introduction to advocacy for greater militarism, and among some Christians it seems to have become a cover-word for maudlin sentimentality or apologetic ecumenism' – see his chapter 'Shalom' in M Polner and N Goodman (eds), *The Challenge of Shalom*, New Society Publishers, 1994, p. 24, n. 4.
23 In most cases this is quite inadequate, depending on how you understand the word 'peace'. Most people's popular conception of 'peace' has simply become:
   • *Personalised:* my own deep inner feeling of peace;
   • *Pacified:* a nice, comfortable, relaxed and tranquil experience;
   • *Marginalised:* peace seen as primarily the absence of war;
   • *Idealised:* a goal to aim for, but not a realistic expectation.
   Shalom, in contrast, cannot be domesticated like this.
24 See Num 6:24–26 and other passages. We shall develop this more when we talk about being a *Values Master*.
25 Isa 9:7. Please note that in my paraphrase of this first couplet of the whole verse I have replaced the word 'government' or 'authority' with 'kingdom', which is mentioned in the second couplet simply to make my point that *shalom* and the 'kingdom of God' are identical, which this verse as a whole illustrates powerfully.
26 Mt 4:23; 9:35; Lk 8:1; Mk 1:14–15 are just a few of numerous examples.
27 These three primary characteristics of *shalom*, and the way I have presented them, are broadly based on drawing together ideas originally found in Perry Yoder, *Shalom: The Bible's Word for Salvation, Justice and Peace*, Faith and Life Press, 1987, pp. 10–23 and Claus Westermann, 'Peace (Shalom) in the Old Testament', in PB Yoder and WM Swartley (eds), *The Meaning of Peace*, 2nd edn, IMS, Elkhart, 2001, pp. 37–70.

28 I have been hesitant to use the word 'salvation'. For me it is a powerful and positive word but I know that for many it is viewed, consciously or unconsciously, with a certain aura of menace; a 'carrot' but in the shadow of a 'big stick'. Generations of popular evangelists and traditional theologians have used the word in contrast to death, judgement, hell and eternal punishment and in doing so have contaminated it with their emphasis on the majority being excluded and the minority included. I want to show that while it does have a sense of saving us from the destructive evil we currently experience in the world, it is primarily about bringing everything and everyone into a 'spacious life-giving environment' (see for example EMB Green, *The Meaning of Salvation*, Hodder, 1965, pp. 11–33). See also endnote 29 in the *New Age Traveller* chapter.

29 Erich Dinkler observes: 'From the beginning one is confronted with whether to translate *shalom* as 'peace' or 'salvation', in 'Eirene – The Early Christian Concept of Peace', in PB Yoder and WM Swartley (eds), *The Meaning of Peace*, 2nd edn, IMS, Elkhart, 2001, p. 74.

30 BBC 'Beautiful Minds', broadcast 12 April 2010. Prof. Jocelyn Bell Burnell is the astrophysicist who discovered 'pulsars'; she is a Quaker.

31 See Mt 19:28 and Acts 3:21. In both cases the same Greek word, *palingenesia*, is used, translated here as 'renewal' and 'restoration' respectively.

32 Isa 65:17–18; cf. 66:22; note that the Hebrew word for 'new' is *chadash* and can express both the ideas of completely new and, as in this case, 'renewed'. The Hebrew phrase 'heaven and earth' is a merism, a figure of speech where naming two opposites, like 'heaven and earth', implies totality, absolutely everything. Here, of course, it has the idea of the totality of the cosmos or universe, but the way the ideas are used shows that it also includes 'heaven' as the dwelling place of God. Hence, the sense of complete totality – everything spiritual and physical, earthly and heavenly, human and divine.

33 2Pt 3:13. There are two words for new in Greek. There is *neos* which refers to something 'completely new, never having existed before', and *kainos* which refers to something 'completely renewed, the old made new again'. It is the word *kainos* that is used here.

34 2Pet 3:12; see also v. 10; we shall be bringing an alternative understanding to these words below.

35 Jn 11:50, the words of the High Priest Caiaphas.

36 Col 1:19–20; the Hebrew word *shalom* and its meaning is implied in the use of the Greek word *eirene* for 'peace' in this text.

37 See 1Pt 2:24; Acts 5.30; 10:39; 13:29; Rev 2:7; 22:2, 14.

38 See Rev 22:2.

39 'Atonement' means 'at one', 'to bring together', 'to reconcile'; it is one of the few Anglo-Saxon words to have found its way into theology. It has become sullied by being used in the many doctrinal views surrounding the death of Jesus. I believe its truest meaning is to be found in its purest original form.

40 The resurrection of Jesus is a huge subject to be handled very sensitively. The traditional attempts to discredit it – a lie made up by early Christians; Jesus swoons on the cross, people thinking he was dead; the body stolen (by the gardener, the disciples, Joseph of Arimathea, the Jews or Romans); the disciples hallucinated, or they went to the wrong tomb – do not explain it. Something profound happened! Literal-historical explanations alone do not begin to do the subject justice. Explanations that stress the spiritual realities at work remind us of the profound mystery we are confronted with that transcends crude explanations. However, a physical event woven into time and space seems important in the light of its link to the events that will ultimately bring about the renewed heaven and earth. See the conversation in Robert B

Stewart, *The Resurrection of Jesus: The Crossan-Wright Dialogue*, SPCK, 2006.

41 The use of the word 'evil' is fraught with difficulty. There is pain and suffering that comes from our inability to live wisely within a challenging world and there is moral evil that comes from our wilfulness in relation to others. The origin of evil is given no direct biblical explanation, but certainly predates human activity in the world. Evil is powerfully personal but we must be cautious in the use of imagery like 'the devil', 'Satan' or 'Lucifer' and the traditional ideas that have grown around them. We are dealing with a mystery – while at the same time a real and serious reality – but a mystery none the less (2Th 2:7 speaks of 'the mystery of lawlessness/ wickedness').

42 Gen 1:2 'the Spirit of God moved across the face of the waters'.

43 Rom 8:11.

44 Rom 8:19, 21.

45 Hag 2:21–22, see also v. 6; and Heb 12:27.

46 2Pt 3:10, see also Mic 1:4; Joel 2:30–31.

47 The phrase 'The Day of the Lord' is mentioned some 200 times in the Hebrew scriptures alone. The Gospels have a number of references to Jesus referring to 'that day' or 'on that day' (cf. Mt 25:13; Lk 17:22–35; 21:34 *et al.*). There are similar expressions such as, 'the day of Jesus Christ' (Phil 1:6 cf. 1Cor 1:8; 5:5; 2Cor 1:14), also 'the day of the Lord' and 'the day of judgement' (cf. 1Th 5:2; 2Th 2:2; Rom 2:16; 1Cor 3:13 *et al.*).

48 The word 'hell' has to be handled very carefully:
- It is likely the English word comes from the Nordic *Hel*, name of the unlovely goddess of the sunless region where souls unworthy of Valhalla were relegated. Others see it as a corruption of *Gehenna* (see below).
- On most occasions 'hell' is used neutrally, to refer to 'the place where the dead are' (i.e. Hebrew: *sheol* and Greek: *hades*).
- It is also used to translate the Hebrew *ge hinnom* (Latin: *gehenna*), literally 'the valley of the sons of Hinnom', on the west side of Jerusalem; the rubbish tip where everything foul was destroyed, including pagan idols during the reforms of Hezekiah and Josiah (cf. Mt 10:28).
- Finally, it becomes the symbol of the total and absolute destruction of evil in all its forms, not of people.

The traditional view of 'hell' gained most of its influence by Christians adopting the Greek idea of the 'immortality of the soul', which is not biblical. We do not '*have* a soul', rather 'we *are* a soul', which is alive only as a body. This is why the resurrection is so important. Only God is immortal (cf. 1Tim 1:17); we are immortal only because God has given us the gift of eternal life, a consequence of resurrection and judgement. This invalidates the traditional understanding of 'hell'.

49 For a very brief overview of my approach and understanding see my short paper on 'Universalism' at <www.galilee.org.uk/Universalism%20PPoints/Universalism2.doc>, and my *Activist Universalism: A Workbook on Living Hope* (forthcoming). A helpful introduction to the subject is Gregory MacDonald, *The Evangelical Universalist*, SPCK, 2008; he does not take my *shalom/ mishpat* approach and I feel that his dealing with judgement/ hell is inadequate, but nevertheless his book is a good place to start.

50 Mt 19:28 and Acts 3:21 and see endnote 30 above.

51 See 1Jn 4:7–8, 16, see also Lam 3:22, 31–33; Ezk 33:11.

52 This love, free of coercion, focuses the challenge against universalism. Some argue that to say every person will be saved demands that some will have to be coerced, because it is inevitable that some will resist God's love. If coercion

were necessary, the outcome would never be *shalom* and God might as well have created us as automatons without the requirement of free will. Others deny universalism because some people will resist God's love and therefore require annihilation along with evil, but Jesus has said, 'If I am lifted up I will draw all things to myself' (Jn 12:32). 'All things' is exactly what it says, 'absolutely everything'. Neither universalism without free will, nor universalism that is not totally successful, is a Jesus-focused understanding of universalism

53 2Sam 14:14, see also Lam 3:22, 31–33 *et al.*
54 These are two very important and widely debated topics. Here are some initial resources:
 Desmond Tutu, *No Future Without Forgiveness*, Rider, 2000. See http://theforgivenessproject.com/
 Howard Zehr, *The Little Book of Restorative Justice*, Intercourse, PA: Good Books, 2002.
 Marian Liebmann, *Restorative Justice: How It Works*, London: Jessica Kingsley, 2007.
55 Ps 30:5.
56 See Temba L Mafico in 'Judge, Judging' and 'Just, Justice' in *The Anchor Bible Dictionary*, vol. 3, Doubleday, 1992, pp. 1106, 1128 – '*mishpat* refers to the restoration of *shalom* ... judges are the restorers of *shalom* ... Originally *mishpat* referred to the restoration of a situation or environment which promoted equity and harmony, that is – *shalom* – in a community'.
57 Exod 18:23; see also Zech 8:16 where the consequence of *mishpat* is to be truth and *shalom.*
58 Rev 7:9.
59 Rev 5:13.
60 2Pt 1:19; see also Num 24:17; Job 38:7; Rev 2:28; 22:16.

Shalom Activist
– working with passion for wholeness

Working for peace is really hard work. Peacemaking means getting up every single day and working hard for global peace. It's not doves or nice paintings or bad poetry; it's very creative hard work every day. And that's the only way to make the world better.[1]

These are the words of Jody Williams – the 1997 Nobel Peace Prize winner for her work to ban landmines.[2]

Jesus declares, 'Blessed are the peacemakers.'[3] The English wording can sound rather sentimental. 'Blessed' translates the Greek *makarios*, which in turn translates the Aramaic *ashray* (from the verb *yashar*), which Jesus would have used. Elias Chacour, the Palestinian Melkite Archbishop of Galilee whose mother tongue is Aramaic, says the word means 'to set yourself up on the right way for the right goal; to turn around, repent; to become straight or righteous'.[4] What Jesus is actually saying is:

> Get up, go ahead, do something, move, you peacemakers, for you shall be called the children of God.

'Get involved! Get your hands dirty!' Only in the activism of peacemaking will you find the true joy and blessings of *shalom*.[5]

We have already seen that *shalom* is actually a verb masquerading as a noun; there is nothing passive about it. It is dynamic, pulsing with energy. Over the years I have tried to shape phrases that draw me closer to both its power and its paradox. *Shalom* is:

> 'Extravagant sufficiency'
> 'Energised wholeness'
> 'Dynamic tranquillity'
> 'Integrated diversity'
> 'Resonating relationships'

'Exuberant fecundity'[6]
'Explosive calm'.

Encountering *shalom* is seismic; I call this 'shalom-shock'. Its impact is always as traumatic as it is life-giving. Jesus illustrates this in his teaching and actions – including his death and resurrection – confronting people with *shalom* in a way that disturbs and challenges.

A wealthy young aristocrat asked to follow Jesus. 'Yes, but sell everything you own first and give it to the poor.' Devastated, he walked away sorrowful; money was too precious to him. The shock of *shalom* hit him hard.[7]

There is a secular Hebrew phrase, *tikkun olam*, which literally means 'repairing the world'.[8] The true task of every person is to work to put right what is wrong in the world. It requires physical hard work, but is profoundly spiritual work. In the words of the Quaker, William Penn: 'True godliness does not turn people out of the world, but enables them to live better in it, and excites their endeavours to mend it.'[9]

Authentic spirituality always gives birth to an activist.

We are told to 'pray for peace'.[10] This opens us up to the divine and makes us sensitive to spiritual possibilities. Yet prayer must lead to work, which is itself also prayer.[11] Tenzin Gyatso (the fourteenth Dali Lama), says, 'I have become sceptical, I do not believe that meditation and prayer will change this world. I think what we need is action.'[12]

We are told that 'Faith without works is dead'.[13] Faith is not about believing a set of abstract propositions; rather it understands certain things to be true and acts on them, proving them to be correct:

> Faith is making the things we hope for become a
> substantial reality,
> it is giving firm evidence for things we cannot yet see.[14]

Clarence Jordan, the activist scholar, translated these words as 'Faith is turning dreams into deeds'.[15] In practice, 'faith is making happen what God wants to happen'.[16]

Faith and hope are welded together almost interchangeably in biblical thought. Both require action; hope refusing to leave any stone unturned to achieve its goal. As Aung San Suu Kyi, the Burmese leader, puts it, 'I don't believe in hope without endeavour.'[17]

We are told to 'seek peace and pursue it'.[18] We are to use all our wit, cunning and wisdom to make *shalom*, however elusive, a reality, learning to read the spiritual, moral, social and political landscape like a hunter–gatherer tracking through an impenetrable wilderness.

So peacemaking requires an enormous amount of physical and emotional hard work, plus creative intellectual skill.[19] Like a blacksmith at the anvil we are to sweat and toil strenuously:

> They shall beat their swords into ploughshares
> and their spears into pruning hooks.[20]

Shalom has to be crafted out of raw and often resistant materials; this requires wisdom soaked in perspiration,[21] shaped by a commitment to love and gentleness and hallmarked by a total absence of violence.[22]

✳ ✳ ✳ ✳ ✳

It is war. An ancient Greek city is paralysed with fear. Every able-bodied man is fighting on a distant battlefield. The citizens are tense. What will be their fate? Watchmen, high on the walls, strain their eyes, searching for a messenger from the conflict bringing news.

Suddenly, far on the horizon sharp eyes identify a runner. Soon his animated gestures are visible – leaping, waving, and clearly shouting with joy. The mood in the city is expectant. The exhausted messenger enters the central forum and in a powerful voice proclaims the single word, 'Peace!' Euphoria overwhelms the population.

This messenger is an 'evangelist' – the Greek word for anyone who brings *good* news.[23] Their message – the *euanggelion* – (translated as 'gospel' in the New Testament) – is peace. The Greeks believed that when the 'evangelist' actually spoke the word, peace physically embraced the community.

I have said that being a '*Shalom* Activist' is our mission.[24] We are to be 'evangelists' proclaiming our message – 'the gospel of peace' – expecting it to become a reality as a result of our words and actions.[25] This was the understanding of the early Jesus-community. They said of him: '[Jesus] came proclaiming peace to you who were far off and peace to those who were near.'[26]

They remembered Jesus sending them out into the towns and villages of the countryside with clear instructions: 'Whatever house you go into, let your first words be, "Peace to this house!" And if a person of peace lives there, your peace will remain upon them.'[27]

They were inspired by the vision of the Hebrew prophet Isaiah who pictures God running, leaping and dancing across hilltops and mountains, leading a group of bedraggled and vulnerable people home from exile proclaiming one single word, '*Shalom!*' It was said of God and all who follow the divine example:

> How beautiful on the mountains,
> are the feet of the one who brings good news,
> who heralds *shalom.*[28]

God is the 'God of peace';[29] we are to be 'people of peace'[30] and our message is the 'gospel of peace'.[31] Notice also the fascinating link across the biblical texts between 'peace' and 'feet'.[32] Our message of peace to the earth is to be a physical reality; the link implies connection, balance and movement – all essential for activism. The '*Shalom* Activist' always leaves footprints of peace.[33]

* * * * *

Before exploring *shalom* activism further we need to pause and consider three potential challenges to what I have said in this chapter so far.

Some people who read these words will already be disappointed and struggling with faith. The call to work to change the world in the light of the *shalom*-vision will seem just another pressure. The challenge remains; however, God always begins where we are and asks only for what we can genuinely offer. Think of 'bite-sized' actions that are personally doable, remembering that Jesus speaks of being like 'yeast' or 'mustard-seeds' that are seemingly insignificant yet dramatic in their impact.[34] However, never let anyone manipulate you by guilt or pressure into any action.

Authentic activism flows from deep inner desire, and always brings joy.

Linked closely to this is a belief by some that the spiritual-heavenly is more important than the physical-earthly. This tension has plagued Christian thinking for most of its history. It was caused by outside influences like Gnosticism, which taught that the physical is evil, and neo-Platonism that saw our material world as an inferior shadow of a greater spiritual reality elsewhere. This has no place in the holistic spirituality of Jesus. Working to change this kind of thinking is part of working to change the world.

Third, others will ask, 'What about all those people from other faiths and beliefs, who work for powerful life-affirming change through activism; often shaming Christians with their passion, courage and achievements?' Jesus is quite clear, 'Whoever is not against us is on our side.'[35] Enough said! Sadly many *will* be against us; including people of faith, indeed some within the church.

So we celebrate all who share our passion for wholeness and embrace them. The title '*Shalom* Activist' is there for all who are working to establish the life-giving values of *shalom* whatever their creed.

Loren Wilkinson, a Christian living on Vancouver Island in Canada, tells how with his wife and daughter he became involved in a protest-blockade against the logging of an ancient forest near their home. The local Pagan community were leading the action, with the nonviolent resistance techniques being taught by a grandmotherly Wiccan priestess. Together they shared the hardship, abuse and daily arrests, bonded by their commitment to save the forest and their love for the earth. He remarks on the beautiful spiritual intensity of the whole event. During times of singing they taught the group the tune to 'You shall go out with joy, and be led forth in peace, and the trees of the field will clap their hands' from Isaiah 55; the protesters were surprised to discover these were biblical words. In return Loren and his family developed a deep respect for the spiritual integrity of the Pagan group.[36]

Jesus himself refers to just such people as 'people of peace'.[37] We honour them and are privileged to work shoulder to shoulder with them, encouraging each other in the task. We shall return to this theme in a later chapter.

* * * * *

From a Jesus perspective, *shalom* is the Christian message in its totality. We have already seen that it is both the centre and the boundary of all that God is, the entirety of what God has to give, and everything God plans to achieve. It is salvation in the most complete sense, the fullness of the kingdom of God. It is very much more than salvation from death; it is life in all its fullness. It declares how things should be and affirms how things shall be. *Shalom* is the 'living hope' of ultimate cosmic destiny. It is the centre of God's purpose for both society and creation. It is everything flowing together in harmony: all peoples, all social structures, and the whole material universe. *Shalom* cascades from the centre of all things, soaking the liminal spaces, saturating the margins and flooding the extremities.[38]

Yet translating *shalom* as 'peace' will mean different things to different people, anything from personal tranquillity to the absence of war. How should we understand it?

We have seen that the root meaning of *shalom* is: 'to make complete' – 'wholeness' 'intactness', 'integratedness' – it is 'holistic', everything fitting perfectly and harmoniously together.[39]

One of the difficulties with a value like 'peace' is it can appear to float above us like a wisp of soft white cloud on a summer's day, beautiful to look at but high above us and simply out of reach. What is exciting about *shalom* is that the biblical text gives very practical ways to measure the extent it is actually present in every area of life – personally, locally, regionally, nationally, globally and cosmically – like a builder using a spirit level, measuring-rule, or plumb line to see if a wall is straight. We have already seen that for *shalom* to be present three essential factors are required, like a three-fold intertwined cord:[40]

- *Shalom* demands physical and material well-being and dignity for all things
- *Shalom* insists that every relationship is just and right
- *Shalom* requires that each person has spiritual integrity and uprightness in character.

Shalom is present only to the extent that each one of these qualities is found; they must shape our work in the world *today* as we live and struggle to establish *shalom*.

We have also stressed that *shalom* is first and foremost about relationships: touching, embracing and energising every possible life-link – our relationship *with* God, our relationship *with* and *within* ourselves, our relationship *with* other people and *with* wild nature. Peacemaking is of course also opposed to every form of violence.

✳ ✳ ✳ ✳ ✳

The 'leper priest' Damien de Veuster died on the Hawaiian island of Molokai in 1889, his body ravaged by the disease. Sixteen years earlier he had chosen to come to this government leper colony where people were forcibly exiled for life for fear of contagion. Given little more than food, with no medical attention, the abandoned group of over 800 people descended into violence, drunkenness and despair. Damien established order, built homes, a school and a hospital; he dressed ulcers, made coffins and dug graves. He organised farming, but above all he created a spiritual focus around which this broken and dying community gathered. He gave both faith and hope to the outcasts, restoring among them a positive sense of identity and dignity. He said, 'My greatest pleasure is to serve the Lord among his poor children rejected by other people.'[41]

It is essential that people's material needs be met.[42]

Every person and all living things must have enough to thrive.

People should have food to eat, clothes to wear, a home to live in, with the ability to provide for themselves and others. They are entitled to enjoy physical health and emotional stability as well as feeling secure. 'A person is bereft of *shalom* when their human dignity is denied.'[43]

Most people first encounter *shalom* as a greeting, '*Shalom aleichem*' ('Peace be upon you'); however, some scholars now believe the word was originally a question, '*Shalom*? – Is everything well with you? Do you have everything you need?'[44] In a world where …

- Half the population live on less than two dollars a day;
- Poverty and starvation are global;
- Millions of children die every year from preventable illnesses;
- Most children are denied an education;

- War and disease leave orphans, widows, refugees and asylum seekers in their wake;
- Millions are degraded by slavery and often trafficked for sex or labour;
- Prisoners are tortured and regularly 'disappeared';
- The poorest people live in huge urban slums with neither sanitation nor employment;
- Unequal political and economic structures benefit the west at the expense of the poor

... the answer to the question is, 'No!'

In forming a *shalom* response these words from the Hebrew scriptures help us to focus: 'Learn to do good; seek justice, rescue the oppressed, defend the orphan, plead for the widow.'[45] Of course similar reflections are found in other faiths as well:

It is a person's obligation always to share with others from whatever they possess – *Hinduism*[46]

Noble people find joy in generosity – *Buddhism*[47]

Worship Allah, and do good to orphans and the needy – *Islam*[48]

Blessed is the godly person and the riches they possess because they can be used for charitable purposes and to give happiness – *Sikhism*[49]

We know that to help the poor and to be merciful is good and pleases God
... we must give the practical help of loving-kindness – *Baha'i*[50]

Jesus travelled Palestine, 'doing good ... for God was with him'[51] – feeding the hungry, healing the sick and resuscitating the dead. He made it quite clear in words and actions:

Blessed are the poor for yours is the kingdom of God.
When you give a feast, invite the poor, the maimed, the lame, the blind,
and you will be blessed because they cannot repay you.[52]

The earliest Christian communities followed Jesus' example in sharing their resources:

...all who believed were together
and had all things in common ...
There was no needy person among them,
for as many as possessed land or houses sold them ...
and distribution was made to each as any had need.[53]

There was no coercion or obligation to act like this, just the joy of
giving to meet the needs of others, an attitude of heart expressed
in the Greek word *koinonia*,[54] which has the sense of 'sharing
equally together'.

During the first three centuries this *shalom-koinonia* continued to
be the hallmark of the early Jesus-community. They gave food and
money to the destitute, widows and orphans and hospitality to
strangers. They would bury the poor when they died, care for
prisoners, fast so that others might eat; some even sold
themselves into slavery to use the money to feed the hungry.
Everyone was treated equally because that is exactly how God
treats us.[55]

What motivates *shalom* to reach out and meet the physical needs
of others is love.

The key biblical Hebrew word is *chesed*, usually translated 'loving-
kindness' or 'mercy', also 'faithfulness' and 'covenant love'. The
early Jesus-community translated it with the Greek word *agape*.
This is first and foremost the love God has for us and we are to
have for God, but it provides the source for every other expression
of love. It is selfless and self-giving, robust yet gentle and all-
embracing.[56]

✳ ✳ ✳ ✳ ✳

Today our world is so changed, yet changed so little. Thousands
are working tirelessly to give the poor and the powerless a 'life
before death'.[57] However, many have come to believe that the real
need is to change the very structures of society in the direction of
social justice, so that the poor, and in fact all humanity, are
empowered and liberated.

This is dramatically and poignantly expressed in the oft-quoted
words of 'the bishop of the slums', the Brazilian Dom Helder
Camara: 'When I feed the poor they call me a saint, when I ask,
'Why are they poor?' they call me a communist.'[58]

Jesus sets the scene by reading his 'manifesto' words from a scroll of the prophet Isaiah in his home synagogue in Nazareth:

> The Spirit of the Lord is upon me,
> because God has anointed me
> to preach good news to the poor.
> I have been sent to proclaim release to the captives
> and recovering of sight to the blind,
> to set at liberty those who are oppressed,
> to proclaim the acceptable year of the Lord.[59]

The phrase, 'acceptable year of the Lord' refers to the 'year of Jubilee', which Jews were expected to practise every fifty years; a time when the soil rested, all debt was cancelled, slaves were released and all property was returned to its rightful owner. Its purpose was to challenge deep selfish attitudes and transform society. However, it was an idea so radical many doubt it was ever practised.[60]

Jesus makes the 'Jubilee' idea central to his work. He demonstrates that social justice – *mishpat* – is at the heart of a biblical understanding of *shalom*,[61] 'putting everything right'; liberating, empowering and healing, establishing just relationships between individuals, within communities, nations and every aspect of creation, both as a present reality and as a future hope. His words are clear: 'Get up, go ahead, do something, move, you who hunger and thirst for justice, for you shall be satisfied.'[62]

An early Christian voice makes another strong link between peacemaking and justice: 'A harvest of justice is sown in peace for those who make peace.'[63] We are urged to roll up our sleeves and 'seek *shalom* and pursue it'.[64] We are to: 'Seek the *shalom* of the city for in its *shalom* you will find your *shalom*.'[65]

Remember the city in question was ancient Babylon. It becomes the biblical symbol to represent every anti-God system and society.[66] So the idea of *shalom* transfiguring Babylon is the promise of the ultimate transformation of all such systems and the goal towards which we work.

God's original plan was for human societies to organise themselves in communities living in harmony with God, within themselves, with one another and wild nature; expressing all the diversity that tribes, nations and languages bring.

The idea of the State – with its centralisation of power in a ruler or system of government, controlling a specific geographical area and guaranteeing order by the use of force – is seen biblically as an act of treachery.[67]

With devastating simplicity Jesus reveals the State for what it is:

Consider the flowers of the field how they grow ...yet I tell you, even Solomon in all his glory was not clothed like one of these.[68]

The phrase 'Solomon in all his glory' is a euphemism for the whole State system and its arrogant promise to meet anxious people's needs. Jesus unmasks it, offering an alternative – a community that trusts in God while living wild and free like nature itself.

The State is about power and the way it connects with the institutions and structures that order society. Biblically these institutions and structures are seen to be an expression of 'principalities and powers' – the point at which the social, political and spiritual interconnect.[69] These powers are part of the natural order of things and originally were good, but have become perverted by both evil and the State, creating a 'domination system' of injustice that *mishpat* challenges. These powers tried to destroy Jesus but his resurrection broke their stranglehold.[70]

The situation is both complex and a paradox. In some countries, the State is openly destructive while in others it appears benign, but the early Christians had no illusions about the status quo.

The State is a servant. We are told all authority comes from God and those who exercise it are responsible to God and unwittingly God's servants. Having usurped power the State carries responsibility for how it uses it. God permits this flawed system in order to provide some temporary stability for societies, 'restraining lawlessness' and so hopefully setting limits on evil. We respect those who carry the responsibilities of power and pray for them. Where governments do good for their citizens they are to be praised and encouraged, but where they fail they are to be called to account. Nevertheless, we work for their overthrow and replace them with God's ultimate rule of *shalom*.[71]

The State is a beast. This is the true nature of all 'domination systems'. The visionary writer of the book of Revelation sees the State as a dragon desiring total power and deification, overstepping all limits. We must recognise this is the actual reality we are dealing with and must always be alert never letting the State's antichrist character seduce us.[72]

Radical political engagement involves devising plans and schemes that confront these concentrations of power in societies that stifle spirituality and humanity; strategies, which are creatively imagined, fearlessly executed and beautiful in their outcome.[73]

- Politics for the '*Shalom* Activist' is spiritual work leading to practical outcomes.
- Politics is about structuring, enabling and empowering community.
- Politics must involve building cultures of *shalom*.
- Politics requires a ferocious love that endeavours to draw difference into dialogue.

This work is costly. Quakers call it being a 'Testimony to the Truth', which leads them to 'speak truth to power'.[74] This creative confrontation has its background in the stories of Hebrew prophets who stood before kings and challenged them, exampling the principle: 'The one who rebukes boldly makes *shalom*.'[75]

Jesus is clear that this is our calling: 'You will stand before governors and kings because of me, as a testimony to them.'[76] The Muslim community quote Muhammad as saying: 'The best kind of *jihad* (struggle) is speaking truth to a tyrant.'[77] To do this requires integrity of character, plus courage in conviction and behaviour. Aung San Suu Kyi has said, 'Courage is grace under pressure ... grace renewed repeatedly under harsh unremitting pressure'.[78]

In 1942 Sophie Scholl was a 21-year-old student at the University of Munich at the heart of Hitler's Germany and at the height of the Third Reich. She joined a secret group, the 'White Rose', made up of eight students and a lecturer carrying out nonviolent resistance to the Nazi regime. Their main strategy was distributing leaflets condemning National Socialism, but they also painted anti-Nazi slogans on walls. The leaflets caused a major stir in many parts of the country. In 1943 Sophie, her brother Hans and their friend Christoph Probst were betrayed to the Gestapo. At their trial the judge raged at them, while they responded with quiet dignity. Their personal faith was clear as they challenged the government. They were condemned to death and beheaded within an hour of sentencing. Walking up to the guillotine Sophie declared, 'How can we expect righteousness to prevail when there is hardly anyone willing to give themselves up individually to a righteous cause? Such a fine, sunny day, and I have to go, but what does my death matter, if through us thousands of people are awakened and stirred to action?'[79]

✳ ✳ ✳ ✳ ✳

There is a moving Jewish legend, the *Lamed Vav Zadikim*,[80] which tells how in every generation there are thirty-six just and righteous people who share the pain of the world with God.[81] Because of them the world exists and without them the world could not continue; their presence prevents God's heart from breaking. Each *zadik* ('righteous one') is marked by humility. They work in secret and are hidden; they would never acknowledge being one of the *Lamed Vav Tzadikim* (and might not even know).[82] Some Jewish thinkers believe the Messiah is probably among them. The reward for their anonymous work is to have direct experience of the *Shekinah* (the unique presence of the Spirit of God) upon them.[83]

For me, one example of a *zadik* is John Woolman,[84] a Quaker who challenged slavery, armed conflict and championed Native American rights. He was an environmentalist with a passion for animal welfare. It has been said of him:

> He wrestled with the knotty issues of war and peace, race and equality, wealth and simplicity, with a striking blend of compassion with courage, tenderness and firmness. And he did this not in some detached, academic way, but right in the midst of the vicissitudes of life. John Woolman was a prophet for his day, a prophet who took the Quaker testimonies for equality, simplicity, and peace and forged them into instruments of social revolution, ever tempering them in the stream of 'Divine Love'.[85]

As '*Shalom* Activists' we are each called to be *zadik*, working to establish *mishpat*; people whose characters are marked by godliness, righteousness and holiness.[86]

Endnotes

1   This is a slightly composite quote from Jody Williams found in John Dear, *Put*

Down Your Sword: Answering the Gospel Call to Creative Nonviolence, Eerdmans, 2008, p. 135 and *Jody Williams: A Realistic Vision for World Peace* video on <www.TED.com>, recorded December 2010.

2   Jody Williams was born in Vermont, USA, in 1950. She learned to hate injustice at an early age when she saw her fellow school children ruthlessly bullying her brother who was deaf and suffered from schizophrenia. In October 1992, after doing humanitarian peace work in Central America, she became the founding coordinator of the International Campaign to Ban Landmines (ICBL) for which she jointly received the Nobel Peace Prize along with the organisation itself.

3   See Matt 5:9.

4   See Elias Chacour, *We Belong to the Land*, HarperCollins, 1992, pp. 143–4. Elias Chacour is the Archbishop of Akko, Haifa, Nazareth and Galilee of the Melkite Greek Catholic Church; born in 1939 in Biram in Upper Galilee, he has dedicated his life to working for peace between Palestinians and Israelis.

5   'Peace is therefore deeply embedded in the teachings and doctrines of the major religious traditions of the world … each of them has proclaimed peace – as an ultimate value, not only as a hallmark of the final eschatological goal that humans could and were destined to reach, but also an individual mental and collective social state that is always worthy to pursue.' See Perry Schmidt-Leukel in *Part of the Problem – Part of the Solution: An Introduction* in *War and Peace in World Religions*, SCM Press, 2004, p. 3.

6   'Fecundity' is a word used in farming to describe fertility and fruitfulness; it is used in art for something that shines with life, is teeming with energy and creativity, is prolific and very much more!

7   See Mk 10:17–22; Mt 19:16–22; cf. Lk 18:18–30.

8   The word *tikkun* comes from a root meaning 'to arrange' or 'to put in order', and *olam* means 'the world'. The phrase *tikkun olam* has its origins in the *Kabbalah*, but in the 1950s it moved from Jewish mysticism to be used by social activists.

9   William Penn, *No Cross, No Crown*, 1771.

10   See for instance Ps 122:6–9; 1Tim 2:1–4.

11   The phrase 'work is prayer' is often erroneously attributed to Benedict of Nursia, founder of the Benedictine order; in fact the origin of the expression remains unknown.

12   Quoted by Jody Williams in *Jody Williams: A Realistic Vision for World Peace* video on <www.TED.com>, recorded December 2010.

13   See Jas 2:17, 20, 26.

14   This is my paraphrase of Heb 11:1, which is usually translated, 'Faith is the assurance (*hypostasis*) of things hoped for, the conviction (*eleuchos*) of things not seen.' I believe that my translation brings out the force of the two key words and illustrates the strong link between faith and activism.

15   This is Clarence Jordan's translation of Heb 11:1 from his *The Cotton Patch Version of Hebrews and the General Epistles*, New Wine Publishing, 1997. Jordan (1912–69) was a farmer, New Testament scholar and a peace and justice activist. He founded the 'Koinonia Farm' (1942) in Georgia, USA, as a multiracial presence in the racist deep south and faced sustained hostility as a result. He was a powerful influence, inspiring among other things the founding of 'Habitat for Humanity', a programme to build homes for the poor all over the world.

16   I coined this phrase in the late 1970s and over decades it has proved its ability to distil the essence of a biblical understanding of faith, in my teaching, like no other definition has been able to do.

17   Quoted by Jody Williams in *Jody Williams: A Realistic Vision for World Peace* video on <www.TED.com>, recorded December 2010.

18   See Ps 34:14; 1Pet 3:11; Rom 14:19.

19 Take note that *shalom* has no concept of 'peacekeeping', which is usually a euphemism for the containment of violence and injustice, not its eradication. The Hebrew prophets are clear, warning of those who proclaim, 'Peace, peace,' when there is no peace (Jer 6:14; 8:11; Ezk 13:10, 16). You may 'keep' or 'contain' or 'control' violence, but *shalom* cannot be contained, only nurtured and allowed to flourish.

20 See Isa 2:4; Mic 4:3; cf. Joel 3:10.

21 Wisdom (Hebrew: *hokma*; Greek: *sophia*) is a primary biblical word used to describe creativity; it is physical, practical and profound; see Prov 8:22–31 *et al*. These ideas will be developed much more fully in our *Wisdom Dancer* chapter. Reflect also on Col 1:28–29.

22 See Matt 5:39, 44; 7:12; we shall develop the understanding of the call of *shalom* to nonviolence in much more detail in our *Meekness Zealot* chapter.

23 The message of the 'evangelist' always had to be good news that brought joy to the hearers: the proclamation of peace, the birth of a child, the announcement of a wedding, etc. A messenger who carried any form of bad news could never be called an 'evangelist'.

24 In 1967 I began exploring and experimenting with universal life-giving values from a Jesus perspective. Early in my search I discovered the biblical Hebrew concept of *shalom*, which has defined and shaped my spirituality and lifestyle ever since. By the early 1970s, people frequently referred to me as a 'pacifist', implying that I advocated being passive in the face of violence (their misunderstanding of the word). This concerned me, along with the peace movement's constant use of the word 'nonviolence' as their primary focus (unwittingly making violence the central feature rather than peace). I was left with the question, 'What is the content of peace?' Struggling with these issues I coined the phrase '*Shalom* Activist' to identify myself, and my self-understanding, and to give focus to my activity and mission. Over subsequent decades I have been surprised and gratified by how many others have also found this phrase helpful.

25 The word 'gospel' is one of the few Anglo-Saxon words to find a place in theology (another being 'atonement' or 'at-one-ment'). 'Gospel' has been given the meaning 'good news' but originally was *god* (good or God) *spel* (story).

26 Eph 2:17; of course the Gospels speak of Jesus proclaiming the kingdom of God (see Mk 1:14–15; Mt 4:23; Lk 4:43–44 *et al*.), but as we have seen the concept of *shalom*-peace and the kingdom of God are identical.

27 See Lk 10:5–6; Mt 10: 12–13.

28 Isa 52:7.

29 See Jg 6:24; Rom 15:33; 16:20; 1Cor 14:33; 2Cor 13:11; Phil 4:9; 1Th 5:23; 2Th 3:16; Heb 13:20.

30 See Ps 37:37; Lk 10:6.

31 See Eph 6:15.

32 See for instance:
- 'How beautiful upon the mountains are the feet of the one ... heralding *shalom*' (Isa 52:7, cf. Nahum 1:15);
- 'Justice makes a path before him, his footsteps bring *shalom*' (Ps 85:13; Jerusalem Bible);
- 'The God of peace will soon crush Satan under your feet' (Rom 16:20);
- 'To guide our feet into the way of peace' (Lk 1:79);
- 'Having shod your feet with the equipment of the gospel of peace' (Eph 6:15).

33 This theme will be further developed in our final chapter, *Footprints of Peace*.

34 See Mt 13:31–33.

35 See Mk 9:40; Lk 9:50; see the contrasting texts Mt 12:30; Lk 11:23.

36 See *Christianity Today*, November 1999
    <http://www.ctlibrary.com/ct/1999/november15/9td54a.html>. I am grateful to
    my friend Liz Ray for drawing this story to my attention. There is a historic
    ignorance and prejudice on the part of Christians towards the Pagan
    community. Many still erroneously link it to Satanism (the worship of evil),
    which most Pagans see as an offshoot of Christianity! Paganism is a vast
    network of groups and ideas about which there is a great deal of helpful
    literature. See the work of Pastor Phil Wyman:
    (http://salemgathering.com/Gathering_Web/NewPages/pagan_talk_signup.
    html), for more on Pagan/ Christian dialogue.
37 See Lk 10:6.
38 Early Quakers spoke of this as 'gospel order', which they believed was the way
    God designed the world to be and the way it will be when we have succeeded
    in making a heaven on earth. See Lloyd Lee Wilson, *Essays on the Quaker
    Vision of Gospel Order*, Pendle Hill Publishers, 1997.
39 Cf. the Akkadian word *salamu* – which means 'to be faultless, healthy,
    complete', and the Amorite texts from Mari where the word *salimum* has the
    sense of 'reconciliation' and 'agreement'.
40 These three primary characteristics of *shalom*, and the way I have presented
    them, are broadly based on drawing together ideas originally found in Perry
    Yoder, *Shalom: The Bible's Word for Salvation, Justice and Peace*, Faith and
    Life Press, 1987, pp. 10–23 and Claus Westermann, 'Peace (Shalom) in the
    Old Testament', in PB Yoder and WM Swartley (eds), *The Meaning of Peace*,
    2nd edn, IMS, Elkhart, 2001, pp. 37–70.
41 The story of Father Damien is found in many sources, the most accessible is
    Hilde Eynikel, *Molokai: The Story of Father Damien*, Hodder, 2000; see also
    the film *Molokai: The True Story of Father Damien*, Prism (PPA 1147), 2001.
42 It is important to make clear that this has nothing whatever to do with popular
    contemporary so-called 'Christian' notions of 'prosperity teaching' where
    individuals believe as a matter of faith that they are entitled to significant wealth
    as a sign of God's blessing. *Shalom* prosperity is always looking for the other,
    the poor and the needy, to receive material blessing, almost always at the
    expense of oneself.
43 Claus Westermann, *Peace (Shalom) in the Old Testament*, in PB Yoder and
    WM Swartley (eds), *The Meaning of Peace*, 2nd edn, IMS, Elkhart, 2001, p. 46.
44 The Chinese have a greeting, 'Have you eaten?' which has the same sense to
    it, the concern for a person's physical well-being; the implication being if you
    have not eaten and are hungry then I will feed you.
45 Isa 1:17; see also Isa 58:3,7; Prov 31:8–9; Job 29:12–17; Lev 19:15; Deut 1:16;
    Ps 72:4, 12–13 and many more.
46 Manusmriti – III, 15–19.
47 Dhammapada 177.
48 Sura 4:36.
49 Guru Amar Das.
50 Abdu'l-Bahá, *Abdu'l-Bahá in London*, Bahá'í Publishing Trust UK, 1982, p. 127.
51 Acts 10:38.
52 Lk 6:20 (cf. Mt 5:3); 14:12–14; for more of Jesus' teaching on the poor see also
    Mk 10:17–27 (*et al.*); 14:3–9 (*et al.*); Lk 14:15–24; 16:19–31; 19:1–10.
53 Acts 2:44; 4:34–35; see also 2:43–7; 4:32–7; 5:1–11; 6:1–7; 11:29 and 2Cor
    8—9.
54 Forms of this word are found forty-five times across the New Testament; see
    especially Acts 2:42; 2Cor 9:13.
55 For texts that illustrate this see E Ferguson, 'Early Christian Acts of Mercy', ch.
    xvii in *Early Christians Speak: Life and Faith in the First Three Centuries*, Bible

Research Press, 1981, pp. 207–18.
56 There are a number of Hebrew words for love. The most widely used is *aheb*, but *chesed* gives the central spiritual and moral focus. Its emphasis on 'commitment' and 'covenant' make it particularly appropriate to link with *shalom*, with its emphasis on relationship. The *rabbis* translated *chesed* with the Greek word *agape* in the LXX (Septuagint), which was the most widely used word for love by the early Christian community.
57 This phrase is taken from the inspiring strap-line used by 'Christian Aid' – 'we believe in life before death'.
58 Dom Helder Camara, Archbishop of Recife and Olinda, Brazil, died on 27 August 1999, at ninety years of age. He worked tirelessly with the poor; a key figure in influencing and interpreting 'Liberation Theology'. He was cold-shouldered by the church hierarchy and threatened by political leaders, living in constant threat of assassination. Paulo Evaristo Arns, Cardinal Archbishop of Sao Paulo, said of him, 'Dom Helder is a poet, a mystic and a missionary. As a poet he knows how to say things and the people understand what he says. As a mystic, he lives praying, and passes his whole life always with God. But he is also a great missionary, a man who brings the ideas of God to the hearts of people' – quoted in <http:totheroots.com/page/34/>.
59 Lk 4:18, quoting Isa 61:1–2.
60 The details of Jubilee are found in Lev 25:8–17. It was called 'Jubilee' from the Hebrew word for 'ram'; the sounding of the 'ram's horn', the *shophar*, heralded the commencement of the year. Imagine how the slaves, the landless and the debtors felt at Jubilee. Imagine how the landowners, the bankers and the slave-owners felt. It sorted out the deep and basic attitudes in the human heart
61 Cf. Exod 18:21–23; 1Kgs 5:12; Isa 60:17; Rom 14:19 and many more.
62 This is Mt 5:6 using the Elias Chacour paraphrase (see note 4 above). Note that the Greek word *dikaiosune*, usually translated 'righteousness', also means 'justice'; the two cannot be separated.
63 Jas 3:18; as in note 62 above, the Greek word is *dikaiosune*, and is usually translated 'righteousness' in this verse, but use of the word 'justice' here seems appropriate.
64 See Ps 34:14 and 1Pt 3:11.
65 See Jer 29:7.
66 Rev 17:5; 18:2–3 are just two of many biblical examples.
67 See 1Sam 8:7–9. Monarchy in ancient Israel is seen as a rejection of the rule of God and is a continuing disaster culminating in the nation being both scattered and exiled in Babylon; it has no place in the divine scheme of things.
68 Mt 6:29; Lk 12:27; for other teaching of Jesus on the State see Mk 12:13–17; Lk 4:5– 8; Jn 18:36.
69 *Exousia* (powers) Rom 13:1–3; 1Cor 15:24; Eph 1:21; 2:2; 3:10; 6:12; Col 1:16; 2:10, 15 *et al. Archai* (principalities, rulers) Rom 8:38; 1Cor 2:8; 15:24; Eph 1:21; 3:10; 6:12. *Stoicheia* (elementals) Gal 4:3, 9; Col 2:8, 20; 2Pt 3:10, 12. *Angeloi* (angels, messengers) Rom 8:38; 1Cor 6:3; 11:10; 1Pt 3:22. See Walter Wink, *Engaging the Powers*, Fortress Press, 1992, where the subject is dealt with in detail, including the practical implications.
70 Christ has triumphed over them (Col 2:15 cf. 1:16–20; Phil 2:10), but he has not finally subjected or subordinated them (1Cor 15:24–28; Heb 10:13), but he will do.
71 See Rom 13:1–7; 2Th 2:7; 1Pt 2:13–17.
72 See Rev 13:1–18; 2Th 2:4.
73 The concept of creative nonviolent strategies in modern times began with Mohandas Gandhi and the movement for political independence from the British in India inspiring Martin Luther King and others. However, the most

developed research and documentation in this area has been done by G Sharp, *The Politics of Nonviolent Action*, Boston: Porter Sargent, 1974, and *Waging Nonviolent Struggle: 20th century Practice and 21st Century Potential*, Boston: Porter Sargent, 2005. For some stories that illustrate the principles see P Ackerman and J Duvall, *A Force More Powerful: A Century of Nonviolent Conflict*, Palgrave/Macmillan, 2000.

74   'Testimony to the Truth', today is most likely to be around the themes of 'Peace, Equality, Simplicity and Truth', possibly adding others such as sustainability, justice and/or community. Testimony is especially about the truth of experience. (This understanding of Quaker Testimony is drawn from an unpublished paper by Simon Hill, *Equipping for Ministry – Testimony and Peace*, 2009.) The phrase 'speaking truth to power' was first coined in the eighteenth century as a charge and encouragement to Quakers, but came into popular use following the publication of a pamphlet, *Speak Truth to Power*, American Friends Service Committee, 1955, which was searching for an alternative to violence during the emergence of the Cold War.

75   Prov 10:10 in the LXX (Greek) translation.

76   Mk 13:9, see also Mt 5:16.

77   This *hadith* (tradition) was quoted by the Islamic scholar, Prof. Mona Siddiqui on BBC Radio 4, *Thought for the Day*, 16 February 2011. The word *jihad* means 'struggle' and it primarily refers to the struggle of inner spiritual growth; it also refers to the struggle to build a good society. It can on occasions refer to the forceful struggle to defend the community.

78   See Aung San Suu Kyi, *Reading 3: Freedom from Fear*, Viking/Penguin, 2010. These words taken from 'Grace under Pressure' in *The Virago Book of Spirituality*, Virago Press, 1997, pp. 269–70.

79   See Annette Dumbach and Jud Newborn, *Sophie Scholl and the White Rose*, Oneworld Publications, 2007; Frank McDonough, *Sophie Scholl: The Real Story of the Woman who Defied Hitler*, History Press, 2010; see the film, *Sophie Scholl – The Final Days*, Drakes Avenue, 2006. For other inspiring stories from the twentieth century begin with G Sharp, *The Politics of Nonviolent Action*, Boston: Porter Sargent, 1974; Dylan Mathews, *War Prevention Works: 50 Stories of People Resolving Conflict*, Oxford Research Group, 2002; D Johnson (ed.), *Religion: The Missing Dimension of Statecraft*, Oxford: OUP, 1994; and many others.

80   The title *Lamed Vav Zadikim* means 'Thirty-Six Righteous Ones'; it is attributed to the teaching of one of the Babylonian Rabbi Abbaye – see Babylonian Talmud, Sanhedrin 97b, Sukkot 45b. In Hebrew script the letter *Lamed* = 30 and the letter *Vav* = 6, hence *Lamed Vav* = 36.

81   Why thirty-six? Where does this number come from? In answer we move into the fascinating realm of Jewish spiritual interpretation and Kabbalic mysticism:
- Zech 11:12 mentions 'thirty shekels of silver' as an allegory for godly people; God ensures there will always be thirty righteous people in every generation;
- Isa 30:18 says 'Blessed are all who wait for Him' (Hebrew: *ashrei kol h.okhei lo*), and the Hebrew word *lo* meaning 'for Him,' is spelled Lamed-Vav and (as we have seen) is numerically equal to 36;
- The 360 degrees of the heavenly circle when divided into units of ten make the number 36.
- The number 36 is twice 18 which in Hebrew letters spells *chai* which means 'life' or 'living' and 72 which is twice 36 makes up the Hebrew name for 'God'.

The idea may have roots in the story of Abraham's efforts to save Sodom (Gen 18), where it becomes evident that any society must have a minimum number of decent people in order to survive.

82 They are also known as the *Zadikim Nistarim*, 'concealed' or 'hidden righteous'.
83 For a detailed description of the Jewish understanding of *shekinah* see JT Marshall, 'Shekinah', in J Hastings (ed.), *A Dictionary of the Bible*, vol. 4, T&T Clark, 1902, pp. 487–9.
84 John Woolman (1720–72) was an American Quaker. See DV Steere, *Quaker Spirituality: Selected Writings*, The Classics of Western Spirituality, SPCK, 1984; and Philip Moulton (ed.) *John Woolman's Journal*, Oxford: OUP, 1971.
85 See R Foster, *Streams of Living Water*, HarperCollins, 1998, p. 144.
86 See Temba L Mafico, 'Judge, Judging' in *The Anchor Bible Dictionary*, vol. 3, Doubleday, 1992, p. 1106.

5 Radical Mystic
– breathing under the open heaven

As peace-activists we seek the *shalom* of the city, working hard to establish justice within society.[1]

As peace-people we seek *shalom* ... and holiness deep within ourselves, hungering and thirsting after righteousness.[2]

We endeavour to be someone in whom the external and internal flows as a single stream, saturating everything with life, letting 'justice flow down like water, and righteousness like an ever-flowing stream'.[3]

This is the mark of true spirituality. To achieve this requires focus, commitment and effort. It will not happen unless we apply ourselves to actually making it happen.

We want to be a *zadik*; a righteous person who stands tall, shoulders squared, facing the world, an activist on the outside balanced by mature spiritual integrity within.

This idea connects directly with the idea of *shanti* – the Indian Sanskrit word for 'peace' – which describes a person who is fully integrated within themselves. In this sense *shanti* is identical to that aspect of *shalom* which points towards an internal spiritual wholeness of character and personality.

A personal experience of peace is very much more than simply inner tranquillity and calm – it is rather the gentle progress towards discovering the complete spiritual and moral integration of everything I am as a person,[4] where 'righteousness and *shalom* kiss each other'.[5]

These hidden inner characteristics and the integrity of the 'person of peace' are revealed in the quality of the lives we live and the sense of hope we inspire in others. As the Hebrew psalmist says:

> Watch the blameless person,
> take note of the upright,
> for destiny lies with the person of *shalom.*[6]

The prophet Micah declares that what is required of a *zadik* is: 'To do justice, to love mercy and to walk humbly before your God'.[7] The phrase, 'walk humbly before your God', refers to 'holiness' – the uniqueness and integrity of *qadosh*. Micah's statement is actually a perfect description of *shalom*; all the essential elements are there.

We have seen that God is the 'God of peace';[8] God's character and Spirit is the source of every aspect of *shalom* for those who seek it. The prophet Isaiah looks to the future and speaks of the 'Prince of Peace', a person who will come from God and rule with 'justice and righteousness'. The title implies this person is 'the very embodiment of peace'.[9]

The Jewish community has always seen this person as the *Messiah*, someone uniquely anointed by God. Christians identify him with Jesus.

＊ ＊ ＊ ＊ ＊

I had invited some Humanist guests to come and talk with my students about their belief-journey. As we sat together in a circle these women and men told how they once identified as being Christian, but now found a non-theist interpretation of life more truthful for them, and how making this choice had changed their lives.

During our warm and stimulating discussion, talk turned to spirituality. This was something they did not want to lose, because for them spirituality embraced ideas and experiences vital to enriching their lives – things that 'lift the spirit'. It touches the higher elements of the human mind and connects with our need for a sense of being part of something much larger than just ourselves.

Their biggest difficulty was using the word 'spirituality' without being misunderstood, because it has become so strongly associated with religion and is used in such a loose way in popular jargon.

Their question to us was: 'What does spirituality *really* mean when shorn of its misleading connotations such as God and the transcendent?'

Can we speak about spirituality in a way that is inclusive?

Yes, the word comes from *spiritus* – Latin for 'breath' or 'wind'. It speaks to that deep intuitive sense we all have, irrespective of culture, that life has a moral and emotional shape to it. Breath and the wind are both physical yet invisible, felt yet intangible; so is the realm of the spiritual.

Spirituality is as natural and essential as breathing.

The vast beauty of wild nature, a significant human relationship, or simply a deep inner sense of well-being might stimulate the spiritual. It brings joy and sometimes awe, giving a fullness, richness and wholeness to everything. Spirituality is where anxiety or sorrow either vanish or find resolve. It touches our highest aspirations and gives us a sense of how things should be.[10] Spirituality may come as fleeting moments, or a sustained awareness. We may explain it in various ways, but here is a vital dimension of being that we all recognise; it is common ground shared by every living person.[11]

* * * * *

I have always loved trees. They have presence and power; branches offering shelter and shade, thick gnarled twisted roots that speak of age, their towering trunks symbols of strength. They stand as timeless sentinels, yet their twig-growth each spring promises the future.

Trees may appear static, but in reality they are a shaft of life thrusting up through rocky soil reaching skyward towards the light, establishing themselves as towering figures in the landscape; while at the same time plunging downwards ever deeper into the darkness of the earth to establish their security and provide nourishment to the whole structure.

A tree is what I picture whenever someone uses the word 'radical'. An overused and devalued word, yet it continues to express something profound. Derived from the Latin *radix*, it means 'of the root', giving the word two main emphases:[12]

- *Going to the root:* discovering what is foundational, fundamental, original, inherent, essential and primal. There is something deep, dark, earthy, hidden and mysterious in this sense of the word.
- *Flowing from the root:* providing what brings structure, nourishment, security, growth and fruitfulness. There is something life-giving, energising, ethereal and eternal in this sense of the word.

This is how I want to be. A person who 'goes to the root' and 'flows from the root' in the quality of my spirituality and the way I engage with society around me.

A great tree has symmetry.

The branches reaching high and visible above the ground are matched exactly by a root system spreading deep and hidden beneath the earth.

This is an important picture of the biblical understanding of reality. For everything that makes up the visible world there is a depth that is invisible; furthermore, the visible is totally dependent on the invisible for its existence and meaning. These are not two parallel universes. There is no 'heaven up there' and 'earth down here', no 'spiritual realm' and 'physical realm'; there is no division, only unity.

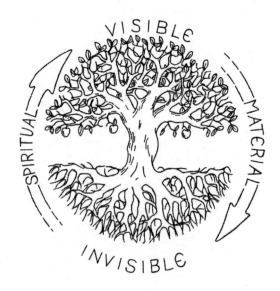

Too many people's experience of spirituality is stunted because their understanding of reality is dualistic and not holistic.

Trees captured the imagination of the earliest peoples; across the globe the idea of a 'Tree of Life' became an icon of spiritual and emotional power. Among different peoples a variety of trees were identified as the 'Tree of Life'; to the Babylonians it was the palm, to the Egyptians the fig, for the Sumerians the vine and the Hebrews the olive; for the Druids it was the oak, for the Chinese the peach and so it continued, each with a story, each with a truth.

We have a remarkable biblical story about a forest grove called 'Eden',[13] a garden heavy with fragrance, taste and beauty, at the centre of which there is *the* 'Tree of Life'. The human couple in the story are invited to feed on it. However, elsewhere in the garden stands another tree, the 'Tree of *all* Knowledge',[14] whose succulent fruit they were forbidden to eat. Why would God forbid them, knowledge is a priceless treasure? The temptation that led them to disobey was a belief that God was preventing them from becoming divine and becoming wise. The reality was the exact opposite. Two things are required to become like God – obedience ('being open to be persuaded'[15]) and actively feeding on the 'Tree of Life' (nurturing spirituality through devotion and action).

Knowledge *alone* may appear to make us like God but in fact leads to death because we don't know how to use it. However, as the 'Tree of Life' and the 'Tree of Knowledge' intertwine they become the 'Wisdom Tree'; feeding on the combined fruit we begin to become like God and also to become a 'Tree of Life' within ourselves: 'The fruit of the righteous is a tree of life.'[16]

To be 'radical' from a Jesus perspective is to connect with the deep moral and spiritual structure of creation, rooted into the very being of God, 'rooted and grounded in love'.[17] It is also to stand tall as a 'Tree of Life' within the world, offering shelter, nourishment, healing, protection and resistance. Being 'radical' embraces both spirituality and activism in one single word.

* * * * *

A mystic is someone with the ability and maturity to understand and communicate spiritual mystery. The popular view of a person who is otherworldly, skilled in secret knowledge ordinary people cannot know, is mistaken.

To explain why, let's begin with a dream.

The biblical story of Jacob's dream finds him asleep at the foot of a stairway reaching up to heaven, with angels ascending and descending.[18] This dream is in fact many people's dream – the ability to move naturally between visible and invisible worlds, between the physical and the spiritual.

This dream is explored across many world cultures where it is believed that at certain times like twilight or midnight, or on special days like Celtic *Samhain* (Halloween), and at special places such as rocks, rivers or forest groves, doors to the spiritual world may open, allowing humans and spiritual beings to intermingle.

Jesus brings fulfilment to this desire beyond anyone's wildest dreams. Using the imagery of the Jacob story, Jesus tells a man called Nathaniel: 'Very truly, I tell you, you will see the heavens opened and the angels of God ascending and descending upon the Son of Man.'[19] With these words Jesus sweeps the perceived barriers between heaven and earth, the spiritual and physical, the human and divine, into oblivion.

So in Jesus every day is Halloween and every place a stairway to heaven.

The implication of what Jesus says destroys forever the whole concept of the 'supernatural'. There is no two-tier universe. The idea of the 'supernatural' is totally human-centred, used in a vain attempt to explain reality in terms of ourselves; so everything we understand is said to be 'natural', while everything beyond our understanding is declared 'supernatural'. This is biblically absurd. God is the centre of reality; reality is rooted in God, not in our perception of it. The biblical writers contrast the 'natural' and 'spiritual' with the 'unnatural' – that which stands in opposition to God – not the 'supernatural'.[20]

All this being so, what appears to us to be miraculous is in reality quite 'natural' to God, and from a Christian perspective Jesus is the first truly 'natural' human being.

This connects exactly with what we said about the branches and roots of a tree providing a biblical understanding of reality, with everything visible having a depth that is invisible, with the visible being totally dependent on the invisible for its existence and meaning. It also makes clear why a mystic should not be seen as otherworldly but rather someone who moves naturally within a reality that flows seamlessly between the visible and invisible.

So, as 'Radical Mystics' we are invited to live and breathe naturally under the open heaven. We are to be 'seers' – people who through the power of the Spirit have greater insight because there are no longer barriers between the human and the divine.

We are entrusted with the mystery that is 'the secret of the kingdom of God'.[21] We must not draw an 'occult circle' that excludes all but the initiated, but rather as Jesus said: 'what you hear whispered, proclaim from the housetops'.[22] Instead we create an 'open circle' that includes all who wish to come and share 'the knowledge of God's mystery, that is Christ himself, in whom are hidden all the treasures of wisdom and knowledge'.[23]

∗ ∗ ∗ ∗ ∗

Go into any bookstore and you will see shelves marked 'Body, Mind, Spirit' exhorting us to 'personal growth' and 'spiritual formation'. These are good phrases, holistic and aspirational, each expressing a desire to develop and mature, achieving our potential.

As mystics and seers, growth and maturity are what we were created for. In fact our starting point is astonishing; we are 'made in the image and likeness of God'. Indeed we are 'little less than God'; Jesus himself said, 'Is it not written … "I said you are gods?"'[24]

This is how blessed we are. It is of course obvious that the reality is not yet fully realised; we are work in progress. Internally we are damaged by our choices and experiences and surrounded by destructive influences, but their power is very dependent on our response to them.[25] The call is to action: 'Work out your own salvation with fear and trembling for it is God at work in you.'[26] As we have seen, 'salvation' is the full experience of *shalom*; 'fear and trembling' is the awe and humility we feel in the presence of true love. Spiritual growth is a collaborative effort; it is taking personal responsibility but it is something we do together in helping one another. It is being embraced by the empowering work of God both among us as a community and deep within each one of us individually.

First there must be desire; like a child looking up at a parent or older sibling and saying, 'When I grow up I want to be like you':

> We shall become mature people,
> reaching the very height of Christ's full stature.[27]

The question at the centre of this book is, 'Who am I?' However, we can begin to answer it only by asking a second question, 'What kind of person do I really want to be?'

This draws my thoughts to words in the book of Revelation:

> To everyone who conquers …
> I will give a white stone, and on the white stone is
> written a new name
> that no one knows except the one who receives it.[28]

The white stone lies in the palm of your hand, a God-given amulet – symbol of victory and a promise of protection.[29] This 'new name' refers to the quality of your character rather than a title by which you are known. It is unique; no one knows it 'except the one who receives it'. The individuality of your identity is a sacred gift from God.

Our spiritual quest is to discover what that 'name' is and with the help of the Spirit see it become a reality in our lives.

✻ ✻ ✻ ✻ ✻

Shalom is first and foremost about relationships, so *shalom*-spirituality begins with our relationship *with* God. However awesome the reality of God truly is, we are invited to share intimacy. *Shalom* with God is about fellowship – the loving reciprocal sharing of *koinonia* – and friendship.[30]

Jesus continually speaks of God as a warm loving parent; he uses the word *Abba* (literally 'Daddy') and the imagery of the wombish compassion of a mother.[31]

A central biblical picture of spiritual intimacy is that of a lover longing for their beloved. This is how *Yahweh* feels for people and Christ for the covenant community.[32] The early Jesus-community used an Aramaic exclamation – '*Maranatha*!' 'Our Lord, come!' – conveying all the yearning of a lover's cry.[33]

The biblical phrase, 'the fear of the Lord', also fits perfectly here. Totally positive, that feeling a lover has towards their beloved of not wanting anything to spoil their relationship; that wholesome 'fear' at the heart of all true love, which liberates the lover from every reason to fear.[34]

The idea of the devotee longing for the divine as a lover is widely used in the history of spirituality. Medieval Christian writers explored it, as do the Vishnu traditions of Hinduism and the mystic poets of Islam, such as Rumi.

Devotion is at the centre of the relationship between the disciple and their *rabbi* or *guru*; they are often called devotees. Yet it must be reciprocal, with the teacher equally devoted to the learner.

Jesus' invitation to 'Follow me' or 'Take my yoke upon you'[35] is always about joining in shared mutual love – journeying, working and growing together. It is out of this relationship that the deep inner transfiguration of *shalom* takes place.

Shalom-spirituality is also about being at peace both *with* and *within* ourselves; as in the *shanti*-focus we spoke about earlier. The call is clear:

Depart from evil and do good; seek *shalom* and pursue it.[36]

Pursue peace with everyone,
and the holiness without which no one will see the Lord.[37]

So when we embrace *shalom* we begin to change. Our deep inner integrity results in *qadosh* – the 'uniqueness of holiness'. God invites everyone to 'be unique as I am unique'.[38] God is the unique one, the 'I am', whose identity and character flow from the depths of divine being and nowhere else.

As a unique individual my holiness will be seen in the quality of the life I live. One such quality is godliness: 'What sort of people ought you to be in leading lives of holiness and godliness?'[39]

Godliness is *eusebeia*, an almost untranslatable Greek word. It describes someone who honours God, holds every person in high esteem, and has strong self-respect.[40] It perfectly distils the greatest commandment:

> You shall love the Lord your God with all your heart,
> and with all your soul, and with all your mind …
> You shall love your neighbour as yourself.[41]

Godliness sums up the early Christian understanding of spirituality in a single word.

The call to love God and our neighbour is often repeated – and rightly so – but the emphasis on self-love, self-respect and self-esteem are neglected. And at what a price – without it spiritual growth is stunted and *shalom* is inhibited.

* * * * * *

The person of peace is called to stand upright, confident in their uniqueness as they learn to image God, self-assured as they explore godliness and holiness. These are all vital steps on the path towards maturity.

Early Jesus-followers encouraged each other with the phrase, 'Let us press on to maturity.'[42] The Greek word for 'mature' is *teleios*; it means being 'complete' or 'whole', and as such expresses *shalom* exactly. Spiritual maturity is inner-*shalom* expressed in outward godliness; this is our goal, and discipleship is the path. Jesus says: 'If you wish to be *mature* … follow me.'[43]

There are at least two problems with how people understand the word 'mature':

- It popularly assumes someone 'has arrived', with no further to go;
- The common translation of *teleios* as 'perfect' suggests it is unattainable.

Maturity is not finality; it is about constant growth and development, like an athlete pushing for a new record, a musician searching for ever more subtle interpretations, or a craftsman honing their skills for ever greater masterpieces.

Eastern Orthodox teaching focuses on the Greek word *epektasis* – 'reaching forward', because there is always deeper and higher perfection to stretch out towards, becoming more and more like God.[44]

A young adult once asked an elderly leader, 'Please tell me, what should I be looking for in a spiritual teacher and mentor?' They replied, 'One who is still learning.'

Remember, maturity has nothing whatever to do with keeping rules or ticking lists. Yes, of course I fail; but there is always forgiveness and instantaneous new beginnings.

A mother only remembers her child's successful steps when they were learning to walk, not how often they fell over.

True maturity has childlikeness at its core. Jesus says:

Be wise as serpents and innocent as doves.[45]

Truly, I say to you, unless you turn and become like children, you will never enter the kingdom of heaven.[46]

Childlikeness is central to true spirituality. Nurturing it opens us out to become more sensitive to God.

A four-year-old girl was overheard whispering into her newborn baby brother's ear. 'Baby,' she said softly, 'tell me what God sounds like. I am starting to forget.'[47]

We shall return to childlikeness again in later chapters. For now, remember it is not 'childishness'; but rather, 'primal personhood'.

Take the time to look at the world with wonder, questions, and awe and quiet confidence, like children do. Touch the world with curiosity, excitement, a sense of discovery and joy. Discover that blend of innocence and truth, which creates emotional and intellectual gentleness and vulnerability. Nurture the remarkable honesty and shrewdness that can be so disarming and terrifying for so-called 'adults'.

Forever childlike, climb the branches of the 'Tree of Life' in eternal playfulness, fill the air with laughter, and delight in the moment, constantly alive to fresh adventures.

* * * * *

I want to conclude this chapter with a few brief reflections on some practical challenges we face living out our spirituality every day.

Spirituality is about growth, but it involves struggle.

On one hand this struggle is positive: like a child's physical development through puberty to adulthood, or an athlete in training.

On the other hand this struggle is challenging: because individuals and society are often hostile to the Spirit and destructive in their responses.

We grow into maturity caught in these tensions.

This is a shared experience with others across the world of faiths – for Muslims this inner spiritual exertion is called 'the great *Jihad* (struggle)'.

One reason we struggle is because we are 're-reflexing' – a reflex is our instinctive physical response to a stimulus.[48] Every day we are trying to learn new life-giving ways to behave to replace old ingrained habits. Developing this 'practical holiness' is hard work and takes time.

Never lose hope.

Remember there is no limit on what the Spirit might achieve in our lives as we cooperate in our choices and desires.

Temptation is another challenge.

Jesus was constantly tempted – there is no sin in that. The Greek word used in early Christian writings is *peirasmos*; it has a double meaning, 'to entice' and 'to test'. Temptation entices me towards wrongdoing and is a real threat, but at the same time it tests out the quality of person I really am by how I respond.[49]

I once heard a Buddhist nun speaking on the radio about temptation.

> It's like sitting in a room on a hot summer's day with a wasp buzzing around, you are alert watching it, hoping it won't land on you with a sting. When I realise I am being tempted I watch the effect it has on me. 'Why do I respond this way?' 'What is this telling me about myself?' Once it is over I take time using meditation to deal with these

vulnerable areas in my life that the temptation has
revealed.

This is practical and profound, positively embracing temptation as
a teacher.

'Spiritual disciplines' – like meditation, prayer, study, fasting and
solitude – rhythms of living that nurture spiritual growth, forming a
'liturgy for life', help in the struggle. 'Discipline' simply means 'to
learn'; it provides a shape to life that is supple and organic – like
the bones of a skeleton that enable the muscles of the body to
move and run and jump.[50]

The goal of spirituality is transformation; each one of us fully
becoming the unique person we were created to be. This is the
work of the Spirit, transfiguring us 'from one degree of glory to
another'.[51] As Abba Joseph of Panephysis said, 'If you will, you
can become all flame.' So we are to be 'ablaze with the Spirit'.[52]
Jesus says, 'the *zadik* will shine like the sun.'[53] The possibilities
and potential are more than we can imagine:

> what we will be has not yet been revealed.
> What we do know is this: when (Jesus) is revealed,
> we will be like him, for we will see him as he is.
> And all who have this hope in him purify themselves,
> just as he is pure.[54]

Purity is a good word with which to finish.

The popular view of purity suggests something uncontaminated
and sealed-off. Jesus has a more robust attitude: 'Get up, go
ahead, do something, move, you pure in heart, for you will see
God.'[55]

Holiness is purity – clean, transparent and unmixed, with a strong
sense of childlike innocence, in which God is seen. However,
Jesus expects the pure to be out in the real world getting their
hands dirty. We are not to be stained by society,[56] but we are to
leave our mark everywhere we go. Religion tries to maintain purity
by restricting and inhibiting; for Jesus purity was about freedom
and healing.

There is a story where a leper approaches Jesus; those around
him were afraid of being polluted. Not Jesus. He steps forward and

touches the man, contaminating him with purity, 'making him clean'.[57]

True purity grasps evil, marking it with good, like a cauterising flame – leaving an indelible fingerprint of fire.

Endnotes

1   See Jer 29:7 and Amos 5:15.

2   See Heb 12:14 and Mt 5:6.

3   Amos 5:24.

4   For peace as moral integrity see Rom 8:6; 14:17; 15:13; Gal 5:22; 2Tim 2:22; 1Pt 3:11; 2Pt 3:14.

5   Ps 85:10.

6   Ps 37:37. In this paraphrase I have used the word 'destiny' in the last line, other translations read 'has a future' or 'has descendants'. The phrase 'person of peace' is also used in Lk 10:6.

7   Mic 6:8.

8   See Jg 6:24; Rom 15:33; 16:20; 1Cor 14:33; 2Cor 13:11; Phil 4:9; 1Th 5:23; 2Th 3:16; Heb 13:20.

9   Isa 9:6–7 and the quote is from EJ Young, *The Book of Isaiah: Volume 1 Chapters 1–18*, Eerdmans, 1965, p. 340.

10 I am struck by the way this expression of spirituality stresses the deep integratedness of everything with a sense of well-being, everything being right and having a subtle inner integrity; another way to describe it would be *shalom*.

11 In forming this reflection on spirituality I am grateful for conversations with Dr Lloyd Pietersen, who also provided me with a definition by Charles Taylor, *A Secular Age*, Cambridge MA/ London: The Bleknap Press of Harvard University Press, 2007, pp 5–6, which gave some helpful pointers. Also for conversations with Marilyn Mason, Rosemary Taylorson, Allan Hayes and Richard Norman. See Richard Norman, *On Humanism: Thinking in Action*, Routledge, 2004, ch. 5; and Marilyn Mason, 'Spirituality –What on Earth Is It?', a paper given at the 7th International Conference on Education, Spirituality and the Whole Child at the University of Surrey, Roehampton, June 2000 – <http://newhumanist.org.uk/456/holy-relics-by-marilyn-mason-summer–2001>.

12 Adapted from the Concise Oxford and Chambers English dictionaries

13 Genesis 2—3.

14 The name, 'Tree of Knowledge – the knowledge of good and evil', has tantalised theologians over the centuries, but is probably best understood as a figure of speech called a 'merism', where naming two opposites, like 'heaven and earth', implies 'the whole cosmos' – totality (see Chapter 3, Note 31). In the same way the 'knowledge of good and evil' implies the 'Tree of *All* Knowledge' – total knowledge.

15 Authentic obedience is never the result of coercion but always the consequence of having a 'pliable heart' (cf. Ezk 11:19) and 'being open to be persuaded' (cf. Heb 13:17); true obedience must always enhance human dignity. The instruction, 'If you eat you will die' (Gen 3:4) was not a threat; it was statement of fact.

16 Prov 11:30.

17 Eph 3:17.

18 Gen 28:10–22.

19   See Jn 1:51; this was however true of every aspect of Jesus' life:
  - At his birth: 'a heavenly host' (Lk 2:13) – notice the message 'shalom on earth'
  - At his baptism: 'heavens torn apart' (Mt 3:16) – inaugurating the new creation
  - In his ministry: 'God visited his people' (Lk 7:16) – the Galilean village of Nain
  - In his words: 'Ephphatha – Be opened!' (Mk 7:34) – the deaf mute
  - At his death: 'temple curtain shredded' (Mt 27:51) – everything changes!

20   Challenging the concept of the 'supernatural' is never going to be easy when it is so embedded in both religious and secular language along with its parallel concept of a 'two-tier/ multi-tier universe' – accepted by theists and rejected by non-theists. We have already argued that the biblical understanding of reality is holistic and rooted in God; here we show that the notion of the 'supernatural' is humanistic. Scientific enquiry itself shows how relative and subjective our understanding of reality is as the more we learn about the world so the horizon line of what we don't know changes. With regard to the miraculous, such experiences may 'break the laws of nature' as we currently understand them, but not as they exist in the person of God 'who holds all things together' (Col 1:17).

21   Mk 4:11.

22   Mt 10:27.

23   Col 2:2.

24   Jn 10:34 quoting Ps 82:6 see Gen 1:27, Ps 8:5 .

25   I am well aware that many people struggle with deep issues that are complex in origin with no simple solutions. Resolving them will take a significant period of time and will often be dependent on the help of experts and a loving supportive environment.

26   Phil 2:12–13.

27   Eph 4:13.

28   Rev 2:17.

29   There has been much discussion as to the meaning of the 'white stone'. It is most likely beryl, (see Rev 21:20; one of the twelve stones in the foundations of the New Jerusalem), a very valuable white stone. In ancient culture it had a range of significance; a jewel, a vote-token of acquittal in court, a sign declaring the keeper victorious, a mark of initiation and more, but in this instance the majority of scholars see it as the symbol of a sacred amulet given by God. See W Barclay, *Letters to Seven Churches*, SCM, 1957pp. 62–63; D Aune, *Revelation: Word Biblical Commentary*, Word, 1997, pp. 189–191.

30   See: fellowship – Phil 2:1; 1Jn 1:3, 6 and friendship – Isa 41:8; Jas 2:23, see also Jn 15:14–15.

31   For '*Abba*-Daddy' see Mk 14:36 where it is explicitly stated, but implied in all Jesus' other references to God as 'Father' especially as this was the understanding of the earliest Christian community; see Rom 8:15; Gal 4:6. For 'wombish compassion' see Lk 6:36 and Marcus Borg, *Jesus: A New Vision*, SPCK, 1993, pp. 102, 130–131 plus footnotes; see also Mt 23:37.

32   See Isa 54:6; 62:5; Hos 2:16; Jer 2:2; 3:20; Ezk 16:8; Eph 5:25–27.

33   See 1Cor 16:22

34   See Eccl 12:13; 2Cor 7:1 and 1Jn 4:18. The phrase 'the fear of the Lord' becomes a synonym for spirituality:
  - It is about awe and wonder, mystery and knowledge, joy and reverence
  - It is given by God (Jer 32:40) and enables people to respond to God (e.g. Gen 22:12)
  - It is the fountain of life (Prov 14:27; 19:23)

- It is clean (Ps 19:9)
- It is the beginning of wisdom (Ps 111:10; Prov 9:10)
- It brings God's favour (Ps 147:11)
- It is one of the qualities of the Messiah (Isa 11:2)
- It is fulfilled in Jesus in his desire only to do the Father's will (e.g. Jn 5:19–20).

35 Examples of Jesus' invitation, 'Follow me', are found in Mt 8:22; 9.9; 19:21; Mk 2:14; Lk 5.27; 9:57. The Greek word *akolouthein* – 'to follow', is found seventy-nine times in the Gospels. The word stresses the relationship between the parties involved. Reference to 'Take my yoke upon you' is found in Mt 11:29.

36 Ps 34:14 quoted in 1Pt 3:11.

37 Heb 12:14

38 Lev 11:44; see 1Pt 1:16 .

39 2Pt 3:11.

40 William Barclay says. 'Clearly this *eusebeia* is a tremendous thing. It never forgets the reverence due to God; it never forgets the rights due to people; it never forgets the respect due to self. It lives forever conscious of duty human and divine. It describes the character of the person who never fails God, others or themselves.' *Daily Study Bible: The Letters to Timothy, Titus, Philemon*, St Andrews Press, 1960, p. 70.

41 Mt 22:37-39.

42 Heb 6:1.

43 Mt 19:21; see also Mt 5:48 and 1Jn 2:5–6.

44 The word comes from Phil 3:13–14.

45 Mt 10:16.

46 Mt 18:3–4.

47 Robert Bensen, *Between the Dreaming and the Coming True*, HarperSanFrancisco, 1997, p. 55, quoted in Michael Yaconelli, *Dangerous Wonder: The Adventure of Childlike Faith*, Navipress, 2003, p. 91.

48 The phrase 're-reflexing' was coined by my friend Dr Alan Kreider to describe the biblical concept of 'sanctification' or the process of developing practical holiness.

49 See Mt 4:1; 19:3; Jas 1:13–15.

50 Two popular books that introduce the subject of the 'disciplines' are: Richard Foster, *Celebration of Discipline: The Path to Spiritual Growth*, Hodder, 1978; and Dallas Willard, *The Spirit of the Disciplines: Understanding How God Changes Lives*, Hodder, 1988.

51 2Cor 3:18.

52 Rom 12:11.

53 Mt 13:43.

54 1Jn 3:2–3.

55 This is Mt 5:8 using the Elias Chacour paraphrase in his *We Belong to the Land*, HarperCollins, 1992.

56 See Jas 1:27.

57 Mk 1:40–42.

6 Creation Companion
– living in harmony with wild nature

The hermit Seraphim of Sarov lived in the forests of the Russian wilderness. For decades visitors were rare, but the few that met him each reported two things: that his face seemed to shine as though full of light and that he had an astonishing rapport with the foxes, hares, wolves and bears that lived around him, with whom he shared his food and played like a child.[1]

A story like this, read from the comfort of an urban home, can seem surreal, remote, irrelevant and frankly sentimental. This is understandable, but reveals the extent to which the Christian community has forgotten that a major biblical mark of a truly spiritual person is that they live in harmony with wild nature.[2]

Two initial examples would be the story of Noah – tightly and peacefully confined with representatives of wild animals during the period of the Flood – and Daniel, who was completely unharmed while imprisoned in a pit of lions, where he had been thrown during an attempt by his enemies to destroy him. Whatever questions the historical background to these stories present, their purpose is to highlight the spirituality of the two characters – both are *zadik*.[3]

Jesus was recognised by his early followers as 'the *Zadik*' – 'the Righteous One'[4]. This being so, it is significant that following his baptism the Spirit drove him into the wilderness, where he was:

> '*with* the wild animals'.[5]

This concise, easily missed little phrase comes in the carefully crafted prologue to Mark's Gospel in which the author paints a picture of exactly what it meant for Jesus to be Messiah. It shows that Jesus' concern for our relationship with God also included concern for our relationship with the rest of creation. The grammar in the phrase, stressing the word 'with', conveys a strong sense of close association in friendship without any hint of hostile confrontation. It is clearly saying that the kingdom of God, inaugurated by Jesus, includes peaceful and personal relationship with wild animals.

The word 'with', stressing friendship and *shalom*-relationship with wild creation, is found in a number of significant biblical passages:

> And every wild animal of every kind
> ... went into the ark *with* Noah.[6]

> and [you] shall not fear the wild animals of the earth.
> For you shall be in covenant *with* the stones of the wilderness,
> and the wild animals shall be at *shalom with* you.[7]

> The wolf shall dwell *with* the lamb, and the leopard shall lie down
> *with* the kid.[8]

> I will make for you a covenant on that day *with* the wild animals of
> the wilderness,
> the birds of the air, and the creeping things of the ground.[9]

Notice that between them the passages refer to the past, the present and the future. They also include the powerful relationship word 'covenant' (*berith*), referring to both inanimate as well as animate creation.

I believe this word 'with' is the single most important and exciting biblical word in terms of ecology and the environment and our relationship with wild nature.

There are many stories of early Christian hermits; women and men who moved away from the towns and cities of their day to seek greater holiness by living in the wilderness.[10] Eyewitnesses leave us these remarkable accounts of the 'Desert Mothers and Fathers' developing close sustained friendships with the animals living around them, including predators like wolves and lions.[11]

Inspired by these stories, Celtic Christians took their pre-Christian traditions with an awareness of the divine in nature and saw that friendship with wild animals was one of the natural marks of a holy person.

The medieval urban imperial church saw salvation between God and humans *alone*. Challenges to this came from Hildegard of Bingen and Francis of Assisi.

Hildegard was a poet, musician, painter, botanist, herbalist, visionary, theologian, and spiritual leader not only of women but also of men, unusual for her time. She brought a liberated sensuous feminine embracing of creation in which there was no hostility between humans and the natural world; only joy, wonder, praise, awe and most of all love.

Francis was a friar–nomad, who saw every creature as a mirror of God's presence. He is remembered for his spirituality, and remarkable bond with animals, birds and the whole of creation. One example was his ability to bring peace between the inhabitants of Gubbio and a marauding wolf that killed sheep and townsfolk, but at Francis' command the problem ceased when the wolf was promised daily food by the citizens.

This relationship between holy people and wild nature is certainly not exclusive to a Jesus perspective.[12] The *Yoga Sutras of Patanjali*, the basic Indian *yoga* texts, clearly state:

> When a person becomes steadfast in their abstention from harming others,
> then all living creatures will cease to feel enmity in their presence.[13]

The key word is *ahimsa* – 'their abstention from harming others' – and those who are mature in its practice discover wild animals become peaceful in their presence;[14] this is another example of the *shanti*-person. There are stories of *yogis* in the forests playfully interacting with tigers, much as Seraphim did with Russian bears.[15]

Another story is of Rabi'a, a former slave girl and Muslim from Basra, southern Iraq, who spent years leading a saintly life in the wilderness, where animals such as deer, gazelles, mountain goats and wild donkeys gathered around her, trusting and fearless.[16]

These stories are popularly dismissed as legends and fables, but there are simply too many of them sharing similar features to be completely ignored. However these stories are told,[17] they provide a strong link with the biblical argument that spirituality involves harmony with nature. They affirm that a clear sign of *shalom*-spirituality is when someone is living in affinity and harmony with wild nature; they also demonstrate how profoundly spiritually sensitive and responsive wild nature itself is in its relationship to God.[18]

In the words of Guthlac, Celtic hermit of the fens, 'Have you never learned in Holy Writ, that someone who has led their life after God's will, the wild beasts and the wild birds will become more intimate with them'?[19]

In contrast, it is also sobering to reflect biblically that one consequence of human wickedness and rebellion against God may involve wild animals becoming destructive and hostile towards individuals and communities.[20]

* * * * *

The *matador* stands erect at the centre of the bullring. His swirling red cape draws the bull into passes close to his body, demonstrating his courageous skill as an artist and athlete. Having established his superiority over an already wounded bull, a single sword-thrust to its heart completes the ritual slaughter. The crowd roars its approval, saluting the bullfighter as a hero.

Apart from the cruelty of this spectacle, its symbolism is profoundly disturbing. It is an ancient drama in which the bull represents wild nature, seen as menacing and hostile, a threat to humanity. The *matador* ('one who kills') is a saviour-figure who rescues the community from this ever-present danger. This imagery is completely anti-Christian (which sees harmony between humans and wild nature), yet the horrific ceremony has flourished for centuries in cultures where the church has been the primary influence. The bullfight is a powerful example of the extent to which Christian understanding has been perverted. Those involved remain compromised until they deliberately choose to behave otherwise.

Jesus quite clearly says: 'Go into all the world and proclaim the good news to the whole creation.'[21] The gospel is green; Jesus does not die just for people, but for the whole 'more than human world':[22]

> through [Jesus] God was pleased to reconcile *all things,*
> whether on earth or in heaven
> making peace by the blood of his cross.[23]

Jesus' death locked him in conflict with cosmic forces of destruction; in the biblical narrative nature convulsed, rocks shattered, the noon sky was as black as night. Jesus' resurrection saw the hold of evil on creation broken forever; an earthquake flung the tombstone aside, a new day dawned – this is a central ecological moment.

The cross was a stake driven into the heart of the earth by evildoers, but in fact it became *the* 'Tree of Life'; symbol of the root-and-branch salvation, which ultimately brings into being the renewed heaven and earth, which in turn embraces the whole of humanity, the totality all living things including inanimate creation, with *shalom*.[24]

Why has the church developed such hostility to wild nature and the wilderness?

Why have the church's teaching and culture become some of the primary reasons behind the current ecological crisis?[25]

The issues are complex. It is easy to be simplistic. However, some of the theological and sociological strands we should reflect on are:[26]

- *Gnosticism:* this teaching is the belief that matter is evil and nature profane, only the spiritual is seen as important; it was officially rejected by the church but is still hugely influential and pervasive;
- *Pessimism:* this is where the church's flawed teaching on 'original sin' and the 'Eden curse' has neutralised the biblical blessings about the natural world and produced a negative mindset that is hostile to creation;
- *Dualism:* this is the idea that God is separate from the world and untouched by creation, that human beings and wild nature are also separate from each other; ultimately only that which is heavenly is important;
- *Technoism:* this is the belief that technology both can and should be used to control nature for human benefit, rather than aiding us to live in harmony with creation; it also describes the cultural attitude that develops from this;[27]
- *Anthropocentrism:* this is the western tendency to place people centre stage to the exclusion of nature, which is pushed to the edges of importance and seen simply as a resource that is there to be exploited;
- *Urbanism:* this is where societies are focused on the built environment with the deliberate intention of protecting themselves from nature; they believe their culture and way of thinking is the only authentic civilisation;

- *Biblicism:* this is where the biblical text is read in such a way that it reinforces all the above attitudes and uses religion to maintain this mindset.

* * * * *

There are two biblical creation stories; the 'Adam–Eden' story, which is told second but is the oldest and simplest,[28] and the priestly 'Creation Hymn' with which the book of Genesis opens.[29] In both stories humans and animals are bound together in unity; both are formed out of the red soil of 'the ground' (*adamah*),[30] they share the same 'life-breath' (*ruach*),[31] as a result both become 'living being-souls' (*nephesh*).[32]

The single feature that distinguishes humans from animals is the fact that we are 'made in the image and likeness of God', meaning we have been given a unique responsibility to 'image God'[33] in the way we live, and in the work we are given to do.

Christians historically have stressed the differences between humans and animals, while science and biblical texts note the similarities. We are astonishingly woven together in a tapestry of life that interconnects each one of us with all others and with God.

This understanding of an interconnection between humans and the 'more than human world' finds close parallels within the majority of indigenous cultures.

One example is the native American Lakota Sioux prayer, *Mitakuye Oyasin*, which means 'all my relatives,' or 'we are all related'; this is a prayer of oneness and harmony with all forms of life: other people, animals, birds, insects, trees and plants, and even rocks, rivers, mountains and valleys.

New Zealand Maoris have a concept called *whakapapa*, which is usually translated 'genealogy'; it suggests a flat foundation, forming a base with layer on layer laid upon it, linking individuals to their kinship group but ultimately connecting the whole creation together as a single cosmic family.

Our problems begin with the God-given instructions spoken to human beings in the two creation narratives and how these have been interpreted.

The 'Adam–Eden' story tells us:

> The Lord God placed the human in the garden of Eden
> to *work* it and *take care* of it.[34]

The word 'work' – *abad* – has the sense of 'to serve like a slave', while the phrase 'take care of it' – *shamar* – means 'to watch over and preserve'. We are to serve wild nature in a way that enables it not only to flourish but also to achieve its full potential in God.

In contrast the opening creation story, presented as a 'Creation Hymn', appears to see things quite differently. Humans are told:

> Be fruitful and multiply, and fill the earth and *subdue* it;
> and have *dominion* over the fish of the sea over the birds of the air
> and over every living thing that moves upon the earth'[35]

The word 'subdue' – *kabash* – has the sense of 'to stamp on something', and 'dominion' – *radah* – 'to rule over', or 'to trample like a winepress'. At first reading these are harsh terms, used by Christians for centuries as a licence to exploit the earth's resources with little regard for the consequences. This is wrong.

These words are from the language of ancient kingship and must be understood and interpreted in terms of humans being called to 'image God' within wild nature, in harmony with the character and values of God's kingship. God rules with love, mercy and compassion. Two primary biblical images that get to the heart of ideal kingship are a 'servant' and a 'shepherd'.[36]

So why is there this apparent harshness of the language?

First, this language originates from the popular notion of kingship at the time, which was coercive. *Yahweh* challenges and completely subverts such thinking throughout the scriptures, exampling authentic 'rule' as 'meekness' – 'strength under perfect control' – that powerful gentleness at the heart of all true 'dominion'.[37] These words call us to be counter-cultural.

Second, these words remind us of the astonishing human capacity to impact creation both for good and harm. *Rabbis* teach that the Hebrew phrase *v'yirdu* – 'have dominion' – also has the sense of 'to descend'. They say when we truly image God, we have appropriate nurturing dominion among animals; otherwise we descend below them and they rule over us. They argue our imaging God in creation raises it up to paradise, but when we do not nature 'descends' into the darkness and hell of an ecological crisis. The phrase also has the sense of 'to go down', 'to wander' and 'to spread', leading some *rabbis* to suggest it is a call to 'descend' from a position of power and 'wander' within wild nature as its equal. These words are a call to us to be wise.

Finally, there are times when wild nature is threatened; whenever that happens these words remind us we have the responsibility to stamp on the threat and eliminate it. This is part of what it means to be *with* creation; this is a call for us to be guardians.

The Hebrew prophet Zechariah gives a powerful meditation on true kingship, 'rule' and 'dominion':

> Behold your king comes to you;
> triumphant and victorious is he,
> *meek* and riding on a donkey,
> on a colt the foal of a donkey.
> He will cut off the chariot from Ephraim
> and the war horse from Jerusalem;
> and the battle bow shall be cut off,
> and he shall command *shalom* to the nations;
> his *dominion* shall be from sea to sea,
> and from the River to the ends of the earth.[38]

Notice how 'dominion' is interpreted as both 'meekness' and *shalom*. We see Jesus illustrating this text when riding into Jerusalem on a donkey.[39] He has already said:

> Get up, go ahead, do something, move, you meek,
> for you will inherit the earth.[40]

In these words Jesus is quoting the psalm:

> The meek shall inherit the land,
> and shall take delight in great *shalom*.[41]

The most popular word used within the Christian community to describe human relationships with creation is 'stewardship'; this is acting responsibly in the absence of a master, anticipating his near return and being prepared to give account.[42] However, this idea is fundamentally flawed.[43]

Built on the Benedictine tradition, it stresses 'respect' and 'responsibility' but fails to challenge established patterns of thinking. It is hierarchical with the earth still subject to humanity. It continues to see humans as *apart* from nature, which needs 'domestication' and control. Creation is viewed as a commodity to be managed, not a relationship to be nurtured. It simply misuses biblical ideas.[44]

We are called instead to 'companionship' with creation – literally, 'those who share bread'; we are not 'stewards' but 'friends'.[45]

This echoes the biblical tradition with a Franciscan interpretation, which is co-existence and inter-dependence with the world, each species retaining its separate identity and freedom. It expresses a love for the environment that is neither confrontational nor adversarial, sharing the planet as a 'community of creation'. Isaac Syrus, seventeenth-century Bishop of Nineveh, said: 'A loving heart is a heart which is burning with love for the whole of creation, for people, for the birds, for the beasts, for the demons – for all creatures.'[46]

In the Song of Songs we read about the bride. In total contrast to the *matador* we met earlier, she lives in peace within the Mount Hermon wilderness where her lover calls her: 'from the dens of lions, from the mountains of leopards'.[47] Here is a woman perfectly exampling companionship and friendship *with* wild nature, revealing her true spirituality. This rare biblical image clearly influenced the visions of the seer John in the book of Revelation, where he speaks of the church as 'the bride'.[48] On one occasion he describes her as 'a woman clothed with the sun', who, when threatened by 'the Beast' of imperialism, flees into the wilderness, her home: 'where she has a place prepared by God'.[49]

✷ ✷ ✷ ✷ ✷

Jacob, travelling across wild country, wearily places his head on a boulder. Asleep under the night sky, his powerful dream-vision evokes the cry:

> Surely the Lord is in this place – and I did not know it!
> … How awesome is this place!
> This is none other than the house of God,
> this is the gate of heaven.[50]

In the Sinai wilderness, Moses stands in front of a desert scrub-bush that is burning without being consumed and hears a voice:

> Remove the sandals from your feet,
> for the place on which you are standing is holy ground.[51]

In both these stories we see how the natural world reveals God directly, the landscape and everything in it is alive with the presence of the divine; we literally stand under an open heaven. The seasons of the year and the cycles of the moon create spiritual rhythms for our lives.[52] Job's wisdom crumbles in awe of wild nature and the creatures that inhabit it.[53] God appears among oak trees and on mountaintops, and is imagined as a roaring lion, nurturing eagle and protective mother bear.[54] For psalmists and prophets, hills 'skip like lambs', trees 'clap their hands' and forests sing along with the rest of creation in praise to God.[55] The earth is seen to be a living entity within itself in its relationship with God – quite apart from human beings.

Why has the church turned away from the power of this truth when my Pagan friends and *shamans* across the indigenous communities of the world are *so* open to it?

In the Gospels Jesus walks on water, commands the wind and waves and rides an ungentled donkey. He illustrates his teaching using seeds, flowers, trees, birds and the rain. His spirituality is constantly expressed using the elemental images of earth, wind, fire and water. He declares that if people are silenced in their celebrations even the stones will cry out their praises to God.[56]

Everything is sacred, because 'The earth is the Lord's and all that is in it'.[57] The first creation story repeats that everything is 'good', concluding that it is 'very good'. The earth is formed and sustained by God's word and Spirit-breath.[58] Orthodox Christians argue that what Moses saw in the burning bush is true of all creation if only we had eyes to see it. The early Jesus-community echoed this:

> Ever since the creation of the world God's eternal power and
> divine nature,
> invisible though they are,
> have been understood and seen through the things God
> has made.[59]

The whole of creation is crafted and sustained by the wisdom of God, whose creative cunning is threaded through every fibre of the cosmos to be discovered as truth by those open and willing to find it. This is 'pan*en*theism' – God *in* everything.[60]

* * * * *

Awe-inspiring and true as all this is, there is another side to the story that is disturbing and challenging, cloaked in mystery and paradox. As an early Christian voice declares:

> The creation waits with eager longing for the revealing of the children of God; for the creation was subject to futility, not of its own will but by the will of the one who subjected it, in hope that the creation itself will be set free from its bondage to decay and will obtain the freedom of the glory of the children of God. We know that the whole creation has been groaning in labour pains until now.[61]

Creation is 'subject to futility'; it is in 'bondage to decay', 'groaning in labour pains' and longing for 'freedom'.

Nature is 'good' but 'groaning'.[62]

Some of this is due to human moral evil we now see climaxing in our current ecological crisis, but it is very much more than this. At the heart of nature a profound struggle is taking place, which today we understand in terms of evolution – the model that makes most sense of our observations of the natural world.[63] It has given us the remarkable beauty and diversity of creation, but at the price of pain, suffering and death – 'nature red in tooth and claw'.[64]

Evolution is popularly viewed as being without design, with 'no purpose, no evil, no good, nothing but blind, pitiless indifference'; if this is so nihilism *is* true.[65]

From a Jesus perspective, evolution should be seen as central to the process that will reach its fulfilment in the renewed heaven and earth.

An objector might ask why a loving God would allow all the pain, suffering and death involved, and couldn't a powerful God have achieved the same goal another way?

We cannot begin to do justice to these huge questions here;[66] however, observing wild nature and reflecting biblically leads me to the conclusion that evolution provided the only way for God to achieve the divine goal of providing an essential freedom and dignity for all things. Also it is a struggle during which God suffers with creation (including humanity) and in the crucifixion takes full responsibility for the pain creation suffers – the resurrection empowering nature's transformation.

The ultimate climax will see every aspect of evolution that did not flourish during the process embraced by *shalom* and made part of the final wholeness of all things; nothing will be lost – this is universalism in its most complete sense.

The earth, like the whole cosmos, is dynamic. It is alive with movement and change, earthquakes, landslides, volcanoes, floods, tsunamis, hurricanes, storms, tornados, forest fires and drought: all popularly seen as hostile. In fact they are part of the very fabric of 'good' creation without which no life on earth could exist.

Humans have a key role in working together with God in this evolutionary process. Part of that role involves respectful cooperation with the earth's natural dynamism – including choosing to live wisely and not populating those areas inclined to tsunamis, volcanoes and other potentially life-threatening evolutionary processes. To live arrogantly as though these natural processes do not occur and then blame God when a crisis happens is outrageous.[67]

Our dynamic earth is made up of 'gifts of God', not 'acts of God'.

How will we choose to live in company with their constant revitalising presence?[68]

Be clear, there never was a bygone paradise we have lost, which we must struggle to regain. Perfection lies in the future, not the past. Biblical creation stories are not attempting to tell us *how* creation took place, but rather *why*; these stories are instead profound meditations on the nature of the earth, its destiny and our role within it for today and into the future.[69] They are also an affirmation that the values of goodness and *shalom* are woven into the very fabric of nature and are playing their part in its unfolding.

* * * * *

Being a 'Creation Companion' takes us into uncharted areas. Again *metanoia* ('think different') is required.[70] In challenging Christian and secular culture at every level, reactions are likely to be either incredulous or even hostile.

Because this territory is so unexplored it means there are more questions than answers. Here are some reflections around four themes.

There is the call to spirituality. Take time to nurture a deep sensitivity, encountering God in every sphere of nature. Embrace the idea that a truly spiritual person lives in *shalom with* all creation. In becoming a *zadik*, develop a *shanti-ahimsa* character where all living creatures cease to feel enmity in your presence. Remember there is no limit to what the Spirit might achieve in your life when you are open and willing to mature.[71] Ours is a feral faith firmly rooted into the sacred wild.[72] Daily I seek to live by the maxim:

Everything is sacred,
live gently in this sacred world with wisdom.[73]

There is the challenge to society.[74] We have already spoken about 'seeking the *shalom* of the city';[75] but our very concept of the city needs transfiguration. Creation not only 'groans' under the struggle of evolution, but also under the burden of human 'civilisation'. The 'Eden Garden', which represents wild nature as God first intended it to be, stands in complete contrast to the city-tower of Babel (Babylon) with its systems of violence, greed, exploitation and arrogance.[76] The biblical story resolves this in the image of the 'New Jerusalem' (literally 'the dwelling place of *shalom*'), symbol of the renewed heaven and earth where wilderness and human habitation flow together in complete integrated harmony.[77] Working with God to make this vision a reality is our inspiration and hope.

There is the importance of activity. Jesus-discipleship involves living as servants, priests and prophets upon the earth, working with wild nature to see evolution climax in God, 'set free from its bondage to decay', obtaining 'the freedom of the glory of the children of God'.[78] Here our role as '*Shalom* Activists' and 'Creation Companions' become one:

- We live at the centre of an ecological crisis of our own making that threatens the very existence of humanity and much of nature. We need to challenge the inertia of the State and society, exampling alternatives in creative thinking and living.
- Jesus calls us away from crippling economic systems to 'consider the birds' who trust God for everything. Wilderness economics has three qualities: to trust God to provide what we need, as with the *manna* in the desert; to make sure we take only what we need, and to display the grace of mutual sharing to meet one another's needs.[79]
- The festivals of Sabbath (rest), Tabernacles (dependence on God) and Jubilee (freedom from debt and slavery) break up the destructive patterns of city-civilisation, calling us back to wilderness living with their rhythms woven into our daily lives.[80]
- The development of agriculture was the foundation of the city-state; also today's agri-business is unsustainable. We have opportunities to explore alternative sources of food production modelled on natural ecosystems.[81]
- We should celebrate science that broadens our understanding of creation, and aids us in living in harmony with it; our technologies should be gentle and wise.
- God is quite clear; 'The land is mine, with me you are but aliens and tenants.'[82] This challenges all the notions of property, ownership and the State; it calls us to live quite differently with true humility (from Latin: *humus* – soil) and meekness of heart.
- We are to live with compassion and love towards the whole of creation. Choosing lifeways that affirm what the Jewish *rabbis* call *tsaar baalei hayyim* ('not to cause pain to living creatures'), and therefore shaped by strong sensitive gentleness.[83]
- The path of 'rewilding' – 'the intentional restoration of wholeness: the integrity of entire ecosystems as well as the integrity of our individual beings' – is *shalom*; this is not returning to a primitive past but rediscovering its lost depths in a 'rewilded' future.[84]
- We work for dramatic change with the subtle power of yeast in flour, from the inside out. The only mark we are to leave, as we touch the earth and live in connection with wild creation, is to be a footprint of peace.

Finally, *there is the question of utility*. We have seen that animals were not created to satisfy human needs and desires, but to have an independent living relationship with God. This led me to ask myself, 'As my companions how can I use them for meat or other food products?'[85] I have found the following words helpful to reflect on:[86]

I have given you every green plant for food.[187]

You will not hurt or destroy on all my holy mountain.[88]

I now choose to eat differently. Of course this subject raises strong emotions, plus the spectre of legalism and guilt.[89] For me it inspires a sense of freedom and celebration.[90] I am often asked, 'Are you allowed to eat this food?' My reply is simple, 'I am allowed to eat anything I like, but freely choose to live gently and eat only a plant-based diet.'

If you make the choice to eat the 'bread of gentleness', do it thoughtfully. Ask yourself, 'What do I really believe? Why am I doing this?' Take your time, one step at a time, experimenting, discovering and celebrating, joyfully deepening your companionship with the 'more than human world'.

✱ ✱ ✱ ✱ ✱

It is likely you live in a city, along with more than half the world population. So some of this chapter may have been hard to relate to. Please don't dismiss it as idealism but rather an invitation to re-imagine.

Remember, as we mentioned above, the final image in the early Christian writings is a city; the 'New Jerusalem', symbol of the renewed heaven and earth where wilderness and human habitation flow together in complete integrated harmony. This is our goal.

Practically, much is already being explored in the areas of urban ecology. City parks are linked to 'green corridors' to encourage wildlife and biodiversity into the heart of the community. Tree planting and 'guerrilla-gardening' on waste ground bring beauty and edible resources, along with allotments for fruit and vegetables and bee-colonies on high-rise buildings, and so much more. All are part of the creative eco-tapestry in many a metropolis.

Personally, let 'creation companionship' nurture your spirituality and inspire your activity; from shaping a gentle lifestyle to involvement with a local green project.

I conclude with a meditation …

Take a red house-brick ... God takes the red clay of the earth and shapes the human form, breathing into it – it becomes a living being.

We take the red clay, shape it into bricks and build cities. Imagine the Spirit-breath of God blowing through the streets of your city, saturating the walls of buildings, soaking the pavements. In the light of our themes, what creative miracles might unfold?

Endnotes

1   St Seraphim (1759–1833) is one of the most renowned Russian monks and mystics in the Orthodox Church; he was recognised as a *staretz* (elder) because of his wisdom and spiritual counsel. See Valentine Zander, *St. Seraphim of Sarov*, St Vladimir's Seminary Press, 1997.

2   Christian writing on ecology and the environment focuses almost entirely on the scientific and the ethical; it contains almost no reflection on the subject from the perspective of personal and community spirituality.

3   For the Noah story see Gen 6—8, for Noah as *zadik* see Gen 6:9; 7:1; 2Pt 2:5. For the Daniel story see Dan 6:10–28. For Noah and Daniel both as *zadik* see Ezk 14:14, 20. Who is 'Daniel'? The Ezekiel 'Daniel' is not the Babylon 'Daniel' unless Ezekiel was finally edited in the post-exile period (though their names are spelt slightly differently). More likely Ezekiel's 'Daniel' is a Phoenician who was 'righteous'. The Babylonian 'Daniel' clearly is *zadik* – called 'blameless'; though the editor may be echoing the Phoenician figure. Another biblical example of a spiritual person living in harmony with nature would be Elijah who lived in the wilderness and was fed by ravens – 1Kgs 17:1–7.

4   See Acts 3:14; 7:52; 22:14.

5   See Mk 1:13. This phrase has been given detailed examination by Richard Bauckham, 'Jesus and the Wild Animals' in Joel Green and Max Turner (eds), *Jesus of Nazareth: Lord and Christ*, Paternoster, 1994, pp. 3–21. This article informs my comments on this phrase. The phrase 'wild animals' distinguished them from domesticated animals and usually implied four-footed animals as opposed to birds, reptiles and fish. It was a phrase usually used of beasts of prey often seen as a threat to human life; cf. Gen 37:20, 33; Lev 26:6, 22; 2Kgs 2:24; 17:25–26; Prov 28:15; Jer 5:6 etc. The Judean wilderness of Jesus' day had leopards, bears, wolves, poisonous snakes (cobras and desert vipers) and scorpions.

6   Gen 7:14–15.

7   Job 5:22–23.

8   Isa 11:6.

9   Hos 2:18.

10   The wilderness, in contrast to cities and civilisation, as the place to encounter God is deeply rooted in the biblical tradition. Moses (Exod 3), the whole of the Exodus journey (the Hebrew name for the book of Numbers is 'in the wilderness'), Elijah (1Kgs 17 and 19) and Amos (Amos 7:14) are just a small sample of 'those of whom the world was not worthy, wandering in deserts, mountains and caves' (Heb 11:38). John the baptist, Jesus and Paul all spent time alone in the wilderness and the church is called to identify with Jesus 'outside the gates' (Heb 13:12).

11 There are a number of intriguing pictures from the catacombs in Rome of early Christians standing in prayer with what appear to be wild animals around them; see Alan Kreider, *Resident But Alien: How the Early Church Grew*, Great Commission Distribution Ltd/ YWAM DVD, 2009. There are also stories of occasions when wild animals in the arena refused to attack Christians who had been thrown to them for execution; while there could be a number of explanations for this the accounts are none the less intriguing, see the Joanne Stefanatos resources mentioned below in Note 17.

12 See the remarkable photography of the Canadian-born artist, Gregory Colbert. He says of his work, 'I am working towards rediscovering the common ground that once existed when people lived in harmony with animals.' Gregory Colbert, *Ashes and Snow: One Thousand Rivers*, Flying Elephants Press, 2007.

13 This is Sutra 2.35 (slightly adapted for gender), for the original see <www.athayoganusasanam.com>.

14 See Kurt A Jacobsen, 'Ahimsa', in Bron Taylor (ed.) *Encyclopedia of Religion and Nature*, vol. 1, Continuum, 2005, pp. 30–31. We shall discuss *ahimsa* in more detail in '*Meekness Zealot*'.

15 One similar figure is the fifteenth-century *sufi*, Taj Baba, from southern India, popularly known as Raja Bagh Sawar – 'The King Astride a Tiger' – he is however claimed by some Hindus to have been a Brahmin *yogi* and not a *sufi*.

16 For Rabi'a of Basra (713–801) see Maria Jaoudi, *Christian and Islamic Spirituality: Sharing a Journey*, Paulist Press International, 1993, p. 85.

17 In the Christian tradition the classic account is Helen Wadell, *Beasts and Saints*, Darton, Longman & Todd, 1995. Many other similar stories are told, particularly from the eastern Orthodox tradition, in Joanne Stefanatos, *Animals and Man: A State of Blessedness*, 1992 and *Animals Sanctified: A Spiritual Journey*, 2001, both published by Light & Life Publishing Company, Minneapolis. While Stefanatos' theological reflection would benefit from more rigour and her storytelling from less saccharine, she has provided a collection of stories difficult to find gathered in one place elsewhere; we are grateful.

18 In Ezekiel 1:4–14, might one aspect of the appearance of the human-like 'living creatures', each with four faces – a human, a lion, an eagle and an ox – symbolise all living things integrated in harmony? See also Ezk 10:14 and Rev 4:7.

19 Edited slightly for gender and contemporary style. See Shirley Toulson, *The Celtic Alternative: A Reminder of the Christianity We Lost*, Century Hutchinson, 1987, p. 66, see also pp. 100–104, 141. Guthlac (673–714) was a hermit on the isle of Croyland in the Cambridgeshire fens.

20 See Lev 26:22; Deut 32:24; 2Kgs 2:23–25; Ezk 39:4.

21 Mk 16:15.

22 This phrase, 'more than human world' is one used by David Abram in his book, *The Spell of the Sensuous*, Vantage/ Random House, 1997, which is a very positive and inclusive way of speaking about the earth and creation.

23 Col 1:20.

24 See Mt 27:45–51; Acts 5:30; 1Pt 2:24; 3: 13; Rev 21:1; 22:2.

25 I am fully aware that many Christians will find these two questions offensive, but that does not make them inappropriate. I am not denying that the majority of Christians, along with most other cultures and peoples, find deep beauty in nature – from a distance – but the way they have chosen to live their everyday lives, with a focus on the work ethic and rampant capitalism, alongside a failure to challenge industrial technology and its physical, social and cultural impact all confirm the significance of my questions. Similar attitudes are not found among people untouched by Christian–western culture. Why do the indigenous populations of the Amazon call Christian missionaries 'the axe carriers'?

26 I am not for a moment suggesting that these issues are exclusively Christian issues – they are not – but I am arguing that they have perverted the gospel because the Christian community has consistently bought into them and failed to challenge them.

27 Beverley J Davies coined the term 'technoism' in 1999 to define the suppressed scepticism and blind compliance towards the uncontrolled and rapid inundation of the technology revolution <www.leadershipeducators.org/Archives/2003/davis.pdf>. I am using it to include this sense, but also the definition I have provided.

28 Gen 2:4b—3:24.

29 Gen 1:1—2:4a.

30 Gen 2:7 (humans from 'the ground' – *adamah*); Gen 2:19 (animals from 'the ground' – *adamah*).

31 Gen 2:7(humans having 'breath of life' – *ruach*); Gen 6:17 (animals having 'breath of life' – *ruach*); see also human and animal 'life-breath' – *ruach* identical in Eccl 3:19.

32 Gen 2:7 (humans as 'living being-souls' – *nephesh*); Gen 1:30 (animals as 'living being-souls' – *nephesh*); the word *nephesh* means to be alive as a physical being. Neither humans nor animals 'have' souls that survive death (this is a non-biblical idea) but 'are' souls that at death await resurrection to achieve their destiny. The word *nephesh* is best translated 'life' rather than 'soul' to reduce misunderstanding.

33 Gen 1:27.

34 Gen 2:15.

35 Gen 1:28, see also 1:26.

36 See Mt 20:28; Phil 2:6–7; 2Sam 5:2; Ezk 34:1–31; Jn 10:11 *et al.*

37 We shall discuss 'meekness' in much more detail when we explore being a '*Meekness Zealot*'.

38 Zech 9:9–10.

39 Mt 21:1–11.

40 This is Mt 5:5 using the Elias Chacour paraphrase in his *We Belong to the Land*, HarperCollins, 1992.

41 Ps 37:11 in the translation of Peter C Craigie, *Word Biblical Commentary: Psalms 1–50*, Word Publishing, 1983, p. 294.

42 See Lev 25:23; Mt 21:33–41; 25:15–30.

43 See Richard Bauckham, *Bible and Ecology: Rediscovering the Community of Creation*, Darton, Longman & Todd, 2010, pp. 1–12 for one of many criticisms of the concept of 'stewardship'.

44 The use of the word 'tenant' in both Lev 25:23 and Mt 21:33–41 is not about our 'role' but about our 'status' (see below); the 'talents' in Mt 25:15–30 are 'commodities', not the 'companion' creation is brought into being to be – 'stewardship' thinking works with inappropriate images.

45 The word 'companion' is from the Latin *com* (with) *panis* (bread), 'one with whom you share bread'.

46 Ian Bradley, *God is Green: Christianity and the Environment*, Darton, Longman & Todd, 1990, p 94, quoting V Lossky, *The Mystical Theology of the Eastern Church*, James Clarke, 1957, pp. 110–111.

47 Song 4:8.

48 See Rev 19:7; 21:2, 9; 22:17.

49 See Rev 12:1–6; this phrase reminds me of the reflections of the Israeli ecologist and theologian, Nogah Hareuveni, who identifies three Hebrew words from the root *D* (dalet), *B* (bet) and *R* (reish) – *DBR*; they are: *miDBaR* – 'desert' or 'wilderness', *DoBRo* – 'a place of pasture (meadow) for gathering and grazing flocks in the wilderness', and *DBiR* – 'Holy of Holies'; there is a

gathering nourishing place at the heart of the wilderness that is the Holy of Holies where God's presence is encountered. See Nogah Hareuveni, *Desert and Shepherd in Our Biblical Heritage*, Neot Kedumim, 1991, pp. 51–52.

50 Gen 28:16–17.
51 Exod 3:5.
52 Gen 1:14–17; 8:22; Ps 74:16–17; 104:19.
53 Job 38:1—42:6.
54 Gen 12:6–7; 18:1; Jg 6:11; Exod 19:1–25; Mk 9:2–8; Hos 11:10; 13:8; Deut 32:11. This sentence is taken (slightly adapted) from Ched Myers (see note 69 below).
55 See Isa 44:23; 55:12. See also Ps 104 and 148.
56 Mk 4:1–9, 35–41; 6:47–51; 11:1–8; 13:28; Lk 12:24, 27; Mt 5:45: earth – Mt 13:44; wind – Jn 3;8; fire – Lk 12:49; water – Jn 4:14; stones – Lk 19:40.
57 Ps 24:1. 'Everything is sacred' is a fundamental truth. The idea of consecrating a piece of land for a church building or a graveyard is an affront to the sacredness of all creation; it is Gnostic in its origins and should be openly resisted. Popular among contemporary contemplative groups is to speak about 'creating a sacred space' for worship; while I understand the sentiments we need to speak differently, such as 'recognising this space as sacred'.
58 Ps 33:6; 104:30.
59 Rom 1:20 see also Acts 14:15–17; 17:24–28.
60 See Ps 104:24; Prov 3:19; 8:22–31; Job 28:25–27; 1Kgs 4:29–34; 'pane*n*theism' is 'God *in* everything' – this is biblical, while 'pantheism' is 'everything is God' (the universe equated with God) – which is not biblical. God's relationship with creation is a mystery difficult to put into words; God is both distinct from creation ('transcendent') yet intimately connected with it ('immanent') – the earth is not divine but it is sacred. God's existence does not depend upon creation, yet creation's existence is totally dependent on God for everything.
61 Rom 8:19–22; for a detailed and excellent study of this passage and Col 1:15–20 (cited above) see DG Horrell, C Hunt and C Southgate, *Greening Paul: Rereading the Apostle in a Time of Ecological Crisis*, Baylor University Press, 2010.
62 See Christopher Southgate, *The Groaning of Creation: God, Evolution and the Problem of Evil*, Westminster John Knox Press, 2008, Introduction, p. 1.
63 I am not suggesting that evolutionary theory is not without its challenges (like most scientific theories!), however it is the most thoroughly tested theory in the history of science and its basic premises seem to have stood up to the rigour of investigation and are accepted by the scientific community as the basis for further enquiry.
64 Alfred Tennyson, *In Memoriam A. H. H.* (1850).'
65 Richard Dawkins, *River out of Eden: A Darwinian View of Life*, Weidenfeld & Nicolson, 1995, p. 133. In rejecting this statement I am not arguing for 'intelligent design' where God is said to intervene in evolution at key points, a view that poses more problems than it tries to solve; nor deism where God leaves creation to its own devices. Rather a long process of exploration under the influence of law and chance, where God continually creates new possibilities for chance without intervening, where freedom and longing and the value to become something greater draws it forward (see Southgate below). Only ultimately will we fully understand the subtle mystery of evolution unfolding in God and wonder at its completion
66 For a clear study of this difficult subject see Christopher Southgate, *The Groaning of Creation: God, Evolution and the Problem of Evil*, Westminster John Knox Press, 2008. While I disagree with some details of his final

conclusions, his overall thesis is excellent, carefully and clearly articulating ideas I held for some time prior to reading this book. The summary of ideas on p. 16 is a good place to start.

67 Do not misunderstand this statement. When the huge tragedies of earthquakes or tsunamis take place with many thousands of deaths it is of course heartbreaking, at times feeling beyond expressing in words or emotions. My point is twofold. First, whenever these kinds of events occur there is an immediate cry, 'How can a good God allow this to happen?' There is no recognition that God has created the best of all possible worlds but we live in both ignorance of and arrogance about this truth. Nor do we recognise that God suffers alongside all those in distress and empowers all those who work to bring rescue and comfort. Second, events like this should stop us in our tracks and lead us to ask the question, 'Shouldn't we be living differently?'

68 Some provocative pointers can be found in reports from the 'Boxing Day Tsunami' (2004) suggesting that, apart from some domestic animals, almost no wildlife died; birds and animals having an awareness of what was about to happen. The primal communities who inhabit the Andaman and Nicobar Islands off the coast of India, who live in sensitive contact with the animal world and the rhythms of nature, appear to have escaped unscathed. For more information see the major online news networks and especially <www.nativeamericanchurch.com>.

69 'Adam' is each one of us at all stages of the human story; we have each rebelled, as Adam did, and we will all die; however the 'final Adam' (Jesus) enables us all to become *zadik* and share the eternal life of God. See Rom 5:12–21; 1Cor 15:20–22.

70 See Rom 12:2.

71 There might be a place to devise a personal 'Vision Quest' with this goal as a focus. For more on a 'Vision Quest' see the Catholic author, Achiel Peelman, *Christ is a Native American*, Orbis Books, 1995, p. 218–221. In my teaching I have created the opportunity for thousands of people to explore a simple 'Vision Quest' exercise in terms of 'dreaming their future' with powerful results. I believe something similar around this focus could prove significant.

72 A powerful exploration of the concept of 'the wild' is Jay Griffiths, *Wild: An Elemental Journey*, Hamish Hamilton, 2007. Using the metaphors of Earth, Ice, Water, Fire and Air to explore indigenous cultures around the world and their relationship with nature, it is strongly anti-Christian for reasons that become clear towards the end of the book; nevertheless it is a remarkable and inspiring reflection on its theme.

73 I coined this maxim in 1998 with the aim of distilling into simple focus the principles I had been endeavouring to live by for some time previously. The key word here is 'wisdom', which we will explore in much more detail when we discuss our identity as a '*Wisdom Dancer*'.

74 This is a huge topic, which we began to discuss in the Shalom *Activist* chapter and will continue when exploring being a *Messianic Anarchist*. Here, from the perspective of the relationship of society/ civilisation to nature, see Ched Myers, 'Anarcho-Primitivism and the Bible' in Bron Taylor (ed.) *Encyclopedia of Religion and Nature*, vol. 1, Continuum 2005, pp. 56–58 for an exciting, radical and insightful critique of the subject. His article has aided my thinking at a number of points in this chapter.

75 Jer 29:7.

76 See the ideas found in R Bauckham and T Hart, *Hope Against Hope*, Darton, Longman & Todd, 1999, pp. 147–153; contrast Gen 2:4–24 with Gen 11:1–9.

77 Rev 21:9—22:7.

78 Rom 8:21.

79 Lk 12:24; Exod 16:1–36 (Jn 6:22–59); see Isa 55:1; Lk 12:22–34; Acts 2:43–47; 2Cor 8–9. I love the way Jesus uses the example of the raven; God provides for the raven (Lk 12:24), but it was the raven that provided for Elijah in the wilderness (1Kgs 17:6) out of the abundance God gave the raven in the first place! What a wonderful example for us.

80 Exod 20:8–11; Deut 5:12–15; Lev 23:33–43; 25:8–55.

81 The most developed of these is 'permaculture'. Two foundational books are David Holmgren, *Permaculture: Principles and Pathways Beyond Sustainability*, Permanent Publications, 2011 and Patrick Whitefield, *The Earth Care Manual: A Permaculture Manual for Britain and Other Temperate Climates*, Permanent Publications, 2004. There are of course many other books available on this subject.

82 Lev 25:23.

83 See Dan Cohn-Sherbok, 'The Jewish Tradition: the Hebrew Bible and the Rabbis' in Andrew Linzey and Dan Cohn-Sherbok, *After Noah: Animals and the Liberation of Theology*, Mowbray, 1997, pp. 27–32.

84 This definition is from Jesse Wolf Harding, 'Rewilding' in Bron Taylor (ed.), *Encyclopedia of Religion and Nature*, .vol 2, Continuum, 2005, pp. 1383–1384; he coined the word and his article is a deeply moving meditation on the subject.

85 This question has nothing to do with sentimentalism but the hard facts as I have presented them. Sadly there is no space to set out a full argument for veganism, so I will restrict myself to what I say in the main text and the few extended observations made in the endnotes below.

86 Taking time to think is very important. Consider also Isa 66:3, 'Whoever slaughters an ox is like one who kills a human being.' I am well aware that these words are spoken in the context of the irrelevance of sacrifice but the ideas behind the words are clearly much more significant than that. Another question to ask is, 'How is it that the arguments used by Christians today to defend meat-eating are identical to those developed by them in the past to justify the continuation of slavery?' It was said that slavery was allowed by God, part of Israel's institutions and was a merciful practice; but one final point might be helpful. It was said that Jesus did not condemn slavery and even healed a slave without demanding his release. For Jesus to have confronted slavery head-on would have been to attack one of the pillars of Mediterranean economics in a way that most people would not have been able to understand. However, we know that justice was such a powerful force at the heart of the gospel that, as it spread around the world of its day, slavery was freely and fundamentally eroded (Philemon vv. 12–16). It is said that Jesus was not a vegetarian; he clearly ate fish (Mk 6:38–41 *et al.*; Lk 24:42; Jn 21:9) and supported catching fish (Mt 17:24–27; Lk 5:4–8; Jn 21:4–8). Different Christian vegetarian responses are given:

• It is argued that the passages that refer to Jesus catching and eating fish were not part of the earliest authentic Jesus' tradition; this is a debatable, weak and inadequate response;

• It is argued that in Jesus' day fish were not considered to be 'meat' (they did not 'breathe' like other animals); whether or not this is true it does not deal with the central issue;

• I believe Jesus recognised that issues around food are very quickly perverted by religion in terms of legalism and purity (as with the Pharisees e.g. Mt 23:23). If Jesus had taught vegetarianism it would have quickly become a 'religious law' rather than a joyful celebration. Jesus rejects religion and focuses on character and spirit: 'There is nothing outside a person that by going in can defile, but the things that come out are what defile' (Mk 7:15). Like slavery, Jesus knew that the gospel properly understood would lead to people freely choosing not to eat meat – sadly this has rarely happened.

87 See Gen 1:29–30; people will immediately quote Gen 9:3, 'Every moving thing that lives shall be food for you; and just as I gave you green plants, I give you everything.' However, this is a concession, like divorce (Deut 24:1–4); God 'hates divorce' (Mal 2:13–16), but divorce was happening and women were being exploited so a concession is given. God's ideal is a vegan diet, both originally (Gen 1:29–30) and ultimately (see Isa 11:9 below). The fact these ideas continue in a centuries-old carnivorous Jewish culture is significant. There is strong rabbinical opinion that the discipline of *kosher* food should be a constant reminder to Jews that God originally wanted them to be vegetarian

88 Isa 11:9.

89 The emotional, psychological and cultural power of food and meat-eating in particular is huge. An African friend of mine told me that a meal without meat was like 'punishment food'. In India and China, as people's economic situation improves their cultural expectation of eating more meat increases.

90 I tease my Orthodox Christian friends that they eat a vegan diet for forty days throughout Lent and call it fasting, while I eat a vegan diet 365 days a year and call it celebrating!

7 Messianic Anarchist
– celebrating the way of freedom

If all men were like Ammon, there would be no need for courts, judges, or police. How strange it is that the anarchists I have met have been the most disciplined of men, lawful and orderly, whilst those who insist that discipline and order must prevail are those who, out of plain contrariness, would refuse to obey and are the ones most unable to regulate themselves.[1]

Dorothy Day, founder of the Catholic Worker Movement, wrote these words about one of the community members; they touch the heart of what this chapter is about.

'What do you think of when you hear the word anarchist?'

When I ask this question the replies are usually the same: 'Molotov cocktails, violence, barricades, anger, dirty, undisciplined, selfish, lazy' – very occasionally someone will say, 'Gentle.'

'Anarchist' is a difficult word, derided from the outside and divided by different ideas within the movements deemd anarchic.[2] The word comes from the Greek: *anarchos* meaning 'without a ruler', and means 'one who is free from powers'. While the mainstream anarchist movements are openly atheist, there is a strong tradition of Christian anarchy, which goes directly back to Jesus himself.[3]

The anarchist embraces the deep dream within every human heart that longs for freedom, to live from within, from the inside out; to live spontaneously, rather than having our behaviour and actions controlled and dictated to from the outside.

When exploring our identity as a *'Shalom Activist'* we saw that God's original dream for human societies was that they would organise themselves in communities living in harmony with the divine, within themselves, with one another and wild nature, displaying the maximum diversity of culture.

All this stands in stark contrast with the idea of 'the State' as a centralised power with a ruler or government, controlling a geographical area and guaranteeing order by the use of force – seen biblically as an act of treachery.[4] The State is about power, controlling the institutions and structures of society, which it has perverted. It creates every injustice that is challenged by the concept of *mishpat*. It also demands that we behave in a way that maintains this status quo. Jesus smashes this stronghold.

True politics is spiritual work that involves building cultures of *shalom* in a way that celebrates all the glorious complexity and diversity seen among people and in the wilderness. It challenges those concentrations of power in societies that stifle spirituality within humanity and creation. We have seen that radical political engagement involves devising plans and schemes that confront these strongholds of power and fear with strategies that are creatively imagined, fearlessly executed and beautiful in their outcome.

But where do we begin? We begin deep within ourselves.

★ ★ ★ ★ ★

I'm standing behind a young mother with two toddlers queuing at the checkout in our local supermarket. Her grocery-laden shopping trolley suggests she has been touring the aisles for some time; her little girls are weary and fractious. Suddenly, one daughter snatches a candy-bar from a low shelf by the till. 'Katie, behave!' her exasperated mother shouts as she replaces it, embarrassed. I felt for the mother in her struggles, but of course Katie *was* behaving – not how her mother wanted her to, but she was *behaving* none the less.

The only people who don't behave are corpses.

While we are alive, everything we do is behaviour; we are incapable of not behaving.[5] The searching questions are 'How do I behave?' and 'Why do I choose to act as I do?' These questions find their focus in what we call 'ethics', which can appear a cold theoretical term, but is at the centre of every breath we take.[6]

How I behave affects the people and natural world around me; but
it also reveals the kind of person I really am. Jesus says, 'By their
fruits you will know them.'[7]

My actions proclaim the real me; they display my character for all
to see.

We may be passionate about radical social and political change
within the world, but the kind of communities and societies we long
to see will be realised only to the extent that each one of us has
the character required to sustain them.

As the quote attributed to Gandhi declares, 'Be the change you
wish to see.'[8]

Spirituality, ethics and politics flow seamlessly together. I work to
weave cultures of *shalom* within the world, while at the same time
working to weave the character of *shalom* within my heart; the two
are interdependent. This reality is at the heart of a Jesus
perspective.

An anonymous second-century Christian was asked, 'What is a
Christian?' They replied:

> You cannot identify Christians from other people by nationality,
> language or customs.
> They do not live in isolated cities, speak some strange dialect,
> or adopt a peculiar lifestyle.
> Their teaching is not the inventive speculation of inquisitive
> minds.
> They are not propagating mere human teaching as some
> people do.
> They live in a Greek or foreign city, wherever chance has
> placed them.
> They follow local customs in clothing, food and other aspects of
> life.
> But at the same time they demonstrate the strangely wonderful
> form of their own citizenship.
> They each live in their native land, but as strangers.
> They shoulder all the duties of citizenship, but are made to
> suffer like aliens.
> Every foreign country is to them a homeland, while every
> homeland is like a foreign country.
> They marry and have children just like everyone else; but they

do not kill unwanted babies.
They share a common table but not a common bed.
They are present 'in the flesh', but they do not live 'according to
the flesh'.
They live upon earth, but they are citizens of heaven.
They obey human laws, but surpass these laws in their
personal lives.
They love everyone, but are persecuted by all.
They are unknown, and yet they are condemned.
They are put to death and yet they are more alive than ever.
They are poor and yet make many rich.
They are short of everything and yet they live in abundance.
They are dishonored and yet their dishonor becomes a glory.
Their names are blackened; nevertheless they stand innocent.
They are mocked and yet they bless in return.
They are treated outrageously and yet behave respectfully to all.
When they do good they are punished as evildoers.
When punished they rejoice as if being given new life.
They are attacked by some as aliens and persecuted by others.
Yet those who hate them cannot give any reason for their
hostility.
To put it simply – life is to the body as Christians are to the
world.
Their life is in the body but is not of the body.
Christians are in the world but not of the world.
Life is locked into the body, yet it holds the body together.
Christians are held like prisoners in the world, yet it is they that
hold the world together.[9]

Notice this early description of a Christian contains no theological
statement, it doesn't even mention Jesus; it simply points to the
character and quality of their lives; lives, which were 'turning the
world upside-down'.[10]

You will remember, the early Jesus-community described
themselves as the 'people of the Way', emphasising godly
behaviour and actions.[11] Jesus-inspired ethics should be
provocative in any society; they are neither easy nor comfortable
and often controversial, but always life-giving and liberating. They
have four essential characteristics:

- *A sign for the present:* my actions offer an alternative, more
  authentic way of living; like a prophecy, my life becomes a
  proclamation of God's character – they are authentic;

- *A symbol for the future:* like a vision my behaviour points beyond the immediate to be a foretaste of the renewed heaven and earth – they are eschatological;[12]
- *A source for empowerment:* like a tree, the way I live points to the God-given values that root me as a person and energise my lifestyle – they are radical;
- *A spur for questions:* like a goad my deeds provoke discussion about the meaning of life and its spiritual, theological and philosophical options – they are disturbing.

What is the key to understanding ethics from a Jesus perspective?

We have already said the single most important question anyone can ask is: 'What kind of person do I want to be?' This question insists that we reach deep within ourselves and dream. Like most people across the countries and cultures of the globe we dream of being free; free within ourselves to achieve our full potential, free to express ourselves in a way that is true, and free from injustice.

Anarchists are one group of people who have endeavoured to live this dream. We have seen they believe that each individual should be free to live their lives out of an inner sense of justice and kindness; and that law, in the way that it imposes other people's desires upon us, is essentially exploitive. People should be free to explore and express their individuality.

There are of course many expressions of anarchy. Small minorities fit the stereotypes of anger, self-interest and violence that besmirch the name; however, most live gently and nonviolently, working to build community. Whatever accusations may be made of a few anarchists, they are all engaging with the God-given truth that we are created to dance to the spirit of freedom. Jesus and the early Christian community put it in these words:

You shall know the truth and the truth will set you free.[13]

It is for freedom that Christ has set you free.[14]

For where the Spirit of the Lord is there is freedom.[15]

Jesus-ethics are a call to live spontaneously in harmony with the character of God in the power of the Spirit; and the first fruit is freedom. The only phrase I can shape that begins to describe such an identity is 'Messianic Anarchist' – nothing else gets close.

Messianic means 'one anointed by God's Spirit'; remember the name 'Christian' is a Greek phrase meaning 'little Messiah':

> You shall receive power when the Holy Spirit has come upon you.[16]

Anarchist means 'one free from the powers'; remember this was the purpose of Jesus' death and resurrection:

He disarmed the powers and authorities … triumphing over them.[17]

The spiritual transformation that Jesus offers turns everything inside out. The source of human behaviour is no longer shaped by external rules but inspired by deep inner values energised by the Spirit. Jesus says: 'Out of your innermost being shall flow rivers of living water.'[18]

* * * * *

The deep dream of the anarchist is seen as too disturbing for most individuals and societies to engage with.

Misunderstood, it is dismissed as an illusion; it would leave society out of control, 'everyone doing what is right in their own eyes'.[19] It seems to be a mandate for lawless self-interest, with the weak crushed by the strong and a perversion of power. Presented with a vision of potential chaos, most people – including the majority of Christians – reach for the law and its embodiment in the State. Here they believe that safety, control, security and continuity will be found.

The concept of law is a slippery thing to define, one that philosophers have wrestled with for millennia without ever reaching a consensus. It can tentatively be defined as 'a rule of action established by authority'[20] – a phrase symbolising everything that is believed to be solid, dependable and appropriate within society. It is also an essential concept at the heart of most religions, whether the 'instructions of Moses' or the 'analects of Confucius'.

For Thomas Aquinas, our human law was simply one in a hierarchy of four kinds of law, flowing from the first precept of the 'natural law': the imperative to do good and avoid evil.[21] In contrast, extreme 'legal positivists', like Hans Kelsen, believe law to be completely disconnected from ethical notions of good and evil, deriving its force simply from authority alone. For Kelsen, this was the purest philosophy of law, unencumbered by constraints of morality.[22]

However, we engage with this topic in the light of the example and teaching of Jesus; we see that the word 'law' arguably has three different understandings:

- 'Law of the Land' – based on legislation – to *control* human behaviour;
- 'Law of the Lord' – based on the *torah* – to *develop* human behaviour;
- 'Law of Liberty' – based on the Spirit – to *free* human behaviour.

Let's explore each of these in turn.[23]

The 'Law of the Land' is to control human behaviour. This is something I remember when a flashing blue light in my rear-view mirror and the whine of a police siren tells me I have broken the speed limit; I have broken the law. Laws, down through history, whether decreed by a monarch, agreed by a community or decided upon by a parliament, are primarily to do with restraint. The temptation to drive too fast on this stretch of road endangering lives had been noted, so the law forbade it, but I have stepped over the mark and will pay the consequences. The 'law of the land' will deal with me.

For all its limitations and frustrations most people accept the law because it is seen to have real value and the alternative is thought too terrible to imagine.

I fully recognise that the subject of the law is profound and complex; it creates a framework within which society functions, very often for good. It protects the vulnerable from the unscrupulous and it provides a means that attempts to put things right when there is wrongdoing.

The law also has a cultural impact that tells everyone, 'In our society we believe this to be right and that to be wrong.' This is why many people will instinctively question a law as 'unjust', as something that *shouldn't* be followed or obeyed, because it does not seem right and therefore not legal.

However, the law also has very real weaknesses. It can only control and restrain people; it cannot change them. It is completely dependent on outside controls – like the police and the courts – to enforce it. Those with influence can manipulate it and it can be used to control populations unjustly. It is also relative, constantly changing depending on those in power and the pressure of public opinion. This is further emphasised by the fact that law is quite different in different cultures.[24]

Finally, the 'law of the land' creates *conformists*. For example, every community has bad laws, these are recognised but – apart from extreme circumstances – people just shrug and live with them; they are simply tolerated. The reality is that law in this form can subtly sap people's moral integrity, responsibility and maturity.

One of the greatest legal jurists of modern times, Ronald Dworkin, continues to wrestle with this question of the duty to obey or disobey unjust laws, demonstrating how the imposition of law, authority and obedience continues to be so vexing and difficult to justify.[25]

The 'Law of the Lord' is to develop human behaviour. Rachel is an orthodox Jewish mother. She prepares food for her family with scrupulous care according to the principles of *kashrut*, a word that means 'fit' – implying that everything is ritually 'clean'. This requires that she will only buy certain foods and prepare them in particular ways, being especially careful never to allow meat and milk foods to contact each other.[26]

Restrictions that would be irksome and irrelevant to most people Rachel joyfully accepts because she sees them as the 'law of the Lord', given by God to foster *qadosh* (the uniqueness of holiness). The directions she follows are based on the 613 commands found among the pages of the *torah* in the Hebrew scriptures. These instructions (the meaning of the word *torah*) are hardly seen as laws, but rather like the words of a loving parent putting their arm around the shoulder of their child to say, 'Let me show you how to live.'

Many of the *kosher*[27] rules are given no explanation, but they are accepted without question as the compassionate wisdom of God with whom she, her family and community are in *berith* (binding covenant relationship).

Talking with Rachel is inspiring as she explains how her pattern of life is all about *grace* (an extravagant gift from God) in which she delights. The same would be true of a conversation with a Muslim, who would tell you that *sharia* law is nothing other than 'the path that leads to the source of life-giving water'.[28]

However, Jesus and the early Christian community teach that God offers much more than rule-based living. Law may have some value but also has fundamental limitations. It is restrictive and cannot change you. It gives instructions like a tutor to children, but it is not a lifestyle for adults.[29]

Laws and rules are provocative but not restorative.

For example, I am walking on the path in a park enjoying the sunshine when I see a sign, 'Don't walk on the grass.' Until that moment I had no interest in walking on the grass; now it is forbidden, there is nothing I want to do more. What is going on? My inner motives have been stirred and revealed but I am given no help dealing with them.[30] Religious laws are external; they may tell the truth but they don't bring freedom. Imagine working in your garden and then coming inside for a meal. The bathroom mirror sends a clear message, 'You are dirty.' It has told you the truth but it is incapable of washing you; you have act yourself to deal with that problem! Once washed you may return to the mirror, and it will proclaim you clean, but it was not part of the solution.

Religious law is just like that: it may tell you the truth but the real answers have to be found elsewhere.

The truth is, the 'law of the Lord' has a strong tendency to create *legalists*; religious people who demand and delight in clear instructions for every situation. There is something in the human psyche that is vulnerable to this; we are all in danger of falling prey to it. Historically the Christian community has arrogantly declared its difference from the *Talmud* and *sharia*, while in practice being every bit as legalistic as either of them, destroying the very essence of Jesus' teaching in the process.

The 'Law of Liberty' is to free human behaviour. Jesus lived in a country controlled by Roman law and within a culture shaped by Jewish law, yet he pointed us beyond the 'law of the land' and the 'law of the Lord' to something more. Does this mean that both of them became irrelevant in the light of his teaching?

The answer is quite simple – 'Yes and No'!

Grappling with this conundrum is the key to Jesus-ethics and living in the way that he taught and exampled. He was very clear:

> Do not think that I have come to abolish
> the law and the prophets;
> I have not come to abolish them
> but to give them real meaning.[31]

He comes to 'fulfil them', to 'draw out their real essence and make them complete', which he does through the power of the Spirit.

For example the 'Ten Commandments'[32] – originally ten two-word phrases – are the basis for covenant; they signpost the character of God ('live like this to begin to be like God'), they are a declaration of human rights, but they are also a prophecy for the future. Examining them closely reveals that the first nine commandments are all about behaviour that is external and visible – you can see if I steal, murder, make idols or commit adultery.

The tenth is different. 'Do not covet' points to my inner attitude, which is invisible to others yet motivates everything I do. People who keep the first nine always fall at the tenth.[33] This is deliberate; the 'Ten Commandments' are just a stepping-stone towards the spiritual maturity God wants everyone to experience.

The Hebrew prophets, Jeremiah and Ezekiel, make this clear:

> 'I will put my law within them and I will write it on their hearts ... No longer shall they teach one another, or say to each other ... for they shall all know me, from the least of them to the greatest,' says the Lord.[34]

> A new heart I will give you, and a new spirit I will put within you, and I will remove from your body the heart of stone and give you a heart of flesh. I will put my spirit within you, and make you follow my statutes and be careful to observe my ordinances.[35]

They envisage a time when people will live *torah* spontaneously, from the inside out, through the power of the Spirit. Jesus makes it clear this time has now come.

Using the two commandments about murder and adultery as an example,[36] Jesus shows that each of the first nine are in fact identical to coveting. I may not have actually murdered or had an adulterous relationship but if my inner attitude is one of anger or lust I am just the same as a murderer or adulterer in the quality of my character.

'So what kind of person am I?'

Jesus offers the opportunity for a process of change and transfiguration to begin through the choices I make and the recreating power of the Spirit.

Jesus brings 'the perfect law, the law of liberty',[37] ethics of the Spirit, to set human behaviour free. It is also called the 'law of Christ' and the 'law of the Spirit of Life',[38] but it is not law as it has ever been conceived of before. The indwelling and empowering of the Spirit is so transforming it is like a new birth with new behaviour.

So what is the relationship between the law and the Spirit?

Let me illustrate this by sharing several reflections from my personal experience of mathematics.

I well remember each of our three children learning to do sums at the kitchen table; enthusiastically adding and subtracting – 'three plus two equals five' – a big tick by the side of their workings and a huge smile of delight on their faces. I was thrilled for them, but my own experience of maths was troubled so I could not help a deep hidden sigh.

'Do they really know what world they are embarking on?'

I have several friends who have done PhDs in mathematics. Talking with them about their research (usually fairly short conversations!) makes it quite clear their work is as different from 'three plus two equals five' as one could imagine. They move in a different conceptual universe.

At school I was told all the angles of a triangle add up to 180 degrees – it was a law you had to accept. For some unexplained reason I was not happy to and would spend hours attempting to draw triangles that did not comply. Though I was unsuccessful it did not leave me convinced. Years later a college lecturer would make the throwaway remark, 'This nonsense about all the angles of a triangle adding up to 180 degrees.' With rapt attention I listened to him explain how, when drawn on a sphere, the sum of the angles of a triangle are quite different. My suspicions were right all along!

In that moment I realised mathematics was not just a set of rules for doing calculations but a different way of thinking about the world using symbols rather than words.

Change the axioms and everything changes.[39]

Living by the law is like a child doing sums; living by the Spirit is like inhabiting the world of PhD mathematics. It is not that sums are wrong or have no value; rather sums are merely a threshold into another vast and thrilling realm. The ethics of the Spirit that Jesus brings are the same; they embrace the essence of the law, fulfil the spirit of the law, and yet transcend the limits of the law in a breathtaking way.

* * * * *

The wind blows where it wants to, you hear its sound
but you known either its origin nor its destination;
so it is with everyone born of the spirit.[40]

This is how Jesus lived, exampling the 'Messianic Anarchist' in every act and action. Like the wind, he was a powerful presence yet moved to rhythms that were a mystery to those around him, akin to wild nature, inspiring and disturbing in equal measure. He invited every person to live the same way, a call to celebrate the way of freedom.

For Jesus, life-giving values not restrictive rules were the key. He met every life situation as fresh and unique, touching it with a fingerprint of fire, creating a masterpiece out of every challenge.

Jesus is someone who lived from the centre, on the edge.

Jesus' life, totally rooted in the divine (the centre) was so free, creative and true that people were constantly shocked as he pushed the boundaries of living towards new and vital possibilities (out on the edge).

The way Jesus lived presented a constant paradox.

His teaching was simple yet unbelievably profound. He displayed self-control but was quite uninhibited. He would affirm individuals yet disturb them as well. There was direction to his life but also spontaneity. While totally reliable, Jesus was quite unpredictable. He was attractive; crowds flocked to hear him yet at the same time he could be shocking and outrageous. With Jesus you never knew what he would do next, yet watching him you realised everything he did was totally consistent.

The essence of Jesus' freedom is like a dance.

The steps are principles everyone can connect with; the music is the fire of the Spirit. His first focus is with words that are found in most world faiths: 'Do to others as you would have them do to you.'[41]

For Jesus the essence of the *torah* and therefore our behaviour must be: 'justice, mercy and faith'.[42]

Asked which is the greatest of the commandments he replies:

> You shall love the Lord your God with all your heart,
> and with all your soul and with all your mind.
> This is the greatest and first commandment.
> And a second is like it, 'You shall love your neighbour as yourself.'
> On these two commandments hang all the Law and the Prophets.[43]

You will recognise this matches exactly the essential relationships that form *shalom*: our relationship *with* God, *with* and *within* ourselves, *with* other people and *with* wild nature. Held in perfect balance they form a spiritual gyroscope to give us equilibrium and points of a compass to guide us.

The early Jesus-community echoes this exactly,

> Owe no one anything, except to love one another;
> for the one who loves another has fulfilled the law.
> The commandments … are summed up in this word,
> 'Love your neighbour as yourself.'
> Love does no wrong to a neighbour;
> therefore, love fulfils the law.[44]

So the first steps along the path to wild freedom have a disturbing simplicity. We begin exactly wherever we are at this moment. As we take the steps we become caught up in the updraft of the Spirit and suddenly whole new dimensions of possibilities open up for us.

This freedom is not simply 'freedom *from'* (sin, guilt, fear, death), but primarily 'freedom *to'* be everything we were created to be. It is dependent on a relationship with God that is uninhibited and exhilarating. This freedom requires me to be responsible and accountable for the way I behave. It is about maturity; it is dependent on my character being able to handle the wisdom and power of choice. This freedom is discovered through the discipline of learning (discipleship); like an athlete, gymnast, artist or musician we are only free to excel if we have put in the time to learn the skills.

It is a new way of thinking (*metanoia*) that leads to this new way of behaving. With rules being replaced by values how do we re-imagine everyday living?

For me, living in the freedom of the Spirit is like a bird migrating. As I watch birds move across the wide-open sky there is the most wonderful sense of freedom, yet at the same time a clear sense of direction. Exactly how a bird can navigate thousands of miles from one fixed point to another remains a mystery to science. What is clear is that many subtle factors combine within the bird's consciousness to enable this to happen. It is possible that a combination of the pattern of the stars, the angle of the horizon line, the position of the sun, the sound of the sea, the pull of magnetic fields, the location of key landmarks, the currents of prevailing winds and a great deal more are all involved.

Like the birds we must learn to use different stimuli to help us live free. We must become sensitive to the inner voice of the Spirit but also use our wisdom-inspired reason, along with love, truth, the example and counsel of others and broad biblical principles, with particular scriptural examples when they are available; and very important, weighing the likely outcome and consequences.

Endnotes

1   Dorothy Day, *Loaves and Fishes*, Orbis Books, 1997, p. 113.
2   There are many books on 'anarchy'; the classic introduction to the different views and thinkers is George Woodcock, *Anarchism*, Broadview Press, 2004.

3 See for example, Leo Tolstoy (trans. C Garnett), *The Kingdom of God is Within You*, Rough Draft Printing, 2010; Jacques Ellul, *Anarchy and Christianity*, Eerdmans, 1991; Vernand Eller, *Christian Anarchy: Jesus' Primacy over the Powers*, Eerdmans, 1987; Alexandre Christoyannopoulos, *Christian Anarchism: A Political Commentary on the Gospel*, Imprint Academic, 2010. See also 'Jesus Radicals' <www.jesusradicals.com>; and *A Pinch of Salt* magazine <editor.apos@gmail.com>.

4 See 1Sam 8:7–9. See the discussion in Chapter 4, Shalom *Activist*.

5 Even doing nothing is behaving! It is a choice of inactivity that we make.

6 The word 'ethics' comes from the Greek word *ethikos*, implying, 'moral character within culture'.

7 Mt 7:16; see also Mt 12:33; Lk 6:44.

8 For an interesting discussion as to the source of this quote see: <www.compassionatespirit.com/Be-the-Change.htm>.

9 This is my own paraphrase of part of *The Epistle to Diognetus*, based on reading a number of translations, see for example CC Richardson, *Early Christian Fathers*, Collier/ Macmillan, 1970, pp. 205–224 and J Stevenson (ed.), *A New Eusebius*, SPCK, 1968, pp. 58–60.

10 Acts 17:6.

11 See Acts 9:2; 19:9, 23; 22:4; 24:14, 22.

12 Helmut Thielicke says, 'Theological ethics is eschatological or it is nothing!' See H Thielicke, *'Theological Ethics*, Eerdmans, 1966, p. x.

13 Jn 8:32.

14 Gal 5:1.

15 2Cor 3:17.

16 Acts 1:8.

17 Col 2:15.

18 Jn 7:38.

19 Jg 17:6.

20 See *Chambers English Dictionary*, Cambridge, 1988, p. 809.

21 Aquinas' elucidation of the philosophy of law is to be found in his treatise of law within *Summa Theologica*, a tour-de-force work of theology and philosophy. This remains the most compelling argument for a 'natural law' with a necessary link between ethical notions of the common good and the final shape of human legislation. For Aquinas, an unjust law was no law at all:, 'Every human law has just so much of the nature of law as is derived from the law of nature. But if in any point it deflects from the law of nature, it is no longer a law but a perversion of law' (ST I-II, Q.95, A.II).

22 Hans Kelsen, *Pure Theory of Law* (1960; Knight trans.), Berkeley, 1967; Union (NJ). 2002. Kelsen's theory of law is deeply hypothetical, and difficult to explain fully here. In its simplest form, it finds the authority for any given law in a hierarchy of orders or 'norms'. The ultimate authority was tied up in the conceptual basic norm or *Grundnorm*. This presupposed basic norm for a particular positive-legal order did not involve any moral or other extra-legal evaluation of the basic norm's requirement of obedience – hence the purity of the system.

23 I am grateful to my friend Drew Worthley, a barrister and a university lecturer in law, for his help in my introductory comments on law and my reflections on 'The Law of the Land' and the information in endnotes 21, 22, 24 and 25.

24 These are all issues that Aquinas was wrestling with back in the thirteenth century; the title of Article 1 in Question 92 of *Summa Theologica* is, 'Is an effect of law to make man good?'

25 Ronald Dworkin, *Law's Empire*, Harvard University Press (Belknap), 1986. Dworkin argues for a community-based, 'associative obligation' in response to

the following questions: 'Do citizens have genuine moral obligations just in virtue *of* law? Does the fact that a legislature has enacted some requirement in itself give citizens a moral as well as a practical reason to obey? Does that moral reason hold even for those citizens who disapprove of the legislation or think it wrong in principle?' (p. 190).

26 See Deut 14:3–21; Exod 23:19; 34:26 and Lev 11:1–46.
27 *Kosher* is the Ashkenazi Jewish pronunciation of the Hebrew word *kasher* meaning 'fit'; as in *kashrut.*
28 This is the meaning of the word *sharia.*
29 Gal 3:24
30 Rom 5:20 see also Rom 7:7–13.
31 Matt 5:17.
32 See Exod 20:1–18 and Deut 5:1–21.
33 For example, the rich young rule-keeper (Lk 18:18–25) and the early Christian leader *rabbi* Saul/ Paul of Tarsus (Rom 7:7–13).
34 Jer 31:33–34.
35 Ezk 36:26–27.
36 See Mt 5:21–30.
37 Jas 1:25.
38 See Gal 6:2 and Rom 8:2.
39 An axioms is a self-evident truth, the basis upon which assumptions and calculations are made.
40 Jn 3:8. These are my most favourite words in the whole of biblical writing and contain the most exciting semi-colon in scripture!
41 Lk 6:31 also Mt 7:12. Some parallels from others faiths are:
*   'Do not do to others what would cause pain if done to you' – *Hinduism*
*   'Do not do to others all that is not well for yourself' – *Zoroastrian-Parsee*
*   'One should treat all creatures in the world as one would like to be treated' – *Jainism*
*   'Treat not others in ways that you yourself would find hurtful' – *Buddhism*
*   'Do not do to others what you would not want done to yourself' – *Confucianism*
*   'Regard your neighbour's gain as your own gain and your neighbour's loss as your own loss' – *Taoism*
*   'Do not do to others that which would anger you if others did it to you' – *Socratics*
*   'What is hateful to you, do not do to your neighbour. This is the whole law' – *Judaism*
*   'Not one of you truly believes until you wish for others what you wish for yourself' – *Islam*
*   'Treat others as you would be treated yourself' – *Sikhism*
*   'Desire not for anyone the things you would not desire for yourself' – *Baha'i*
Adapted from Symon Hill, *The No-Nonsense Guide to Religion*, New Internationalist Publications, 2010, p. 31.
42 Mt 23:23; see also Mt 9:13 and 12:7.
43 Mt 22:36–40.
44 Rom 13:8–10.

8 Values Master
– handling dangerous treasure

April 1994 saw three months of genocide sweep like a wave across the central and east African country of Rwanda in which an estimated one million Tutsi and moderate Hutu died at the hands of the majority Hutu population. During the height of the massacre Paul Rusesabagina, a hotel manager in the capital city, Kigali, saved the lives of 1,268 people who fled to his building for safety. He succeeded because of his skilful negotiation, personal ingenuity and astonishing courage, in the face of constant threats from the *Interahamwe* militia on the outside. He described himself simply as 'an ordinary man' who did what he did saying, 'I don't ever want to regret.'[1]

This story illustrates powerfully the words of Jesus: 'The good person out of the good treasure of their heart brings out good.'[2]

We have heard Jesus calling us to live by the ethics of the Spirit; to be people who are free and rooted in life-giving values, not rules.

The 'treasure' that Jesus speaks about here refers to these 'values'.[3]

Maori Marsden, a tribal elder and pastor from New Zealand, comments

> There is no specific term in Maori for value. With our holistic view of the universe the Maori idea of value is incorporated into the holistic term *taonga* – 'a treasure, something precious'; hence an object of good or value.[4]

The foundation and essence of all culture is found in values.

So what are values?[5]

A simple compact definition might be:

> A conception held by an individual or a group of what is good
> and desirable, which influences their choices and their actions.[6]

Values are about beliefs and behaviour.

They develop in earliest childhood, becoming our 'moral mother
tongue' with powerful emotional connections. Deeply internalised,
they are shaped out of our experiences with those closest to us –
inspired by their behaviour as much as by their words. Usually
intuitive, values are instinctive rather than carefully thought out,
and are strongly resistant to change.

We treasure them.

Values define what we believe to be right and wrong, providing the
moral framework within which we move. They are the bridge
between what we believe and how we act, shaping who and what
we are.

They form the spiritual core at the heart of culture, guiding and
motivating the behaviour and attitudes of those within it. It is
impossible to exaggerate their significance. They are subtle and
subversive, yet dramatic in their impact.

Imagine values forming our internal moral–spiritual structure; like
the bones and muscles that give our body its strength and
flexibility. Living by values we engage the challenges of life, like a
gymnast or a dancer with fluid movement, poise, balance and
creative rhythm. Legalism, in contrast, can offer only an outer shell
for structure and protection, leaving us like a spiritual snail or moral
armadillo.

Please note: this next point is very important.

It is quite possible for people to value things that are destructive
and bad (revenge, selfishness, indulgence, injustice, to name a
few).

Jesus actually speaks about a 'bad tree', 'bad fruit' and 'evil
treasure'.

> No good tree bears bad fruit, nor again does a bad tree
> bear good fruit; for each tree is known by its own fruit. Figs
> are not gathered from thorns, nor are grapes picked from a

bramble bush. The good person out of the good treasure of the heart produces good, and the evil person out of the evil treasure produces evil; for it is out of the abundance of the heart that the mouth speaks.[7]

We are to be a good tree, producing good fruit, someone in whom good treasure is found. This is true godliness.

✻ ✻ ✻ ✻ ✻

This being so, we are each invited to become a 'Values Master', skilled in the art of living.[8]

Jesus perfectly examples what this means. He shows us the quality and content of each value and then demonstrates how to apply them creatively in the way we live. This is at the heart of his uniqueness. He is the 'master' from whom we have the opportunity to learn; empowered by the Spirit this way of living can become a personal reality.

So if values are akin to 'treasure', we should learn to approach them like an expert in antique jewellery or a connoisseur of fine wines.

If values are like our moral–spiritual 'bones and muscle' we need to become like an athletics coach or choreographer who works with runners or dancers to develop their core strength, flexibility and ability to win. We need to deepen our understanding of values.

How do they interconnect with each other?
How can they be developed like muscles?
What strategies can we use to make the most of them?

To achieve this goal we need to be able to draw on deep resources to meet the challenges we encounter. Jesus gives a powerful picture:

> Therefore every scribe who has been trained for the
> kingdom of heaven
> is like a householder who brings out of their treasure
> what is new and what is old.[9]

Here is a person with a storeroom filled with astonishing 'treasure'. Whatever the need the resource is there. Sometimes it is something old, trustworthy, tried, tested and honoured; on other occasions it is fresh, new, surprising and unexpected.[10]

Every time it is appropriate, exactly what we need.

Jesus is clear that in order to access these value-resources we need to be 'trained'; there needs to be learning before there can be living. This is part of discipleship – becoming skilled in knowing values and practising their craft.

As every athlete and artist knows, to become skilled you must learn, and this always involves a cost.

A shopper in New York inadvertently walked into a jewellery store for the mega-rich. Browsing the items she noticed there were no price tags. Enquiring, she was told dismissively by the assistant, 'If you have to ask how much it costs, you can't afford it!'

The language of value inevitably raises the question of price. Jesus tells a story about two quite different people for whom the price of treasure cost them everything. One stumbled on it by chance, for the other it was the result of a long search. Both recognised its value instantly and paid the price:

> The kingdom of heaven is like a treasure hidden in a field,
> which someone found and reburied;
> then in their joy they went and sold all that they had and
> bought the field.

> The kingdom of heaven is like a merchant in search of fine pearls;
> on finding one pearl of great value,
> he went and sold all that he had and bought it.[11]

Living by values has a cost. It may be in public opinion; it will certainly be in personal discipline. It may cost you in money and time; there will be a price in your commitment to others. The treasure itself will cost you everything, but because it is priceless what you gain in return far exceeds the price you pay.

* * * * *

A young child picks up a Rubick's Cube, attracted by the array of brightly coloured squares scattered across its surfaces, further intrigued by the fact she can turn them in seemingly every possible direction with such delightful clicking sounds; the perfect toy. For an adult it is a nightmare. Aligning the six colours across each of the six faces seems simple enough, but once you actually try the complexity can seem overwhelming, with frustration and anger often the only result. This is a parable about encountering values.

On the one hand, talking with children about love, kindness, beauty and joy is easy: quite at home among storybooks, chunky building blocks and splashes of brightly coloured paint. On the other hand, discussing justice, truth, wisdom and forgiveness with adults can be uncomfortable. They can seem to clash rather than connect; creating problems rather than solving them and touching deeply embedded attitudes.

Engaging with values takes us into a complicated and challenging world.

Values are something we feel instinctive about; we take them for granted, rarely giving them a second thought. Surely we 'just know' what is good or bad? Yet when we do reflect on them they often become nebulous and vague. One of the reasons for this complexity is that values are both very practical yet deeply philosophical, all at the same time.

Once again the personal challenge is to become mature and wise.

The call to live by values is an invitation to live life in a way that is free, spontaneous, and creative, yet always leaving footprints of peace. Because, at the same time it is a summons to face the cruel realities of life, with all the pain and suffering endured by so many every day and to open our lives to others and do something about it.

Embrace life with spontaneous goodness, guerrilla kindness and lawless love.

Live like a free-runner.

Free-runners move across the cityscape using acrobatics that are both athletic and aesthetic. Always travelling forward, they continually test their physical and mental ability, showing everyone that the built environment presents no obstacles and holds no fears for them. They take our breath away as we watch their awesome skill.

Live from an inner freedom and flow, move with strength, leaving a trail of joy.

* * * * *

My elderly parents were flying home from Indonesia. My mother sent me a postcard, 'Our luggage weight exceeds the limit, but we are trusting to our grey hair.' She was right. They came through 'Arrivals' with bulging suitcases, having paid no excess baggage charge. No self-respecting Indonesian would have insulted a silver-haired couple by demanding they pay extra at the check-in. I am certain the compliment would not have been returned at any airport in the west.

This reminds us how different values are understood and interpreted in contrasting cultures – in this case the value of 'respect'.

So what is the source and origin of values?

It is popular to argue that thinking about values is overrated; that values are simply created by different cultures to meet their specific needs. Spinoza famously said,

> We don't strive for things because they are good but call the things we strive for good. [12]

If this sceptical position is true then all value thinking is entirely relative, with serious negative implications for a spiritual understanding of behaviour across all faiths. Values become nothing more than interesting human ideas with no spiritual source or dimension.

Is this correct?
Can we really speak of universal core-values at the foundation of all cultures that are shared and understood across humanity?

These are big and complex questions, but here are a few reflections. [13]

Of course it is true that many things valued by a particular culture are simply the product of that culture. Binding of women's feet in ancient China to keep them 'baby-like' and dainty would be one example of this.

However, it is also true there are values shared across all cultures; 'love' is one obvious example. It is a central concept and emotion found in every society and healthy individual on earth.[14] It may be understood and expressed in a variety of ways but the core-value is always there. This would be true of peace, courage, wisdom and many others too. These values also possess an objective quality; we can say, 'Simon is a good person', which everyone can agree or disagree with, irrespective of their particular cultural background.

Values are also always related to a 'centre of value', which will be different depending on the culture concerned. For example, among indigenous people it may be the surrounding natural environment, while for the Humanist it is the human person. These 'centres of value' for particular cultures are not exclusive to those cultures, which strongly implies there is a source of values that transcends any particular culture.

The debate will continue. However, for the reasons just mentioned I believe we can speak of universal core-values and of a 'primal morality' embedded deep inside every human heart, irrespective of culture. Jesus and most world spiritual teachers make this assumption; their hearers from across different cultures accept this also, so we have every reason to do the same.

* * * * *

In the autumn of 2003 in Leeds in the north of England, a citywide festival called 'Together for Peace' attracted large numbers of people from across the different faith and culture groups in the area and the wider population as a whole, celebrating around this central theme. Now a charity, 'Together for Peace' continues to have an ongoing impact through its project work in local communities and with a diverse range of organisations from grassroots to local government.[15]

Here is just one of many examples of the power of universal core-values to provide a focus to draw different faith and culture groups together around central issues. These may be anything from forgiveness and compassion to justice or peace. I believe the fact that shared values can provide a gathering-place for people, irrespective of culture and faith, is possible because we are each made in the image and likeness of God with an awareness and sensitivity to core-values that are part of our shared spiritual DNA.

I would argue it also demonstrates that, parallel to the physical structure to the universe, values provide a corresponding moral and spiritual shape to the cosmos as well, to which we are all open and able to connect. This would also explain why all values – including meekness, courage and trust – flow over quite naturally into wild nature and find a response there (as we discussed being a '*Creation Companion*').

On one occasion I was leading a discussion about living by values when a person in the group pointed out, 'Have you noticed how every core-value we have mentioned is related to our basic needs?'[16] Reflecting on this profound insight it became clear to me that life-giving values represent not only something every human being and every living creature needs, but also that they have the right to experience and enjoy.

The subjects of 'human rights' and 'animal rights' are matters of some debate with strong feelings on either side. Nevertheless, it seems quite clear to me that what God desires for every human being and the whole of creation – in the light of core-values – is in fact *their right*. Our mission is quite simply to work to see that every person, and the whole 'more than human world', experiences their rights, even if in the short term it is necessary for me to forgo my own personal rights to achieve this.

We have all heard politicians use phrases like, 'family values', 'political values' and 'national values', while preachers proclaim 'Christian values' and 'biblical values'. They rarely say more; they assume we know what these values are. They also subtly imply that because we hold these values others do not.

This needs to be challenged.

We must insist that speakers who use phrases like 'national values' or 'Christian values' identify in detail what they understand these values to be. What will be revealed is that most of these values are shared equally by other nations and other faiths. Yes, there will be cultural and spiritual differences in understanding but substantially we all stand together on common ground.

We have much to learn from each other's unique and rich encounter with values. Every insight and perspective from other cultures helps us. This being so, we should no longer speak of 'national values' or 'Christian values' but refer instead to 'our nation's understanding of values' or 'a Christian understanding of values', acknowledging that we are dealing with something that is shared by all and – as we learn from one another – it will enrich us all.

This is well illustrated by a conversation I had with a Christian leader in Bethlehem. He told me how he had recently travelled through the West Bank in Palestine, looking for Christians who might be living in poverty to see if he could offer them financial help and support. He arrived at an isolated village where he found an elderly brother and sister; the man had severe physical disabilities. To his offer of money they replied, 'Perhaps just a little to help us buy more medicine would be helpful.' He said, 'But what about your need for food, clothes, fuel, and rent for your house?' To which they replied, 'Oh, our Muslim neighbours provide all that.'

Here was a community reaching across the culture–faith divide, meeting the needs of their vulnerable neighbours; it is also an example of the poor caring for the poor. Across the globe there are so many stories of the kindness and hospitality of the poor; people living generously, compassionately, and joyfully sharing what little they have with others. They are a challenging example to those of us who have so much more.

* * * * *

There is a delightful *rabbinic* legend that tells how God created every blessing that could ever be imagined or would ever be created; they lay like a huge pile of treasure. God needed a container, a bag, a box or a jar, in which to put them, but could find nothing – so God created *shalom*.

The Jewish *rabbis* declare, '*Gadol hashalom*' – '*shalom* is the highest of values'.[17] Here is the centre of value to which all values are related and the source in God from which all other values flow. Imagine a cascade of values saturating the world, with *shalom* as the headwaters:

> Let justice roll down like waters,
> and righteousness like an ever-flowing stream.[18]

Out of your innermost being shall flow rivers of living water.[19]

We have already seen that values are also spoken of as fruit: 'For the fruit of light is found in all that is good, right and true.'[20]

```
                        ──  SHALOM  ──
                  joy      LIFE       awe
            purity    zeal  HOPE   clean   mercy
         integrity   beauty  LOVE  sharing   humility
       steadfast    modest   FAITH    wonder    maturity
      goodness    healing    TRUTH    honour    boldness
    kindness      strength   GRACE    perfect    godliness
   patience      belonging   WISDOM   authority   obedience
  acceptance     endurance   JUSTICE   devotion    generosity
 gentleness     friendship   FREEDOM   genuine    innocence
faithfulness    meekness     HOLINESS   hospitable   selfcontrol
forgiveness    fruitfulness  COVENANT   repentance   contentment
encouragement   forbearance  SALVATION  reconciliation  childlikeness
thanksgiving    compassion   SPIRITUALITY  overcomer  tenderhearted
perseverance              RIGHTEOUSNESS           mutual-affection
```

On occasions they are imagined as a beautiful fragrance:

> Their beauty shall be like the olive
> and fragrance like the cedars of Lebanon.[21]

Values are frequently spoken of as clothing, which interestingly is often more revealing than nakedness:

> I put on righteousness and it clothed me;
> my justice was like a robe and a turban.[22]

So life-giving values are the flow, the fruit, the fragrance and the fabric of authentic spiritual life and they are always good.

How often do we focus on single values like justice, love or wisdom, imagining each like a solitary pearl on a necklace? This is not wrong because each has exquisite worth and beauty, but neither is it the whole truth. All values are holistic; completely integrated and interconnected together, each inseparably linked to every other one, creating a single whole.

I believe that within each individual value you will find every other value.

Notice the reference to 'the *fruit* of the Spirit' – it is clearly singular and not plural – yet the writer then proceeds to identify nine distinct values:

> The *fruit* of the Spirit is love, joy, peace, patience, kindness, generosity, faithfulness, gentleness and self-control.[23]

It is interesting how often biblical writers present us with 'clusters' of values, for example.

> Make every effort to support your faith with goodness ... knowledge ... self-control ... endurance ... godliness ... mutual affection ... love.[24]

There is no pick-and-mix here; life-giving values are a unity, which is important to remember when thinking about behaviour. Of course we all have strengths and weaknesses that we struggle with, but that is never an excuse for quietly excluding certain qualities because we find them challenging. The fully integrated person embraces values in their totality.

There is something wonderfully free, spontaneous, creative and certain about living by values. They challenge all forms of legalism and ethical styles that begin with the word – 'No!' While they are perfectly capable of stopping people in their tracks and challenging behaviour, they always do it in a way that is positive by offering creative alternatives.

Living by values is about living by 'Yes!'

All this undermines, sabotages and liberates us from traditional thinking because life-giving values are fundamentally subversive. They move into the cracks and crevices of our lives and the structures of society with powerful effect. Jesus speaks of them as functioning like weeds in a farmer's field:

> The kingdom of heaven is like a mustard seed,
> which planted in a field grows into a great shrub that
> birds nest in.[25]

Or the yeast used in bread making:

> The kingdom of heaven is like yeast ...
> hidden in flour until it was all leavened.[26]

At first glance both seem insignificant, but once embedded in their environment they are powerfully transforming, changing everything.

We have already seen that most values are verbs masquerading as nouns. They are dynamic and full of energy. Most people imagine values to be simple and straightforward, warm and engaging like children's brightly coloured bricks, or pastel-coloured flowers.

They need to wake up!

Values are a high-explosive and volatile cocktail.

Touching them is handling dangerous treasure. When you begin to realise just how powerful values are, how deep their significance and potential for astonishing transfiguration once they are activated, everything changes.

The truth is, if life-giving values don't disturb me, if they don't actually terrify me with their possibilities, then I simply haven't begun to understand them yet.

* * * * *

Finally, exactly how do we imagine these values affecting every area of life, through our relationships and the work that we do?

Notice how we expect lawyers to focus on justice, nurses to be motivated by compassion, and teachers to be concerned with knowledge and truth. We associate certain values with particular occupations; this is understandable but regrettable. If every value contains every other value and all values are essential for *shalom*, then every value should be at work in every situation all the time.

How can we expand our thinking?

Recognise that you have at your disposal these powerful interconnected values, which when placed strategically within the relationships and structures within which you move – once ignited by the Spirit – have the potential for astonishing impact and change.

When teaching on values I like to gather people into small groups, each with two packs of well-shuffled cards; one pack names a different value on each card, the other pack identifies a different occupation. A card from each pack is turned over prompting the question. 'How does this value relate to that occupation?' The discussions continue until all the ideas are exhausted, when the next two cards are revealed. There are of course numerous permutations, each revealing new possibilities.

- How might joy influence architecture?
- How might beauty influence medicine?
- How might forgiveness influence cooking?
- How might justice influence house-building?
- How might truth influence marketing?
- How might hope influence news media?
- How might freedom influence law enforcement?

Endnotes

1 See Paul Rusesabagina, *An Ordinary Man: The True Story behind Hotel Rwanda*, Bloomsbury, 2007 and the film, *Hotel Rwanda*, produced by United Artists/ Lions Gate Films, directed by Tony George.
2 Lk 6:45.
3 Other passages that refer to 'treasure' are Mt 19:21; Mk 10:21; Lk 18:22; 2Cor 4:7.
4 M Marsden,*The Woven Universe: Selected Writings of Rev Maori Marsden*, Marsden Estate, New Zealand, 2003, pp. 38 – quote slightly adapted for gender.
5 Among the range of responses to this question some of the most obvious ones would be:
- *Assumptions* that we make about value and worth;
- *Beliefs* that direct our actions;
- *Concepts* to which we aspire and wish to emulate;
- *Connections* that link people together as a group;
- *Convictions* that shape decisions;
- *Criteria* by which we make those decisions;
- *Directions* that point towards practical achievements and results;
- *Evaluations* by which we judge ourselves and others;
- *Guides* to behaviour for individuals and communities;
- *Ideas* of what is intrinsically good, desirable and right;
- *Ideals* that inspire a person towards perfection;
- *Motivations* towards achieving 'ends' and 'goals';
- *Principles* that form a guide for conduct and belief;
- *Qualities* that make something desirable or valuable;
- *Standards* against which to check or measure things.
6 I formed this definition myself after reviewing a number of academic definitions.
7 Lk 6:43–45.
8 I am fully aware of the masculine bias of this term, but I am using it with the sense of one (female or male) who is skilled, knowledgeable, and displaying outstanding ability as with 'chess master' or '*Zen* master'.
9 Mt 13:52.
10 My father used to tell a story about a remarkable shopkeeper called Bachhi Ram who had a tiny store high in the Himalaya yet always seemed to have whatever he needed. 'I was there twenty years, I don't want to give the impression he always had what I wanted. But the thing I never thought he'd

stock – somewhere in the back of that shop, there it was. Oh, we had some fun. In fact over the years it's been a bit of a competition as to whether he had everything I needed. I will be honest; 80% of what I wanted, he had in that shop. How he got that stock list, don't ask me.' See Pat Wraight, *On to the Summit: The Len Moules Story*, Kingsway 1981, pp. 63–66.

11 Mt 13:45–46.

12 See Spinoza, 'Ethics Part 3: 'On the origin and nature of the mind', 1677 – a note on proposition 9.

13 These ideas are freely adapted from RH Neibuhr, *The Responsible Self*, Harper Row, 1963.

14 I say 'healthy individual' because I am aware that this is not apparent among psychopaths and sociopaths, who of course have serious mental conditions.

15 For more information about 'Together for Peace' see <www.t4p.org.uk>.

16 I am grateful to my friend Jill Mann for making this insightful observation and for the 'Peace School' group for the conversation that developed from it.

17 See Rabbi J Milgrom, 'Let Your Love for Me Vanquish Your Hatred for Him', in DL Smith-Christopher (ed.), *Subverting Hatred*, Orbis Books, 2007, p. 156.

18 Amos 5:24.

19 Jn 7:38.

20 Eph 5:9, see also Gal 5:22–23; Phil 1:11; Mt 7:16; 12:33; Lk 6:44.

21 Hos 14:6 see also 2Cor 2:14–16; Phil 4:18.

22 Job 29:14 see also Isa 11:5; 59:17, 61:10; Eph 4:23–24; 6:14–17.

23 Gal 5:22–23.

24 2Pt 1:5–8.

25 Mt 13:31–32; remember that the mustard plant was considered a weed by Palestinian farmers.

26 Mt 13:33.

Meekness Zealot
– grappling with assertive gentleness

'The word "enemy" no longer has any meaning for me.' The speaker was the diminutive figure of Fr Ibrahim Nairouz, pastor of a church in Nablus, in West Bank, Palestine. These are remarkable words in themselves; but all the more so coming from a Christian living in a community that is overwhelmingly Muslim, and under the grip of the occupying Jewish Israelis. The integrity of both his words and whole demeanor were inspiring: for him building bridges into the hearts and lives of others – however hostile – was a passion.[1]

Listening to him I thought of the Hebrew prophet Jonah, whose message can be summarised as, 'God loves those you hate the most.'[2] I also reflected back to a conclusion I had reached decades before; that Jesus' teaching and example show there are no circumstances in which the use of violence can ever be justified. His words are clear:

But I say to you. Do not resist one who is evil.
If anyone strikes you on the right cheek, turn to them the other also;
and if anyone would sue you and take your coat, let them have your shirt as well;
and if anyone forces you to go one mile, go with them two miles.[3]

The Son of Man has not come to destroy the lives of human beings but to save them.[4]

Put your sword back into its place;
for all who use the sword will perish by the sword.[5]

Let anyone among you who is without sin be the first to throw a stone.[6]

I recognise that this a very controversial topic, but that is because it is very important. Deep emotions are at play here, as well as real practical issues. My choices will also influence my sense of identity. Let me try to explain why I have arrived at the decisions I have made.

* * * * *

What is violence?

We use the word frequently, make so many assumptions about it, and yet rarely reflect on it.[7] I find this a helpful definition:

> Violence is emotional, verbal, or physical behaviour that dominates,
> diminishes, dehumanises or destroys ourselves or others.[8]

Violence crosses boundaries without permission, disrupts authentic relationships and separates us from others. It often has the deliberate intention of hurting, perhaps even killing others. It is frequently motivated by fear, unrestrained anger, or greed with the aim of increasing power or control.

However, it is important to remember violence can also be stirred by a desire for justice in the face of injustice: a longing to put things right, to overcome an imbalance of power, to end victimisation or oppression. Those who use violence for these reasons often do so with a conviction that they are putting right a prior violence or injustice.

Nevertheless, the reality is that acts of violence almost always provoke new violence, creating a spiral of retaliation.[9]

Violence towards another human being damages or destroys someone made in the image and likeness of God.

A person can be violated by:

- *A thought chosen:* violence begins in the heart and mind.[10] Destructive thoughts dehumanise me; they break my relationship with the other person and communicate negative feelings – the cold shoulder is powerful – even if nothing more is said or done;
- *A look given:* we say, 'if looks could kill' or speak of 'the evil eye'. A glance, like the cold attitude, can communicate destructive feelings to others. They sense them, take them into

themselves, and are essentially violated, self-imprisoned and often tortured by them;

- A *word spoken:* we talk about someone using 'a cutting phrase'. So many people are deeply harmed by words alone without physical aggression. They can destroy self-esteem, creating fear and anxiety, exposing the victim to shame and ridicule;
- A *harmful action:* a physical attack that damages the body is the most obvious expression of violence. The fist, the boot, the blade or the bullet, all leave pain, injury and often death in their wake.

There are many dimensions to violence; it can span everything from personal self-harming to international threat and war. There can be the interpersonal violence of bullying and racism, alongside the powerful but often hidden faces of structural and cultural violence, where economics and social class or local customs and tradition can cause untold suffering.

When actually faced with violence people usually make one of three responses:

- *Accommodation:* they accept violence with a shrug; it is part of the status quo, so perhaps they endure it, maybe they support it; in all likelihood they turn a blind eye;
- *Avoidance:* this is 'flight'; they physically remove themselves from the scene of the violence to avoid suffering harm and seek a place of safety;
- *Attack:* this is 'fight'; they stand up to their attacker and use violence as a response with the clear aim of physically defeating their assailant.

I wish to offer a fourth possible reply to violence, *assertive meekness.* This involves taking the path of *most* resistance in the face of an attack without using violence in response to the hostility. We shall deal with this approach to violence in much more detail in the rest of this chapter.

I have never liked the word 'pacifist'. Although it means 'someone who makes peace', the way it sounds when spoken gives the impression of a quite different word – 'passivist'. That is also how it is popularly understood – someone who is passive, inactive and would do nothing in the face of violence. No matter how often this meaning is challenged it stubbornly remains.[11] Such a response to violence would be immoral and at odds with the teaching and example of Jesus.

I equally dislike the word 'nonviolence', though it communicates much more effectively than 'pacifism'. I dislike the word because it makes violence the primary point of reference rather than *shalom*. It implies that the absence of violence is both sufficient and the equivalent to establishing peace, which we know from our reflections on *shalom* to be far from the truth.[12] However, nonviolence is the word of choice across the global peace movement.[13] Its current understanding has been shaped by Mohandas Gandhi's use of the Sanskrit word *ahimsa*,[14] which we have mentioned previously:

- The word *hims* means 'to desire to do harm';
- The word *ahimsa* means 'to renounce the desire to kill or harm'.

Much as I dislike the word 'nonviolence' I recognise that its use in certain circumstances has real value.[15] Confronted with violence a person may not know how to respond other than violently; in their confusion the single word 'nonviolence' gives them an immediate alternative focus – don't use violence. It is a first step with very practical strategies, a holding position until they can deepen their understanding as to what peace really means.[16]

So, in the place of both pacifism and nonviolence I have coined the phrase 'assertive meekness' (mentioned above) – resisting violence without using violence, grappling with violence against the backdrop of '*shalom* activism'. I have already written about meekness as 'strength under perfect control' – that powerful gentleness which is the true dominion of human companionship with wild nature. Here we see it as the central quality required if our response in the face of violence is to be in harmony with the character of Jesus.

People think 'meekness is weakness'; a biblical perspective is quite different.

The Hebrew word is *anaw*, but it is the Greek word *praus* used in the early writings of the Jesus-community that significantly deepens our understanding. Scholars comment on it being so remarkable as to be almost untranslatable. *Praus* brings together three contrasting ideas:[17]

- *Anger:* meekness holds this explosive yet vital emotion in perfect balance between the two extremes of blind rage and spinelessness. It is the ability to express appropriate anger with positive effect;[18]
- *Control:* meekness would describe a wild animal that has learned to respond to a word of command or instruction. It is also like a powerful war horse prior to battle being held in check by reins in the hands of the warrior on its back;
- *Gentleness:* meekness is moving with serenity and poise. It is having humility and dignity along with kindness, inner stillness and calm. It has openness towards others and a willingness to learn from them.

So there is something wild and raw about meekness while at the same time it is saturated in tranquillity and maturity, 'strength under perfect control'. It is an essential quality for authentic leadership and a mark of someone who is wise.[19] Meekness fuses the identities of the '*Shalom* Activist' and 'Messianic Anarchist' perfectly and shows why it is at the heart of being a 'Creation Companion'. To show these ideas in action I now want to use the controversial story of Jesus cleansing the Temple as a master-class in meekness.[20]

＊ ＊ ＊ ＊ ＊

I have had thousands of conversations about 'assertive meekness' over the years: I doubt there has been one when someone has not said, '… but Jesus used violence when cleansing the Temple'. I believe this comes from a misunderstanding of meekness and a careless reading of the story. To help us I have put together a composite retelling of the event, based on Matthew's account, with additions taken from the Gospels of Mark and John.[21]

> Then Jesus entered the Temple and found people selling cattle, sheep and doves, and the moneychangers seated at their tables. Making a whip of cords he drove out all who were selling and buying in the Temple, [as well as] the sheep and the cattle, and he overturned the tables of the moneychangers and the seats of those who sold doves; and he would not allow anyone to carry anything through the Temple. He told them, 'Take these things out of here! Stop making my Father's house a marketplace!'[22] His disciples remembered it was written, 'Zeal for your house will consume me.'[23] [Jesus] said to them, 'It is written,

"My house shall be called a house of prayer;[24]
but you have made it a den of insurrectionists."[25]

The blind and the lame came to him in the Temple, and he
cured them. But when the chief priests and the scribes saw
the things that he did, and heard the children crying out in
the Temple, 'Hosanna to the Son of David', they became
angry and said to him, 'Do you hear what they are saying?'
Jesus said to them, 'Yes, have you never read,

"Out of the mouths of infants and nursing babies
you have prepared praise for yourself"?'[26]

The Jews then said to him, 'What sign can you show us for
doing this?' Jesus answered them, 'Destroy this Temple and
in three days I will raise it up.' [They said], 'This Temple has
been under construction for forty-six years and you will raise
it up in three days?' But he was speaking of the temple of
his body.

They kept looking for a way to kill him; for they were afraid
of him, because the whole crowd was spellbound by his
teaching. He left them, went out of the city to Bethany, and
spent the night there.

This story is the climax of Jesus' entry into Jerusalem on a donkey
prior to his arrest and crucifixion;[27] he is staking his claim as
Messiah at the very heart of the nation.

He planned for prime-time and maximum exposure, a
demonstration calculated to interrupt business as usual and
bring the imminence of God's reign abruptly, forcefully, to
the attention of all ... It was at once a demonstration, a
prophetic act, a fulfilment event and a sign of the future.[28]

Jesus chose the place and time with care: this was a calculated
act, not a spur-of-the-moment response.

Please note: the key to understanding this story is recognising it is
'acted prophecy'.

Biblical prophecy proclaims the character of God; it *forth*tells the
truth, it does not *fore*tell the future.[29] An acted prophecy is a public

demonstration of truth with memorable and disturbing impact, exactly like we have here.[30]

What Jesus sees happening in the Temple enrages him; he sees the religious-political hierarchy of the day involved in spiritual and social corruption that must not go unchallenged. He will not be silent or restrained. In that moment, every word, action and fibre of Jesus' being communicates vehement passion against the prevailing injustices of the power system displayed in the Temple.

'Zeal for God's house consumed him.'[31]
Jesus' meekness displays anger on behalf of truth and justice; this is real righteousness.
For Jesus the wrath of God is 'wild but it is good'.[32]

However, the central question remains: 'Was this an act of violence on Jesus' part?' A glance at the text suggests, 'Yes', but careful reading and reflection affirm, 'No'. It is instead a perfect display of 'assertive meekness'. Yes, Jesus is angry, but he displays supreme self-control. He creates a storm in which he is the central calm. He throws over tables and brandishes a whip *but* harms no one, other than the pride and greed of traders. The whip has a certain symbolism, but is a practical necessity for guiding agitated cattle out of the crowded precinct. Here we see rage and restraint in exquisite balance, yes it is a fine line – but a clear one.

The written story clearly has a theological purpose, but contains strong eyewitness accounts that are key to our conclusion. Try to relive the story imagining you were there.

Why didn't they instantly lock-down the Temple precinct?
Where were the Temple guards?
Why do we have children singing rather than clinging to their mothers in fear?
Why are the blind and lame drawn into this forbidden territory towards Jesus?
Why do the crowd stand spellbound rather than restraining Jesus or fleeing in panic?
Why do the authorities so eager to arrest Jesus miss this perfect opportunity?

I sense a presence about Jesus that is disturbing yet transfixing. What is happening is very physical but no one is violated. Descriptions are inadequate; I am certain had we been there we would have witnessed something awesome, but the word 'violence' would not have been one we would have used to describe it.

Here we see every aspect of meekness on display: anger, control and gentleness.

Jesus is *the* 'Meekness Zealot' and calls us to be the same, grappling with assertive gentleness. We are to stand tall, shoulders squared, facing the world of violence robustly from a place of deep inner strength, touching hostility with fingerprints of fire.

* * * * *

There are many challenges to the idea of 'assertive meekness'; two in particular merit more detailed discussion here.

'What about *the 'texts of terror' and 'God's genocide' passages?'*

In the Hebrew scriptures there are significant passages where God is presented as commanding Israel, led by Joshua, to carry out genocide against Canaanites.[33] This is a complex subject we can reflect on only briefly here.[34]

Notice first that these texts were written for liturgy – not as history. Their purpose was to focus on holiness; they are to be taken seriously but not literally.[35] Canaanite religion threatened to destroy the Hebrew faith; these texts are about the ruthless avoidance of moral and spiritual contamination, not the destruction of people. These stories are similar to the example of the instruction 'an eye for an eye', which always meant 'compensation' and never violence. Jesus said, 'If your eye/ hand offend you … cut it off' and an early Christian instruction says, 'Put to death in you what is earthly …' All such extreme language is to focus the mind on moral and spiritual realities, never implying actual physical harm.[36]

Archaeology suggests the Hebrew people settled in the land by assimilation, not conquest; and other biblical accounts do not support the idea of genocide.[37] The Israelites may well have been involved in conflict and massacre but God did not order it.

In a key passage Joshua encounters a mysterious warrior with a drawn sword and he challenges him:

'Are you for us, or one of our adversaries?'
'Neither, but as commander of the army of the Lord I now come.'
'What do you command your servant?'
'Remove your sandals, for the place where you are
standing is holy.'[38]

God is a warrior ('Lord of Hosts', sometimes used of God, is a warrior title) who fights for *neither* side but only for what is right and to put things right. God is about holiness, not holocaust.

From a Christian perspective there is a contrast between two Joshuas:[39]

- *Joshua*, who occupies the land of another people, builds a geo-political entity, uses the sword and takes vengeance on his enemies. He is a symbol of the religious-political fanaticism that besmirches God's name. He did not achieve salvation (Joshua means 'saviour') and historically his work was a spiritual-moral failure.[40]
- *Joshua–Jesus* (Jesus is 'Joshua' in Greek), who lives in an occupied land, building a God-centred community, declaring, 'My kingdom is not like the kingdoms of this world; if it were my followers would fight.'[41] Instead he commands, 'Love your enemies.'[42] He achieves cosmic salvation through an apparent defeat by violence.

I am not suggesting my brief comments resolve the issues presented by the 'genocide passages', but I hope they emphasise the need to read them with maturity and wisdom in the light of the full breadth of biblical revelation and careful historical evidence.

This reminds us that just because something is biblical it is not necessarily Christian.

∗ ∗ ∗ ∗ ∗

'What about the Christian tradition of "Just War"?'

Since the fifth century CE[43] the majority of Christians from most denominations have believed that war in at least some circumstances is just and right as a last resort.[44] This 'Just War' idea has as its aim: 'To limit war in the pursuit of justice, but only if certain conditions are met.'

These conditions are:

- A *just cause*: there must be a clear wrong, action must be authorised by a legitimate authority, and it must have clear objectives with a good chance of success;
- A *just means*: armies must use only the minimum force necessary to accomplish a victory, it must be proportional, also making sure only the military are attacked;
- A *just intention*: on the battlefield there must be respect for the enemy; they must never be humiliated and soldiers must fight with the spirit of a peacemaker;
- A *just disobedience*: if a soldier sees any of the terms of the 'Just War' being violated they have a moral responsibility to leave the battlefield and cease fighting.

While these restrictions may have minimised some atrocities on history's battlefields, in reality 'Just War' is exactly what it says – it is *just war*.

It is nothing more than a reworking of the ancient 'myth of redemptive violence', which argues it is essential to use violence to avoid being overwhelmed by the greater violence of chaos and evil.[45]

'Just War' theology began to develop once Christians started to identify the church with the State as a centralised power under the Roman Emperor Constantine in 312, controlling a geographical area, protecting its boundaries and guaranteeing order by the use of force.

Throughout the first three centuries Jews challenged Christians that Jesus could not be the Messiah because scripture prophesied Messiah would establish worldwide peace, which clearly did not happen. The Christians replied by saying this biblical vision of peace had indeed begun *within* the church, a community that refused all use of violence.[46]

Fast-forward to 1263. A Jewish *rabbi*, Nachmanides, stood before the Spanish King James I of Aragon, arguing that the Christian faith could not be true for all the reasons previously given, but with this devastating twist, 'It was prophesied the Messiah would usher in an age of universal peace and yet the church has never ceased to engage in warfare and extol military virtues.'[47] What a change from the first three centuries. What a terrible indictment of the church's 'Just War' doctrine.

I have already said that violence can be stirred by a desire for justice in the face of injustice: a longing to put things right. Many see World War Two as a 'Just War' in this category. In reality, while it technically met the first of the conditions required, it failed to meet all the others, so cannot be seen as a 'Just War'. It is perfectly understandable why people turn to violence in the face of injustice or threat, but Jesus reveals its deception and offers an alternative, which historically the majority of the Christian church has rejected.

This reminds us that just because something is Christian it is not necessarily biblical.

As a 'Meekness Zealot' we have three tasks:

- To unmask and confront injustice and evil;
- To respond to violence with 'assertive meekness';
- To turn the hearts of our enemies towards friendship;

Jesus gives us three examples.[48] In each case the disciple faces humiliation, abuse or exploitation, but turns the situation into creative confrontation with the possibility of reconciliation.

If anyone strikes you on the *right* cheek, turn the other also.[49]

In the Orient the only hand ever used to strike someone would be the right one; the left was the unclean toilet hand, never *ever* used in public. The natural way to hit someone on the *right* cheek would be to use the back of the right hand as an insult to an inferior. To turn your other cheek, your *left* cheek, to your attacker would force them to use the open palm or fist of the right hand, which would be done only to someone who was an equal. To 'turn the other cheek' is therefore to assert your equality with your attacker, saying, 'You cannot demean me, I am a human being like you, your status or superior strength or advantage does not change that fact.' It is an act of fearless dignity with a love that hopes to change their attitude towards you also.

From anyone who takes away even your coat
do not withhold even your shirt.[50]

In this second example, the setting is the law court. Only the poorest peasant would be sued for their outer garment, their coat.[51] Why does Jesus say, 'Give them you undergarment as well'? This would leave them stark naked. In Judaism nakedness was a taboo, but the shame was always with those who were looking on. By this act the poor disciple shows the creditor up for who and what they really are: their exploitation has led to the debtor being left with nothing. The disciple takes the initiative, greed has been unmasked, and the dignity of the poor has been affirmed, but again the aim is to change the oppressor's heart as well.

If anyone forces you to go one mile, go also the second mile.[52]

Finally, in occupied Israel, a Roman soldier could legally command a civilian to carry his pack for a single mile, but no further. To insist on walking for a second mile shifted the balance of power. The soldier was now under pressure; forbidden to allow a civilian to backpack for him more than a mile he could face very serious reprimand. This instruction of Jesus was to deliberately challenge the command and humiliation system of the oppressor. It also confronts the soldier with the humanity of the oppressed person who seeks to have a positive relationship with him.

We see from these teachings 'assertive meekness' requires courage and creativity. It improvises and keeps the oppressor off-balance. In its own way it is also an acted prophecy – making a public demonstration of truth with memorable and disturbing impact. At the same time it also recognises the image and likeness of God in every other person; that being so, it hopes to change their hearts and minds.

Violence appears to offer people simple solutions; you hurt the person who offends you, and if you feel you have been successful, your anger and fear are rewarded with a sense of immediate gratification. 'Assertive meekness' does not offer a simple alternative to this – each challenge requires maturity, creativity and wisdom (the theme of our next chapter, *Wisdom Dancer*).

There is however dignity and beauty in this alternative.

I delight in the fact that Jesus gives us numerous examples of how to respond – like the three discussed above – but none of them are relevant to our culture today. The principles clearly remain, but we have to find our own fresh imaginative ways of applying them to our particular situation.

In the light of this, let's conclude with a brief comment on the classic challenge to those who oppose all use of violence:

What would you do if a violent person broke into your home and threatened to kill your family?[53]

First, it is important to state there is no guarantee that 'assertive meekness' will bring a satisfactory solution (though it very often does), just as there is no certainty using violence will be successful either (and it very often isn't). With regard to the suggestions below we see Jesus using most of them, with many others finding them very effective.[54]

Every violent encounter will be different, so it is important to think creatively. What unexpected and surprising responses might take the initiative and enable a peaceful resolution to the threat? Clear thinking with reason and subtle logic opens possibilities.

Attackers always expect their victims to be afraid, so responding with calm fearlessness can be disarming. Speaking with quiet self-assurance in an authoritative manner can unsettle their confidence and shift the balance of power.

Diminutive Gladys Aylward walked into the middle of a Chinese prison riot demanding the ringleader hand over his axe. Dumbfounded at her fearless authority, he obeyed. She calmed the rioters and then negotiated their complaints with the authorities.[55]

On many occasions the attacker will have practical needs: they are hungry, they want money or drugs, they are suffering emotional or psychological distress. Is there an opportunity to meet their needs? Winsome kindness and genuine compassion can turn the tide of violence.

Facing violence calls for us to be tactical and practical, developing a careful plan or ruse. On one occasion Jesus hid from those threatening him![56] Creating a physical obstruction with obstacles or even using nonviolent restraint both have their place, as does alerting others to the threat.

One night a crazed junkie demanding cash held Dorothy Samuel and a friend at knifepoint on the streets of Philadelphia. They had no money, so spoke to him quietly and walked with him to their flat where they gave him some dollar bills – he left apologising he didn't have any change![57]

At all times expect the unexpected to happen, even a miracle.[58] While our responses are vital, as a spiritual person we are aware that there are many factors at play and the most astonishing outcomes are possible.

Finally, if my life was taken, I pray the fearless dignity of my death and forgiving love in my eyes towards my killer would never be erased from their mind and might one day lead them to seek forgiveness and choose a different path.[59]

'Assertive meekness' is an art form to be learned. Each day we all face violence at some level in our lives; choose to identify it and then engage with it creatively. This makes us sensitive to possibilities, our thinking begins to change (*metanoia*) and so does our behaviour. Then when the bigger challenges come we are more likely to be prepared.

Keep remembering the ultimate aim is to turn all conflict into positive relationships – this is the vision of *shalom*. Jesus could not be clearer: 'Love your enemies.'[60]

The early Christians were clear:

> If your enemies are hungry, feed them;
> if they are thirsty, give them something to drink;
> … overcome evil with good.[61]

Ultimately we too, in all truthfulness as 'Meekness Zealots', can join Fr Ibrahim Nairouz in saying: 'The word "enemy" no longer has any meaning for me.'

Endnotes

1   Fr Ibrahim Nairouz is the priest of St Philip's Episcopal Church, Nablus, in Palestine. Among his many activities he runs a school and holiday clubs for Christian, Muslim, Samaritan and Druze children, also for a whole day every month he hosts sixty Muslim *imams* in the church building, providing hospitality, building relationships and discussing community matters
2   It is not explicitly stated in these terms in the book of Jonah, but the words of 3:10 and 4:2, 9–11 make it clear that this is the message, remembering that at this time the Assyrians (inhabitants of Nineveh) were the cruellest nation ever known, feared above all others and the greatest threat to Israel. Ironically today

almost all the descendents of the Assyrians (most of whom live in Iraq) are Christians!

3   Mt 5:39–41; cf. Lk 6:27–31.

4   Lk 9:56 – footnote in the NRSV.

5   Mt 26:52.

6   Jn 8:7.

7   Combining the *Concise Oxford English Dictionary* and the *Chambers English Dictionary* we get the following range of definitions:
    - *Violate:* to do violence, to disregard, to act against, to fail to comply with, to ravish, to profane, to defile, to break in upon, to disturb;
    - *Violent:* the use of physical force, intensely forcible, impetuous, unrestrained in action, overmastering, vehement, wrested;
    - *Violence:* being violent, unlawful exercise of physical force, excessive, unrestrained, unjustifiable force, outrage, profanity, injury, rape.

8   This definition of violence comes from Ken Butigan, *From Violence to Wholeness*, Pace e Bene Nonviolence Service, 2002, p. 13. The observations that immediately follow the definition are also stimulated by this source.

9   This provocation of violence is arguably part of the bigger picture of human 'memesis' (to copy or imitate). The French philosopher, historian and literary critic, René Girard, has written extensively of memesis as the fundamental anthropological characteristic of human behaviour. In his work, *Things Hidden Since the Foundation of the World* (Stanford: Stanford University Press, 1987), Girard argued that religious rituals initially limited these cycles of violence through the role of the scapegoat, but that this scapegoating was then exposed and defeated by Christ. Ultimately then for Girard, salvation from cycles of violence comes through the cross, which unveils and defeats the deception of ritualised violence, rather than giving into imitated patterns of violence. The passion of Christ is the permanent exposé of the 'the things hidden from the foundation of the world' – that both the order and disorder of human life are founded on the clashes of mimetic desire relieved by the lie of the scapegoat mechanism. The gospel of peace is responsible for the 'collapse' of patterns of violence, sacred or otherwise. I am grateful to my friend Drew Worthley for these reflections.

10 Mt 5:21–22.

11 Ironically United States President Barack Obama, in his acceptance speech for the Nobel Peace Prize, December 2009, illustrates this. Having honoured Gandhi and Martin Luther King he says however, 'I face the world as it is, I cannot stand idle in the face of threats.' Once again someone you would expect to know better sadly perceives 'pacifism' as 'idleness'. Quoted in JR Krabill and S Murray (eds), *Forming Christian Habits in Post-Christendom: The Legacy of Alan and Eleanor Kreider*, Herald Press, 2011, p. 83.

12 I make these observations from a position of deep respect for all those members of peace movements who continually show the most astonishing courage and creativity in working to bring an end to war, violence and injustice. It is only that I know from personal experience for many the whole understanding of the concept of 'peace' is astonishingly un-thought-through and that Christian *shalom* thinking has much to offer.

13 It may seem trivial but to many the removal of the hyphen from the word 'non-violence', to create the single word 'nonviolence' is seen as a significant peace-concept; whatever the intention it still only says what peace is *not* and still singularly fails to communicate anything creative or positive about the concept of peace.

14 This word is central to Jain philosophy and is also found in Hinduism (as we have seen); it was highlighted within mainstream by Gandhi (1869–1948), who

was also deeply influenced by the teaching of Jesus, particularly as interpreted by Tolstoy (1828–1910). Gandhi's peace-witness inspired many, including Martin Luther King Jr (1929–68) and the American Civil Rights Movement in the 1960s. All these facts have combined to give the idea of 'nonviolence' such a prominent place in peace thinking and vocabulary.

15 I am grateful to a conversation with Simon Barrow of 'Ekklesia' when we reflected on these points together in July 2006.

16 The subject of strategies regarding nonviolent action is immense. The classic work on the subject is by Gene Sharp in his three-volume book, *The Politics of Nonviolent Action*, Porter Sergeant, 1973, where he categorizes 198 examples and the principles behind them; this is well worth careful study.

17 See F Hauck and S Schulz, 'Praus', in G Kittel and G Friedrich (eds), *Theological Dictionary of the New Testament*, Eerdmans, 1968, pp. 645–651 and William Barclay, *Gospel of Matthew (Vol 1): The Daily Study Bible*, St Andrew Press, Edinburgh, 1956, pp. 91–93.

18 This was particularly the view of the Greek philosopher Aristotle who saw *praus* as a central ethical quality.

19 Num 12:3 it is used of Moses as leader, used in Zech 9:9 and Mt 21:1–11 of the victorious warrior king enacted by Jesus' entry into Jerusalem on a donkey. It is the quality of those who inherit the earth – Ps 37:11; and in Ps 18:35 it is used of God.

20 I recognise that properly understood the word 'meekness' does not need the prefix 'assertive', but because meekness is so completely misunderstood I believe it is essential to use it in the context of violence.

21 See Mt 21:12–17; Mk 11:15–19; Jn 2:13–22.

22 Zech 6:12–13.

23 Ps 69:9.

24 Isa 56:7.

25 Jer 7:11.

26 Ps 8:2 (LXX).

27 See Mt 21:1–11. We recognise that in John's Gospel this story is placed early in Jesus' public ministry; whether this is done as a literary technique or for other reasons is uncertain and much debated.

28 BF Mayer, *The Aims of Jesus*, SCM, 1979, p. 197.

29 On the rare occasions that biblical prophecy does foretell the future, it does so only to support the central message about the character of God and how we should respond to it. It interprets the times and how we should behave in the present; it is not about giving details so we can predict the future.

30 There are numerous biblical examples of acted prophecy, with people like Ahijah (1Kgs 11:29–39), Hosea (1:3–8), Isaiah (8:1–3; 20:1–6) and Ezekiel (4:1–3; 12:1–16; 24:15–24) and others as prime examples.

31 Quoted from Ps 69:9.

32 Phrase adapted from CS Lewis' comment about Aslan in the words of Mr Beaver in *The Lion, the Witch and the Wardrobe*, Penguin Books, 1959. 'Then he isn't safe?' said Lucy. 'Safe?' said Mr Beaver ... 'Who said anything about safe? Of course he isn't safe. But he is good ...' (p. 75). 'He's wild you know. Not like a *tame* lion' (p. 166).

33 See for example Deut 7:2; 20:16 and Josh 6:2, 21. It is estimated that in the Hebrew scriptures alone there are 600 passages of explicit violence, 1,000 verses describing God's own acts of violent punishment, 100 passages where God commands others to kill and several stories where God appears to irrationally kill or try to kill someone. We have a problem!

34 Early attempts to resolve the issue suggest the Hebrews *thought* God had asked them to commit these acts, so they retell the stories believing this had

been required of them – they were mistaken. Or, edited in the exile, the stories reflect how the Jews *wished* they had acted towards the Canaanites; if only they had removed the temptation to sin that eventually led them to be driven from the land into Babylon.

35 The 'genocide passages' or 'texts of terror' are mainly found in:
- Deuteronomy – which is for spiritual teaching (*Torah*)
- Joshua - which is part of the 'former prophets' (*Nebim*)
- Psalms - which were written for worship (*Kethubim*).

Recognise them as stories being retold with a liturgical purpose (teaching, declaration, meditation, worship). There are no 'historical' books in scripture; the stories are retold with the deliberate purpose of drawing out their spiritual meaning, not as a historical reconstruction.

36 See Deut 30:15–20; Exod 21:24; Mt 5:29–30; Col 3:5.

37 Reconstructing the period of settlement and judges is complex. Archaeology does not support the wholesale destruction of towns at this time as the text suggests; the evidence points to settlement by assimilation, not conquest. Some fighting probably took place, but not genocide. Ancient warfare was ruthless and merciless, even more so when driven by theological ideology like Israel's. It is also clear all 'Canaanites' were not actually destroyed (see Jg 1:1); the widespread presence of Canaanites throughout Israel's history is a case in point and the reason for the continuing significance of these texts.

38 Josh 5:13–15.

39 I am grateful to my friend Joe Baker for this insight.

40 Despite Josh 11:23 see Jg 1:1 and the fact that Canaanite influence continued throughout Israel's history and in the end led to her destruction and exile from the land. Had Joshua not used violence how different the story might have been. Note also how for René Girard, the violent deliverance of the Israelites from Egypt did not cure them of their own problems with mimetic rivalry and collective violence because, during the journey through the desert, violence, rivalry and aggression continued to flare into destructive patterns of behaviour. Sometimes the people ganged up on Moses and Aaron, or otherwise the people ganged up on somebody else in an effort to create a scapegoat for violent sacrifice. Many of these Old Testament narratives reveal how new victims are created in the effort to save other victims by violent means. I am again grateful to my friend Drew Worthley for this reflection.

41 Jn 18:36.

42 Mt 5:44.

43 Thinkers like Augustine (5th century CE) and Aquinus (13th century CE) developed the idea out of concepts that had been discussed by Greek philosophers like Aristotle, and interwove them with ideas about war from the Hebrew scriptures. Then certain New Testament passages (eg Rom 13) were read in the light of these findings. 'Just War' thinking subsequently became the basis of international law

44 There have of course been notable exceptions with the Anabaptists, Quakers and the Brethren.

45 This is an ancient Mesopotamian myth from the Babylonian creation story, the *Enuma Elish*. *Tiamat*, the goddess of chaos, is murdered by her son, *Marduk*. He dismembers her body and creates the universe out of her cadaver. Creation is an act of violence, order is established by means of disorder. Forms of this myth have influenced cultures from India to Ireland. It is no coincidence that the Roman (Latin: *pax*) and Greek (*eirene*) words for 'peace' mean a 'truce', implying the fundamental nature of the universe is chaos, violence and evil. Any experience of peace must be short-lived and inevitably engulfed once more by violence. This myth is deeply embedded in western culture; whether in

TV cartoons or major films you see the 'good guy' using violence to hold back the tide of chaos and evil which threatens to triumph. Violence is the means of redemption. It is a clear influence on Christian 'Just War' thinking.

46 For the Christian response see G Lohfink, *Jesus and Community*, Paulist Press, 1984, pp. 168–176.

47 Nachmanides was also known as Moses ben Nachman; for further details see Joan Comay, *The Diaspora Story*, Steimatzky, 1981, pp. 132–133.

48 See Mt 5:38–42; Lk 6:29–30; the reflections on these three sayings of Jesus are a simplified adaptation from Walter Wink, *Engaging the Powers*, Fortress Press, 1992, pp. 175–182.

49 Mt 5:39.

50 Lk 6: 29.

51 Cf. Exod 22:25–27; Deut 24:10–13, 17.

52 Mt 5:41.

53 For a full discussion of this question see John Howard Yoder, *What Would You Do?* Herald Press, 1983.

54 For a discussion as to how Jesus handled violence and conflict, see my 'Jesus: The Peacemaker' in Dana Mills-Powell (ed.), *Decide for Peace: Evangelicals and the Bomb*, Marshall Pickering, 1986, pp. 74–85.

55 See Alan Burgess, *The Small Woman*, Pan Books, 1969.

56 See Jn 12:36.

57 See Dorothy Samuel, *Safe Passage on the Streets*, Abingdon, 1975.

58 See Lk 21:13–15; 1Cor 10:13.

59 Remember that 'martyrdom' means 'witness'; I am to be a martyr–witness in both how I live and how I die.

60 Mt 5:44.

61 Rom 12:20–21.

10 Wisdom Dancer
– exploring the rhythms of creativity

A wise woman who lived in the wilderness found a precious stone in a mountain stream. The following day she met a traveller; the man was hungry so she stopped to share her food with him. As she opened her bag he saw the stone and, on impulse, he asked the woman to give it to him. She did so without hesitation. Having eaten the traveller left, rejoicing in his good fortune, for he knew the gemstone was worth enough to give him security for the rest of his life. However, a few days later, he returned to give the precious stone back to the wise woman. 'I've been thinking', he said, looking earnestly into her face. 'I know how valuable this stone is, but I give it back in the hope that you can give me something even more precious.' He paused, 'Please tell me what you have deep within you that enabled you to give me this gemstone so freely.'[1]

As a 'Values Master', wisdom is one of the great jewels we have to work with; it is treasure indeed.

How much better to get wisdom than gold.[2]

In a world obsessed with facts, figures, data and information there is a disturbing absence of wisdom, almost an indifference to it. It is rarely spoken of on the streets, in the popular media or even in church;[3] the new spiritualities are possibly the one exception to this sad reality.

A dictionary would define wisdom as: ' the possession of experience and knowledge together with the power of applying them critically or practically'.[4]

A brief biblical definition would be the skill and discipline of applying truth to the experience of life; the art of being successful, of forming the correct plan to gain the desired results.[5]

Alongside a Jesus perspective the pursuit of wisdom is the focus
of many cultures and faiths; several examples are:

By three methods we may learn wisdom:
first, by reflection, which is noblest; second, by imitation,
which is easiest;
and third, by experience, which is the most bitter. –
Confucius[6]

A person is not wise merely because they talk much.
But one who is calm, free from hatred and fear,
is truly called a wise person. – *Buddha*[7]

Allah gives wisdom to whom Allah wills,
and whoever has been given wisdom
has certainly been given much good. – *Quran*[8]

It is also interesting that scientific classification of modern
humans has chosen to identify us as *Homo sapiens* – 'wise
person'.[9]

* * * * *

There they were in front of me, street dancers – leg-splitting,
somersaulting, head-spinning – in the city precinct, improvising
rhythms and moves to express their joy, show their skill, raise the
momentum of the group and draw us bystanders into the tempo.
Dance seems to spring up out of the very earth and pulsate
through nature, a symbol of life itself. It is movement that matches
the rhythm of music or simply the thrill of the moment. Dance can
express every mood; intimate or exuberant, celebrating and
storytelling; it can bring healing to individuals and peace to
communities. For years dance has been for me a symbol of
creativity and the skills at its heart a picture of wisdom.

This dance and craft of wisdom, properly understood, is the means
by which *shalom* becomes a reality; so it is essential we grasp a
biblical insight into *hokma* in Hebrew and *sophia* in Greek. There
are a number of different facets to this jewel of biblical wisdom.

Wisdom is personal: like all values wisdom only becomes a reality
in as much as it is incarnated in our thoughts and actions.
Interestingly on occasions the words *zadik* (someone who is just
and righteous) and *hokma* are almost interchangeable:[10]

The mouth of the righteous flows with wisdom.[11]

We are told that the 'fear of the Lord is the beginning of wisdom',[12] a fear like the feeling a lover has towards their beloved – not wanting anything to spoil their relationship.

Wisdom is practical: wisdom is the central biblical word for creativity. Even professional mourners are viewed as wise, as they expertly guide a family gently through the experience of grief.[13] You capture something of the breadth of wisdom if you think of someone imagining a boat, drawing up the plans, physically building it, and then having the skill to set sail, and navigate by the stars to a predetermined destination. Wisdom is the discipline of conceiving and achieving practical results.

Wisdom is pastoral: sensitive to the needs of others, wisdom enables someone to 'sustain with a word a person who was weary'.[14] In the same way wise leaders formulate plans that help others enjoy all the benefits of life; not unlike a sea captain, they navigate the community through unpredictable waters to a safe harbour.

The complete opposite to a wise leader is 'the fool'.[15] In most cases this is as far removed from the idea of a 'village idiot' as it is possible to get. The fool is intelligent, educated and sophisticated but has put together an understanding of life in which every possible question can be answered without any reference to God.[16] This of course does *not* include atheists whose views are the only honest position for them to hold. No, the fool is about arrogance; fools are 'wise in their own eyes' (so can include religious people too).[17] They increasingly hold positions of leadership and influence in our society with the inevitable negative effects on a population looking to them for direction.

Wisdom is philosophical: the Greek word *philosophos* has the wonderful meaning, 'friend of wisdom'. Like much ancient Greek philosophy, the biblical understanding of wisdom recognises that life is full of paradox, ambiguity, puzzle and enigma, however unlike ancient Greek philosophy the biblical understanding of wisdom goes beyond the theoretical and abstract. It is deep. However, it is not just practical; we are urged to reflect on life, to meditate and actively contemplate experience,[18] to think, question and reason, to 'see, know, consider and understand'.[19] Several biblical wisdom writers wrestle with the overwhelming and perplexing questions of life, such as the nature of God, the problem of suffering and the meaning of existence.[20] All this brings about a 'largeness of mind',[21] but also has practical implications for how we live our daily lives.

Are you wise?
How do you become wise?
What is it about wisdom that most attracts you?

True wisdom in its complete sense belongs to God alone;[22] the only one who has the most complete knowledge about all things and can accomplish everything. God's wisdom is ultimately inscrutable and a mystery quite beyond human grasp.[23]

Biblical writers use a number of strong images to describe wisdom.

Wisdom is like a woman: both *hokma* and *sophia* are feminine in gender, and across world cultures wisdom is a gift in which women constantly excel.[24] Biblically we are introduced to this mysterious and beautiful woman, 'Wisdom', speaking out on the streets and in the town square like a typical Hebrew prophet, but we also find her at the city gate giving counsel as a respected elder. She opens her home as a place of hospitality, offering a feast to all those who are hungry for maturity and insight into life. More intimately she comes as a lover and covenanted life-companion bringing erotic delight – not unlike 'the Beloved' in Song of Songs, in contrast to the seductive emptiness of the prostitute 'Ignorance'. 'Wisdom', this beautiful voluptuous woman, is to be sought after, found, wooed and married.[25] There is every reason to believe she is clothed in *shekinah* (also feminine in gender) – 'the full expression of the presence of God'.[26]

Wisdom is like a child: there is a tantalising and charming passage picturing wisdom as God's little girl and favourite child; the first of all things to exist, still to be weaned, she plays in her father's workshop while the task of creating the cosmos is taking place. You hear her laughter and childlike delight as the complexity of the world and humanity are brought into being:

> The Lord brought me into being at the beginning of the
> divine work,
> the first of God's acts long ago …
> then I was beside God like a nursing child;
> delighting God day after day,

always at play in the divine presence,
at play everywhere in God's world,
enchanted to be with the human race.[27]

At the heart of wisdom there is childlike playfulness and sheer joy;
something we must never forget and to which we shall return.

Wisdom is like a craftswoman: wisdom is about the skills, craft and
cunning of creativity: 'The Lord by wisdom founded the earth.'[28]

Here is 'Wisdom' in the heat of the divine forge and the demands
of God's workshop, bringing creation into being; she is as capable
at working tough metals, shaping rough timber and carving stone
as at doing intricate embroidery or subtle colour-work. She
provides the technique that enables God's creative word to
become reality.[29]

Wisdom is like a treasure: we have already seen this is an
important image. In founding creation 'Wisdom' has been woven
into the very fabric of the cosmos;[30] she lies there like precious
stones or seams of gold, silver and other valuable metals waiting
to be found. We are to be like prospectors or miners, searching the
wilderness or the dark depths underground with the single aim of
finding her:[31]

... for wisdom is better than jewels,
and all that you may desire cannot compare with her.[32]

✳ ✳ ✳ ✳ ✳

The sculptor Michelangelo was stripped to the waist, bathed in
sweat, his hammer pounding a chisel that tore into beautiful
white marble, stone chips flying everywhere. A passer-by
stopped to watch and then asked, 'Sir, why do you work with such
terrible speed and frenzy?' Michelangelo replied, 'Because there is
an angel imprisoned in this rock and it is crying out to be set
free.'[33]

This story is an intriguing reflection on the biblical understanding of
creativity at the core of wisdom; seeing what others do not see,
zealous for truth, incarnating imagination and eager to bring
liberation to lives in a hard unyielding society.

How do we nurture this?

What liberates creativity and wisdom?

Three words closely linked to the Hebrew word *hokma* highlight the nature of wisdom's creativity:

- *Tbuma – insight*:[34] as on the occasion when the Israelite King Solomon was confronted with two women both claiming to be the rightful mother of a baby – he ordered the living child to be sliced in half to be divided between them; in the horror of the moment the true mother screamed, 'No, she can have it!'[35] Or how in the 1890s the Swedish chemist, Savante Arrhenius, became the first to understand that CO_2 emissions, global warming and potential climate change were all linked together.[36]
- *Bina – understanding*:[37] like a child joining up dots on a page to reveal a hidden picture. The ability to make unexpected connections between things seemingly unrelated; this can be beautiful, disturbing, revolutionary, practical, and humorous – sometimes quite shocking. Arthur Koestler saw it as central to all creativity whether artistic, scientific or comic. He called it 'bisociative thinking', a creative leap or flash of insight bringing together previously quite unconnected points of reference, enabling us to experience reality on several planes at once.[38]
- *Yada – knowledge*:[39] this is full experience of life, not just information about it; the actual raw encounter that enables creative wisdom to be true. Often used to describe sexual intimacy where the couple 'know' each other in a way that is only possible as a result of sexual intercourse; this would connect with the erotic images linked to *hokma* already mentioned. Only the knowledge of experience can bring wisdom that is authentic.

However, turning to reflect on all this in terms of Jesus and our own identity and mission, note that his liberating dance of creativity with its new ways of understanding is often met with hostility – people prefer the comfort of what they know to the freedom of new possibilities. As Ayn Rand once said: 'The person who invented fire was probably burnt at the stake.'[40]

* * * * *

We meet Jesus on the dusty Palestinian roads as a maverick rabbinic teacher but creative to his fingertips. He is referred to as 'a carpenter's son';[41] the Greek word *tekton* implies someone who works with hard materials such as wood, metal, stone or iron, so might best be described as a builder.[42] The Hebrew behind the Greek possibly suggests a furniture maker (chests, cupboards, stools, benches). Another tradition speaks of Jesus making yokes and ploughs.[43] His father, Joseph, was a skilled craftsman and there is every reason to believe that he apprenticed Jesus in these skills and they worked together in the Nazareth area.[44]

Early writers reveal Jesus' remarkable rhythms of creativity as a quite natural facet of his everyday life. This is riddled with enigma; you cannot pin it down or explain precisely what is going on. He was ruthless, relentless and unsparing in his pursuit to confront people with truth wherever he went. He did it with integrity while using every means available, leaving footprints of peace everywhere he moved; he was *the* 'Wisdom Dancer'.

There is a story that at the height of the Cold War a schoolteacher in eastern Europe wanted to do something to challenge Communism. Uncertain, he finally decided to become a stand-up comedian in a local nightclub telling jokes about the regime. His act was hugely popular and he was soon arrested. On the day of his trial the only evidence against him was his little book of jokes, which was read out in the courtroom with great solemnity by the clerk. The result was uncontrollable laughter among the guards and everyone else present. The judge, apoplectic with rage, had to halt the trial; these 'little revolutionaries' – as the schoolteacher called his jokes – were doing their work.[45]

Jesus' parables were 'little revolutionaries'; exceptional stories that created humour, surprise and shock, confronting the hearer with truth about themselves and God, challenging them to think and act differently.

Many of Jesus' parables work exactly like a comedian's joke; they are stories that draw people in, encouraging them to relax, and then with that final punch line confront them in a way that disturbs or liberates – the truth once embedded like shrapnel works its way towards their heart. Like a joke they divide hearers into those who 'get it' and those who don't, or who choose not to be amused. You have to 'get' parables, but in reality parables 'get' you.

Can you remember a story or a joke that had this impact on you? What other 'little revolutionaries' have you encountered?

Stories with the level of impact of a parable have to be crafted to an astonishing standard. They must be culturally appropriate and sensitive, working with a sophisticated understanding of human psychology; pared down to the minimum so there are no extraneous elements, while at the same time being able to carry, communicate and focus core ideas that can be delivered with maximum impact as the story reaches its climax. That is creative communication at its best.[46]

Jesus' miracles are of course another remarkable example of creativity; both in their ability to make something happen beyond normal human expectations, and the way in which they are also used to illustrate a particular truth Jesus is teaching.[47]

* * * * *

Jesus was a master craftsman both as carpenter and communicator. What qualities marked him out as someone with a 'spirit of wisdom'?[48]

Humour seems close to the surface most of the time. There is a sense of frequent spontaneous joy and playful laughter, with a little gentle teasing, all intermingled with deep serious focus. What were Jesus' jokes like? Humour is so subtle and culturally nuanced we are certainly missing a great deal reading an English text based on a Greek account of memories that were originally in Aramaic. But we get flashes when he speaks about camels going through a needle's eye,[49] or trying to take a speck of sawdust from someone's else's eye while having a log of wood in your own;[50] not to mention referring to God as 'a daddy with a womb'![51]

We have already seen playful childlikeness at the heart of creative wisdom. Not only did Jesus have delightful humour but he also looked at the world through the eyes of a child. He insisted the ability to truly receive his message is open to people only to the extent they were childlike.[52] He also tells stories and uses images and ideas that children can relate to as easily as adults. As the anarchic Chinese philosopher, Lao Tze, once said, 'Wise people hear and see as little children do.'[53] Visiting an exhibition of children's drawings, Picasso once remarked: 'When I was their age I could draw like Raphael, but it took me a lifetime to learn to draw like them.'[54] Jesus' personality has the same feel to it.

Jesus' creativity is shaped and textured by wild nature around him. The Greek philosopher, Aristotle, said, 'Wisdom begins in wonder.'[55] Jesus shares this wonder; it flows from his wide-eyed childlikeness. Hebrew sages saw wisdom woven into the fabric of the world, like a thread holding the web of creation together; they called us to learn from animals, birds, fish and plants.[56] King Solomon, a legend in wisdom and creativity, spoke of trees, plants, animals, birds, reptiles and fish;[57] in Jesus someone far 'greater than Solomon' was present.[58] He moved freely within the natural world, exploring its rhythms of creativity, using its images to illustrate his ideas. For him the words and the ways of wild wisdom sprung quite naturally within him.[59]

What do children see that adults don't, and why?
How does wisdom begin in wonder?

For all his love of wilderness Jesus was a people-person, an insightful observer of human nature with a keen eye for the lives of people across the whole of the society in which he lived. People he met on his travels and the characters that illustrate his stories; from farmers to homemakers, day labourers to prostitutes, the blind and lepers, rulers and merchants, and so very many more ...

Jesus often acted like modern-day 'Adbusters', who subvert mainstream society by counter advertising using billboard graffiti. Like them Jesus used culture to challenge culture, exposing hypocrisy, waking people up to the illusions they live with, then revealing and demonstrating alternatives. His powerful pithy sayings, highly memorable, often increased their impact by juxtaposing ideas, such as: 'Sabbath was created for people, not people for the Sabbath'.[60]

Time and again Jesus quite intentionally created tension in a situation before he acted. He seems to have done it for different reasons: to heighten expectations, to create unexpected space, to test faith; it is part of his creative technique.[61] For example when a foreign woman begs Jesus to heal her daughter, to everyone's horror he replies: 'It is not fair to take the children's food and throw it to dogs!' He was actually creating space for this woman's astonishing faith and tenacity to be revealed, with her response: 'But even the puppies eat the scraps that fall from the children's table!'[62]

Watching Jesus move within his tightly regulated society is like watching a chess-master at work; a player of such skill they can usually beat the experts. Like them Jesus works within a tightly defined space with strict rules on his moves; yet he himself is not under pressure, but rather he creates pressure by turning obstacles into opportunities. We see careful thinking, with flashes of brilliance and finally checkmate – the shock of the true.[63] Like the occasion when a woman was caught in the very act of adultery; the authorities said, 'The law commands us to stone such women'. Jesus replies: 'So be it, but just make sure it is someone without sin who throws the first stone.'[64]

Where culture crushes justice, what 'chess-move' would you make? What current marketing slogan offends you; how would you 'Adbust' it?

We have discussed at length Jesus' commitment to 'assertive meekness'; it finds its dexterity and rhythm within creative wisdom. The Hebrew sage Qoheleth said:

> Wisdom is better than might ...
> Wisdom is better than weapons of war.[65]

Jesus warns his disciples of possible persecution:

> I will give you words and a wisdom
> that none of your opponents will be able to withstand or contradict.[66]

An early Christian voice speaks of: 'gentleness born of wisdom'.[67] For Jesus conflict had to count for something, as in the case of cleansing the Temple, or else it was a useless or dangerous diversion. Sometimes he defused the situation by his teaching; at other times he simply walked off and left them standing.[68] On other occasions wisdom dictated that he hide in the Temple or escape across the Jordan.[69]

On each occasion he had to decide whether what faced him was a creative crisis. His work was not to be endangered or frustrated. Nevertheless, when the time was right he would allow himself to be engulfed by the mob as a means of winning the greatest victory of all.[70]

Jesus does not fight to win, but rather to proclaim the truth and expose evil. He is always looking to find that space in the human heart and mind. Some of Jesus' most powerful statements about

God's love come in response to the bitterest attacks against him.[71] Opponents may be silenced but never humiliated; the door to God's *shalom* is always open.[72]

* * * * *

To me Jesus was like a guerrilla gardener: an activist who reclaims waste ground from neglect and derelict land from misuse by planting it, bringing flowers where there was rubbish and food-crops where there was rubble; using 'seed-bombs' to get flowers into hard-to-reach spaces. Like them Jesus' creative wisdom cultivates neglected spaces in people's lives, bringing beauty secretly, taking communities by surprise, working for 'the sheer joy of it' and not for reward.

There is much here to ponder and learn: the challenge of nurturing playful childlikeness alongside seasoned creative skills. Remembering that wisdom is a gift,[73] given generously if we ask for it,[74] but we must also be prepared to think and work at it to make it our own.

We are told in no uncertain terms to, 'Get wisdom!'[75]

Here is a call to develop a maturity of character illuminated by joy and wonder – a key to unlock the infinite possibilities woven into the fabric of a God-created world; a world, however, that is also broken, but in which creative wisdom is to play a vital healing role.

I am inspired by the fact that Michelangelo's masterpiece, 'the David', was carved from a block of marble so damaged by a previous sculptor it was considered unusable by every other artist of his day.[76]

In a similar way, I am challenged by the way that the wisdom of dance can give a voice to a woman so traumatised by violence she is incapable of telling her story through words, or how drama and play can return once brutalised boy-soldiers to a measure of childhood. How the rhythm of a drumming-circle or even paint on paper can provide significant steps for many towards wholeness. How the laughter of clowning can bring healing. The way storytelling, meaningful rituals and shared meals have been used to draw hostile groups together and bond communities together ... the examples and possibilities are endless.

Endnotes

1   This story, by an unknown author, has been slightly adapted from
    <www.wow4u.com/wisewoman/index.html>.
2   Prov 16:16; see also 8:10, 19; Job 28:15–19
3   With reference to the church, in all my years I have no memory of ever hearing
    a sermon on this subject – trust me, I have heard many thousands of sermons!
4   See *The Concise Oxford Dictionary*, Oxford University Press, 1982.
5   The second half of the definition is a quote from DA Hubbard, 'Wisdom', in JD
    Douglas (ed.), *New Bible Dictionary*, Inter-Varsity Press, 1982 (2nd edn), pp.
    1255–1257.
6   Taken from <http//en.wikiquote.org/wiki/Wisdom>.
7   *Dhammapada* v.258.
8   Sura 2:269 (slightly adapted for gender).
9   By Carolus Linnaeus (1707–78).
10 See RE Murphy, 'Wisdom in the OT', in DN Freedman (ed.), *The Anchor Bible
    Dictionary*, vol. 6, Doubleday, 1992, pp. 920–931.
11 Prov 10:31; see also Ps 37:30.
12 Prov 9:10; Ps 111:10.
13 See Jer 9:17–18.
14 Isa 50:4 (adapted).
15 See Prov 12:15; 14:16; 18:2 and many others.
16 See for example Ps 14:1; 53:1; Prov 18:2, Lk 12:16–21.
17 Isa 5:21.
18 See Josh 1:8; Ps 77:12; 143:5.
19 Isa 41:20, see also Job 37:14.
20 Job and Qoheleth are two examples.
21 1Kgs 4:29 (KJV) – a wonderful Hebraism expressed in Jacobean English!
22 See Isa 28:29; 31:2; Dan 2:20–23; Rom 11:23; 16:27.
23 Job 28:12–21; 1Cor 2:7.
24 I find the reference to 'a wise woman' from Tekoa (2Sam 14:2) intriguing, she
    clearly had a reputation for her wisdom.
25 This description of the beautiful woman 'Wisdom' is drawn from across the
    pages of Proverbs 1—9.
26 As mentioned previously, for a detailed description of the Jewish understanding
    of *shekinah* see JT Marshall, 'Shekinah', in J Hastings (ed.), *A Dictionary of the
    Bible*, vol. 4, T&T Clark, 1902, pp. 487–489.
27 Prov 8:22, 30–31; this is a much debated passage, especially over whether the
    word *qana* means 'created' here or something less specific and whether the
    rare word *amon* should be read as 'workman' (later Jewish sense) or 'nurseling'
    (more natural sense). For a more detailed discussion see RE Murphy, 'Wisdom
    in the OT', in DN Freedman (ed.), *The Anchor Bible Dictionary*, vol. 6,
    Doubleday, 1992, pp. 920–931; and G Forhrer, 'Sophia', in G Kittel and G
    Friedrich (eds), *Theological Dictionary of the New Testament*, vol. 7,
    Eerdmans, 1971, p. 491. On the subject of 'playfulness' also see Ps 104:24–26
    where God creates 'Leviathan' the whale to play with.
28 Prov 3:19.
29 Working with metaphor must always be done carefully. I am of course not
    suggesting that either wisdom or the word of God are somehow separate from
    divine being, but ways of attempting to understand aspects that are ultimately
    beyond full understanding.
30 As we will mention below, 'Hebrew sages saw wisdom woven into the fabric of
    the world as the thread holding the web of creation together', not unlike the
    logos in Greek thinking, the creative 'word–reason' that held the universe

together and was so important in the early Christian understanding of Jesus' relation to creation and the destiny of the universe (see Jn 1:1–5).

31 Job 28:1–22 gives a powerful meditation on wisdom using just this imagery.

32 Prov 8:11.

33 This story of Michelangelo (1475–1564) comes in different forms from many sources, some accounts identify the passer-by as Pope Julius II.

34 See for example Ps 136:5; Exod 35:31.

35 See 1Kgs 3:16–28.

36 See for example <http://www.guardian.co.uk/environment/2005/jun/30/climatechange.climatechangeenvironment2>.

37 See for example Prov 8:9; Dan 9:22.

38 See A Koestler, *The Act of Creation*, Picador, 1964, pp. 27; 33–36, wonderfully illustrated throughout the whole book.

39 See for example Prov 1:2; Exod 29:46, also Gen 24:16; 1Sam 1:19–20 as a sexual reference.

40 Ayn Rand, *The Fountainhead*, Harper Collins, 1961; and <www.goodreads.com/author/quotes/432.Ayn_Rand?page=4>.

41 Mt 13:55; Mk 6:3.

42 Traditionally the eastern (Greek) church tended to stress his working with wood, while the western (Latin) church tended to speak of an iron worker.

43 See WL Lane, *New International Commentary on the New Testament: the Gospel of Mark*, Eerdmans, 1974, pp. 202–203.

44 It is believed by many scholars that they both may have worked on the extensive building programme at Sepphoris just a few miles north of Nazareth. Note that Jewish *rabbis* usually had training in a manual craft; the early Christian leader *rabbi* Paul was a tentmaker (Acts 18:3).

45 This story was the subject of a film called *Little Revolutionaries*, broadcast by the BBC in the 1970s in their *Wednesday Play* or *Play for Today* series. Sadly I have never been able to trace the details of the author or the actual events on which it was based, but it made a lasting impression on me.

46 I am fully aware that each parable of Jesus was astonishingly sophisticated and each one has to be read in its historical context, cultural environment and literary form, for which you will have to turn to reputable commentaries and resources, but I hope my general observations provide some initial value.

47 Jesus' miracles are seen as a continuation of the creative work of God (Jn 14:10). The Gospel writers use a range of Greek words to describe the significance of the miracles:
- *Dunamis* – a demonstration of the powers of the age to come, now!
- *Erga* – the works of God who continues to act through the Messiah;
- *Semeion* – signs of the presence, power and character of God's kingdom;
- *Exousia* – actions that demonstrate God's rule and authority are present;
- *Thaumasios* – events that fill people with a sense of awe and wonder.

Jesus' words and works must not be separated, they support each other and illustrate and explained each other at every stage (Jn 10:37–38).

48 See Isa 11:2.

49 Mk 10:23–27.

50 Lk 6:41–42.

51 Jesus words, 'Be merciful as your heavenly father is merciful' (Lk 6:36), is using an Aramaic word for 'mercy' which is the plural form for the word 'womb', so it would be better translated, 'Be wombish as your heavenly father is wombish.' See Marcus Borg, *Jesus: A New Vision*, SPCK, 1993, pp. 102, 130–131 plus footnotes.

52 See Mt 18:2–5; Mk 9:36–37; 10:13–16; Lk 9:46–48; 18:15–17.

53 Taken from <http//en.wikiquote.org/wiki/Wisdom>.

54 R Penrose, *Picasso: His Life and Work*, New York: Harper, 1958, p. 275.
55 Aristotle's *Metaphysics* 1.ii.19.
56 Job 12:7–8; see also Prov 30:18–20, 24.
57 1Kgs 4:33.
58 Mt 12:42; Lk 11:31.
59 See Lk 9:28; Mt 5:1; 6:26–29; 7:15; 11:7; Mk 1:13; 6:35; Jn 10:12.
60 Mk 2:27; some other examples are Mt 4:19; 5:5, 36, 41, 44; 10:16; 11:12;
    19:12; Lk 6:21; 9:60; 10:3; 14:11; Mk 8:35; 10:31.
61 Some other examples are Mt 14:22–33; 22:19–21; 17:24–27; Mk 6:30–42; Lk
    5:1–8 (cf. Jn 21:1–8); Jn 2:1–11; 11:1–44.
62 Mk 7:24–30.
63 Some other examples are Mt 5:27–28; 9:9–13; 12:9–14; Lk 7:36–50; Jn 2:13–
    25; 4:1–42; 6:22–59; 13:1–20.
64 Jn 8:1–11.
65 Eccl 9:16, 18, see the whole section, vv. 13–18.
66 Lk 21:15.
67 Jas 3:13.
68 Jn 7:25–31; Lk 4:30.
69 Jn 8:59; 10:39–40.
70 Mk 15:11–14.
71 See for example the whole of Lk 15, but set against the background of vv. 1–2.
72 See Mt 23:37–39; Lk13:34–35; cf. Mt 22:34–40.
73 2Chr 1:10; Eccl 2;26; Dan 2:21.
74 Jas 1:5.
75 Prov 4:5; 19:8; 23:23 (read Prov 4:1–9 for a powerful instruction to make
    wisdom your own).
76 The story is well told in <http://100swallows.wordpress.com/2008/02/04/
    david-and-the-bad-block/>.

11 Subversive Celebrant
– feeding at the table of conspirators

Sara Miles was a chef, a left-wing journalist, war correspondent and an atheist; she is a lesbian. This is her story:

I walked into the church out of curiosity. I had no earthly reason to be there. I had never heard a gospel reading, never said the Lord's Prayer. I was certainly not interested in becoming a Christian. I walked in, took a chair, and tried not to catch anyone's eye. We sat down, stood up, sang, sat down, waited and listened and stood up and sang. 'Jesus invites everyone to his table' a woman announced.

We gathered around the table. Someone was putting a piece of fresh crumbly bread into my hands, saying 'This is the body of Christ' and handing me the goblet of sweet wine, saying 'the blood of Christ' and then something outrageous and terrifying happened. Jesus happened to me. I still can't explain. It made no sense. I felt as if I had just stepped off a curb or been knocked over painlessly, from behind. The disconnect between what I thought was happening – I was eating a piece of bread; what I heard someone else say was happening – the bread was 'the body of Christ'; and what I *knew* was happening – God, named 'Christ' or 'Jesus' was real, and in my mouth!

'All the way home, shocked, I scrambled for explanations. Maybe I was hypersuggestible, surrounded by believers pushing me into accepting their superstitions. My tears were just pent-up sadness after a long hard decade, spilling out because I was in a place where I could cry anonymously. Really the whole thing must have been about emotion: the music, the movement, the light …

'Yet that impossible word, *Jesus*, lodged in me like a crumb. I said it over and over to myself, as if repetition would help me understand. I had no idea what it meant; I did not know what to do with it. But it was more real than any thought of mine, or any subjective emotion: it was as real as the actual taste of bread and wine. And the word was indisputable in my body now, as if I had swallowed a radioactive pellet that would outlive my own flesh.'[*1]

As a result of this experience Sara went on to found the Food Pantry, which currently provides free groceries to about 500 hungry families a week, from around the altar at St Gregory of Nyssa Episcopal Church in San Francisco. It buys in between six and eight tons of food each week, and offers it free to everyone who comes. Families select the food they need from a wide variety of fresh fruits and vegetables, bread, rice, pasta, beans, cereal and dry goods. The Food Pantry is run entirely by volunteers, most of them people who came to get food and stayed to help out.[2]

Sara insists The Food Pantry is not an act of outreach but expresses gratitude to God who meets the needs of our own hunger in abundance. The bags full of macaroni and peanut butter that are given to strangers are in remembrance of him.[3] The fact that it takes place around the central table of the altar is crucial. This is neither a charity nor a food-kitchen for the poor; it is a Eucharist community.

* * * * *

The stories about Jesus and the earliest community gathered around him make one thing very clear: the only physical thing Jesus leaves us, with which to build the church, is a table with food on it.[4]

Taking the daily Palestinian peasant meal, giving it focus in terms of himself and his message of *shalom*, and placing it as the cornerstone of the new community was an act of creative genius. The truth is that the most inclusive image of the life, death, resurrection of Jesus is not the cross but a meal.

Why did Jesus choose a meal table as the cornerstone of being church?

In making the meal central, Jesus connects with something deeply primal. One of the first things to identify human beings within wild

---

nature was the hearth. More than 30,000 years ago the cooking fire enabled people to prepare food that was no longer raw. It became the centre around which the family or community gathered to eat face to face, talking, smiling, laughing, storytelling and sharing food. Initially fire would have been a threat and danger, and eye contact across a central food source being encircled by individuals with open mouths and exposed teeth would have suggested hostility. At some point these danger signals were transformed into the very essence of welcome and acceptance.[5]

So the shared meal now marks the stages of the day, moments for celebration, communication and the expression of acceptance. The hearth and the food table have become the very womb of all human culture.[6]

How would you explain the miracle of the meal in human development?

Watching a documentary series about the people of eastern Europe, I was struck how while travelling from country to country the reporter's most significant moments all took place around a meal table, with a family or community sharing bread, wine and local dishes in abundance.[7] There was intimate and animated conversation, laughter and sometimes tears and respectful silence for a storyteller. Many times a sudden spontaneous voice would begin to sing beautifully above the clamorous talking. Initially a solo, others would soon join in; as the tempo rose chairs would be pushed aside, musical instruments would seem to appear from nowhere and dancing would begin. As the rhythm slowed, people returned to the table and the eating and conversation would be resumed. Reflecting on the series I kept thinking, 'This is how Jesus intended church to be, this is the essence of the Peacemeal.'

＊ ＊ ＊ ＊ ＊

I love the word 'conspiracy'; it literally means 'breathing together'. It emphasises being connected and committed in a shared moment, breathing as one; like a rowing team pulling the last few metres towards the winning line, a choir singing in unison at the climax of a great oratorio, or a couple making love. Yet our modern use of the word has given the shared connection and commitment of 'conspiracy' a subversive twist. For me it sparks the image of a small group of people in the dark cellar of a tavern or alehouse, huddled around an oak beer-keg with a candle or storm lantern at the centre, breathing together as they plot and plan a new political order.

We have seen that 'breath' and 'breathing' are the universal picture of spirituality.

I have long felt this is how we should visualise church: a community of faith committed to the shared cosmic vision of *shalom*, gathered round a table with food, connected to each other in love, breathing together the life and power of the Spirit as we scheme and organise in very practical ways how to play our part in the transfiguration of the status quo.

This is the Peacemeal and it is explosive.

The simplicity of this meal disguises its depth and astonishing power. Every single aspect of what it means to live from a Jesus perspective is embedded within this meal; every element of truth is there to be discovered and shared. It can also find authentic expression in any and every culture of the world without importing any alien elements. It offers both the reality and mystery of profound spiritual encounter, touching us with the fingerprint of fire, as we saw in Sara Miles' story, while at the same time the opportunity and challenge of meeting the very physical needs of the hungry and destitute. This ordinary meal when celebrated authentically should provoke our society to look hard at its attitudes and become a means – as we have said before – of 'turning the world upside down'.[8] Placing this meal at the centre of our understanding of community and society – a meal that is seemingly so simple and innocuous, yet in the light of the person of Jesus, so explosive and disturbing – is why I see myself as a 'Subversive Celebrant'.

What is your reaction to church as a community of conspirators?

This meal is also vital in our search for identity. It is never found in individuality, only in community. This truth is powerfully expressed in the Xhosa word *ubuntu*, from southern Africa, which Archbishop Desmond Tutu among others has highlighted.[9] *Ubuntu* describes an approach to life that can be translated as, 'a person is a person only through other people', or that 'I am because we are'; sharing the Peacemeal emphatically makes this point. *Ubuntu* also recognises the worth of all others and acts for their benefit; it is generous, hospitable and compassionate, caring and sharing, it is about friendship and reconciliation; relationships are priority. Each interconnected person is unique and of great worth – in biblical terms 'made in the image and likeness of God'. It also touches the essence of what we understand about being 'the Body of Christ', which is so important to this meal.[10] The parallels between *ubuntu* and *shalom* are exciting; we shall discover them woven throughout the fabric of the Peacemeal as we continue.

∗ ∗ ∗ ∗ ∗

Each summer in Britain there is a huge Christian music and arts festival called 'Greenbelt', the centrepiece of which is a Sunday morning communion service, always inspiring, wonderfully creative, but understandably restricted to a small piece of bread and sip of wine due to the many thousands of people participating. Over the years of attending I have endeavoured to subvert proceedings by arriving with bags filled with large loaves of bread, piles of soft fruit, and boxes of red wine with pint beer glasses to serve it in. At the point when we gather in small groups to share the bread and wine I encourage everyone around to rip up the loaves and along with the fruit and wine to share it within the group and then as widely as possible among other groups. On one occasion a Baptist minister got caught up in the eucharistic mayhem we were creating; he later reflected:

> Large loaves of bread, fresh fruit and a wine box, no less, were being passed around us: 'have more' being the refrain. Any sense of unfamiliarity or even guilty irreverence soon dissolved into joyous liberation. Growing up conservative evangelical, my singular experience of communion was the ubiquitous grape juice shot glasses and a tiny cube of bread. As a pastor I have always struggled with the rather stilted or artificial nature of the 'meal', so being invited to 'have more' of the bread, the fruit and the wine, of Christ's presence in me, of fellowship was truly a wonderful experience. The fact we didn't all know each other yet we celebrated in abundance the unity of the body, the wholeness in knowing Christ as a group: the reality of communion became dramatic. No longer was it about 'nip and sip' in solemnity; it was about joyous abundance, a celebration of what Christ has done for us.[11]

How can this communal meal, given by Jesus to his community, have been reduced to 'nip and sip' in almost every Christian tradition?

Why is it no longer a proper meal?
Why have we forgotten that all the stories of Jesus feeding multitudes say, 'they all had as much as they wanted', being 'filled' and 'satisfied'?
Why has the sense of abundance evaporated?[12]
What were the influences behind the original Peacemeal and where has it gone so wrong?

The early Jesus-community understood the Peacemeal to be foundational, based on the example of Jesus himself for whom 'table fellowship' was central.[13] He clearly loved the whole eating experience; you simply cannot be called 'a glutton and a drunkard', however unkind its intention, without there being some basis for it.[14] Notice how often we see Jesus at the meal table – sometimes just with his disciples, on other occasions as an invited guest or even inviting himself as a guest.

Much of his teaching took place during a shared meal; among other things he used its imagery as a picture of the future. He scandalised public opinion by regularly 'eating with tax collectors and sinners',[15] shattering social boundaries, affirming access to God without intermediaries and revolutionising the popular ideas of holiness and purity.[16]

One Jewish scholar has noted that this activity above all others is what marked Jesus out from his contempories: 'He took his stand among the pariahs of his world, those despised by the respectable. Sinners were his table companions and the ostracised tax collector and prostitute his friends.'[17]

To sit at table with someone is an expression of intimacy and fellowship, to invite someone to a meal is to honour them and express trust and acceptance. In this way prostitutes find forgiveness; tax collectors are liberated from their ill-gotten wealth and inspired to distribute it to the poor and the hungry are fed. This is our example.

What would subversive table fellowship in your neighbourhood look like?

＊ ＊ ＊ ＊ ＊

Just hours before his arrest and execution, Jesus shared *Pesach* – the Passover meal – with his closest friends in Jerusalem.[18] This centuries-old tradition is shaped around drinking four cups of wine – each with a distinctive name and theme – with a full meal as its centrepiece.[19] Jesus gave it a completely new meaning.

The meal started in the time-honoured custom of sharing the first two cups of wine with their respective themes of 'to life' and then 'to freedom' along with the retelling the Exodus story. Then Jesus began the main meal by taking unleavened *matzos* and breaking it, dividing it among the group, not with the usual words, but the astonishing declaration, 'This is my body.' The meal concludes with a beautiful blessing and everyone sharing the third cup of wine with its theme, 'to *shalom*'. Again Jesus startles the group, saying, 'This is my blood.' After singing Psalm 118 together they left the room, crossed the Kidron valley to the olive groves of Gethsemane where later that night Jesus would be arrested. The fourth cup of wine, with its theme 'to Jerusalem' – 'the dwelling place of *shalom*' – and its message of future hope was left on the table untouched, hinting at events yet to unfold. Jesus' actions and words were shocking and disturbing, but they become the vital catalyst in the birth of the Peacemeal.

Following Jesus' crucifixion and burial, those women and men closest to him encountered him in resurrection power on several occasions in the context of a meal. Travelling home from Jerusalem one night two disciples met a stranger on the open road; inviting him to share supper they realise it is Jesus – 'he was known to them in the breaking of bread'.[20]

At dawn on the shore of Lake Galilee a stranger calls to a group of his followers in a fishing boat, 'Come and have breakfast'; we are told – 'they knew it was the Lord'.[21]

The Peacemeal does not simply remember Jesus' life and death but celebrates his resurrection and all its implications, which is why it so often took place 'on the first day of the week', Sunday, the day of the resurrection.[22]

Seven weeks later, at the Jewish feast of *Shavuoth*,[23] the bewildered Jesus-community received the promised empowering gift of the Spirit. These *Pentecost*[24] events transfigured them and once more found their focus around the sharing of food and the material resources they had:

> All who believed were together and had all things in common;
> they would sell their possessions and goods
> and distribute the proceeds to all, as any had need …
> they broke bread in one another's homes
> and ate their food with glad and generous hearts,
> praising God and enjoying the goodwill of all the people.[25]

The meal became the cornerstone of the community. Jesus' teaching and example were at its core; but it also built on the foundation of four important Hebrew meals, which were eaten:

- *Daily:* this was 'supper', the main family meal of the day. It had *koinonia* – 'a relationship of sharing' – as its focus, from which the word 'communion' would later develop. It is also picked up in the frequently used phrase, 'the Lord's supper'.[26]
- *Weekly:* this was the Friday evening *Shabbat* meal. It had 'covenant' (*berith*) and 'steadfast love' (*chesed*) as its theme, which the *rabbis* translated with the little-used Greek word *agape* – as 'unconditional love'. The early Jesus-community often called the meal 'the *Agape*', and gave deeper meaning to the traditional declaration of that evening – '*Shabbat Shalom*'.
- *Annually:* this was the *Pesach*–Passover spring festival meal, remembering the *exodus* from Egypt, from slavery to freedom. This was 'thanksgiving' – as in the Greek word *eucharisteo* – from which Christians developed the name 'Eucharist', which has *charis* – meaning 'grace' – at its heart: an 'extravagant beautiful gift'.
- *Finally:* this looks forward to the 'Messianic banquet' yet to come, when all the nations and peoples of the earth will participate.[27] Later the Latin word *missio* – 'to send' – was used to emphasise this, a 'missionary meal' – sent out to invite others in – eventually revocalised as 'the Mass'.

The Peacemeal is most frequently referred to by the Hebrew phrase *paras lechem* – 'breaking bread' – which refers to the Palestinian custom of breaking a loaf of bread with the hands at the beginning of a meal along with words of thanksgiving and then tearing and sharing the bread together while eating the meal (never cutting it with a knife).[28] The phrase came to denote 'sharing a meal together'. Occasionally the Peacemeal was referred to as a 'love feast', fusing *agape* and *paras lechem* together.[29]

From the very beginning the meal was seen not only as a celebration of the life, death and resurrection of Jesus but also as a way of making sure the poor and needy in the community had sufficient food. This is why the Christians in Corinth were condemned when they failed to share their food with the poor. They corrupted the 'Lord's supper' and as a result 'many were weak and ill and some died' – due to malnutrition.[30]

A Peacemeal that does not feed the poor cannot claim to proclaim Jesus.[31]

At the beginning of the third century CE the Peacemeal was still being shared both as a family meal at home and also as a wider community meal.[32] However, by the end of the same century the heart had been ripped out of it by church authorities; the bread and wine were isolated, put on a pedestal and called 'the Eucharist', while the meal itself was relegated to a charity supper, which the rich gave to the poor and called 'the *Agape*'.[33]

This act of vandalism not only destroyed the Peacemeal but also fractured the very understanding of what it means to be church, something from which we have never recovered.[34]

* * * * *

All food is sacred because it enables life. Across world faiths it is understood to have a source beyond itself; it is a God-given gift and a point of connection with the spirit.

This truth is at the heart of the Peacemeal; it is a mystery but no less a reality. The word used in relation to this is 'sacrament', from the Latin *sacramentum*, which in its contemporary sense means making invisible truth physically tangible.[35] This meal is Jesus-centred; our bodies should not only be physically nourished with the food but also spiritually energised.

The words of Jesus, 'This is my body' and 'This is my blood' are clearly the starting point for encounter. The tragedy is not only have the bread and wine been ripped from their place at the heart of a full meal, but also their understanding has become polarised. Some Christians insisting only special words by special people can enable them to *become* the body and blood of Jesus,[36] while others argue the bread and wine only *represent* them.[37] Neither view stands up to scrutiny. Jesus could not be clearer, 'This *is* my

body–blood'; it does not *become*, it does not *represent*, it simply *is*.
A mystery, yes, but also a demonstration of the power and
presence of the Spirit and the holistic nature of reality we
discussed previously, with the spiritual and physical seamlessly
and potently interfused.

When Jesus makes his 'bread–body' and 'wine–blood'
declarations he is primarily saying, 'This is me.'[38] The physical act
of sharing is vital because in doing so we become interwoven with
him and one another as we eat, through the presence of the Spirit,
even if all the participants don't recognise it. There is something
simple, beautiful truthful and powerful in this enigma, yet it is also
disquieting. Jesus had previously said:

> Unless you chew the flesh of the son of man and
> drink his blood you have no life in you.[39]

This is a vegan meal with cannibalistic overtones; so typical of
Jesus to disturb and shock us into really thinking deeply about the
true intensity of experiencing oneness.[40]

Why can't the simplicity and mystery of Jesus' words just be
accepted?

In using bread and wine to say, 'This is me', what do you think he
is implying?

This meal is about relationship, vertical and horizontal, with God
and one another; a family meal with covenant at its heart. It has
been said, 'If I break bread with you, I am telling you I'm prepared
to die for you.' This is not unlike *diyafa*, the hospitality covenant of
the desert *Bedouin*, where no traveller, even a sworn enemy, is
ever turned away but given food, shelter and protection and then is
able to leave in peace. Once food and drink are shared the host
would give his life to keep the guest safe if there was an attack on
them.

The dimensions and possibilities of this meal are infinite. Jesus is
remembered and his body is re-membered in reconciliation,
forgiveness and healing in the wholeness of atonement-*shalom*.
This meal is for a 'society of friends' who, sharing 'the kiss of
peace', declare that each relationship is right.[41]

Here are people who are breathing together.

It is also a lovers' tryst around a table of devotion. Andrei Rublev's sublime icon of *The Holy Trinity* – based on the story of Abraham welcoming God in the form of three strangers at the Oaks of Mamre, where he prepares them food – captures this; I have heard it described as each figure with the beautiful face of an identical sister and the body of a young man looking into each other's eyes.[42] On the table between them is a goblet of wine with space for another to join them – we are invited to be that person. The Peacemeal is a response to that invitation and another means by which *epektasis* takes place, enabling us to 'reach forward' and become more and more like God.[43]

This really is feeding on the Tree of Life.

This meal combines the present with the future, it is 'until he comes';[44] it is the hors d'oeuvres of messianic banquet. It is filled with anticipation and wild hope. Jesus asks us to pray: 'Give us today our daily bread.'[45] The word *epiousion*, translated 'daily', is an intriguing word, with a possible double meaning, not only 'sufficient' for today but also the bread of 'tomorrow'.[46] The Peacemeal not only empowers us for the *shalom* activism needed today and provides the food with which to feed the needy, but it is also energised by the life of the age to come and is a sign about tomorrow and the renewed creation.

✷ ✷ ✷ ✷ ✷

The conspiracy of the Peacemeal leads to both compassion and action; it involves the community in sharing and declaring as we work towards the transfiguration of the status quo.

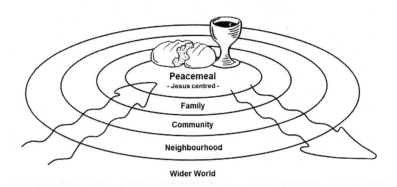

Peacemeal
- Jesus centred -

Family

Community

Neighbourhood

Wider World

The Peacemeal is *centripetal* – from the Latin: 'to seek the centre', or 'drawn towards the centre'. The word is, 'Come!' It is an open circle with the risen Jesus at its centre, welcoming everyone.[47]

> Come, eat my bread and drink my wine I have mixed.[48]

> Come, for everything is now ready now.[49]

There is only one table and it is open to all. What each guest experiences will depend on their relationship to the host and their spiritual openness; some may simply have their physical hunger satisfied, while others discover transformation. In each case something significant is happening. It is the place and space where God is at work.

As it is a family meal children must be at its heart, participating as soon as they are physically able to do so. Jesus is uncompromising on the subject:

> Let the little children come to me;
> do not stop them;
> for it is as to such as these the kingdom of God belongs.[50]

The whole community will learn from them. Some of my most significant experiences of breaking bread have been in the company of children; their innocence, enthusiasm, openness and innate spiritual understanding of the significance of the meal is always astonishing.[51]

Hospitality is expressing kindness to strangers, being welcoming and generous towards guests. It is about the extravagant expression of grace towards others. There is a blurring of the line between host and guest; giving and receiving become a continuous whole. It is, of course, a challenging path, because we come up against our own fears and insecurities, yet each step is an adventure of trust and vulnerability. We create sanctuary for the insecure, a place of acceptance, healing and forgiveness for the broken; somewhere we can serve the needs of others.

Take note also of Desmond Tutu's words, 'When you are feeding the people, you are feeding God.'[52]

How can we nurture a culture of hospitality and welcome?

It was a Sunday evening. I will never forget the look on their faces. They were a young homeless couple, living in a derelict council house on a tough south London estate, a few doors down from someone in our community. Discovering they hadn't eaten for four days she said, 'Come to church with me tonight and have a good meal.' They walked nervously through the door into a room set out for a feast – our Sunday service. 'Wow' they gasped. 'We didn't know church was like this!' Sadly, most times it isn't – but it should be.

What do you think of the declaration, 'No eating, no meeting'?

The Peacemeal is *centrifugal* – from the Latin: 'to flee the centre', or 'dispersed from the centre'. The word is, 'Go!' Jesus sends us out into society; this is a 'missionary meal'.

Go … into the streets and lanes of the town,
bring in the poor, the crippled, the blind and lame …
Go, out into the roads and byways,
and compel people to come in, so my house may be filled.[54]

Here being a 'Wisdom Dancer' and 'Subversive Celebrant' intertwine. We take the invitation to the meal out to where people are; we feed them where we find them, we embrace them in their need. We need creative and imaginative approaches, everywhere leaving footprints of peace.

SPEAK – the student and young adult's peace and justice network[54] – planned a day of action on one of London's busiest streets outside a UK government agency that funds private arms deals across the globe; activity aiding repression, harming development and fueling conflict. The day climaxed with a huge crowd of us celebrating 'Peacemeal on the Pavement', a liturgy they had invited me to write and lead, which involved declaring the truth, covering a large cardboard tank with beautiful flowers, singing and dancing and sharing bread and wine among ourselves but also with passers-by. As one participant on the day reflected:

We were highlighting the injustice of our government's complicity in suffering caused by its arms sales around the globe, and our mustard-seed-scale demonstration in front of their offices was laden with symbolism, a glimpse of the kingdom. The bread–body of Jesus' weakness became our strength; the wine–blood of Jesus' despair became our joy.

I remember feeling liberated from my English repression by three times shouting '*Shalom!*' at the towering office block. The flowers – a symbol of peace and justice – prophesied over the seeds and deeds sown within that building.[55]

More and more people are discovering the creative and provocative possibilities of the Peacemeal, this subversive celebration that feeds Jesus to the world, feeding the hungry, sharing food with our enemies, eating in a way that is gentle with animals and wild nature, anticipating the messianic banquet.

In what other ways can we use the Peacemeal as a voice for justice on the streets?

★ ★ ★ ★ ★

Halfway between the two great cathedrals facing each other across the seaport city of Liverpool, above a radical community bookshop, is 'Somewhere Else' – better known to everyone as 'Bread Church'.[56]

We arrived a little late; the large room was already full of people standing at rows of long trestle tables kneading dough – children, parents, young adults and senior citizens. This morning there was also a group with learning difficulties participating, accompanied by their tutors from a local college. Warmly greeted by Barbara Glasson,[57] the Methodist minister whose vision brought it all into being, we put on aprons, filled a large plastic bowl with flour and began mixing our dough and talking with those around us. Once the bread was in the oven we shared a simple liturgy together. Tables were then cleared, soup bowls set out for a nourishing meal accompanied by hot fresh bread rolls. Everyone shared the washing-up and cleaning the room. This space is home to 'Bread Church' every Tuesday and Thursday morning with Sunday worship once a month; it is also a spiritual sanctuary for lesbian, gay, bisexual and transgendered people, the survivors of abuse and the homeless from the city streets.

We left, taking our two loaves of bread, one to eat at home and the other to give away. I was reminded of the early Celtic tradition, 'Whenever you break bread make sure you take a piece of the loaf away with you to share with a stranger on the way home.'

Endnotes

1   From Sara Miles, *Take This Bread*, Ballantine Books, 2008, pp. 57–59; edited for focus and space.
2   See <http://www.saramiles.net/food_pantry>.
3   See Sara Miles, *Take This Bread*, Ballantine Books, 2008, p. 116.
4   I am using the word 'table' here, not only with specific reference to food and eating a meal, but also as a symbol/ metaphor of relationship and community that is expressed by it and flows from it as this whole chapter will make clear. I also recognise that to build church Jesus also leaves us with the memories of his teaching and the empowering of the Spirit, but the only physical thing is the table.
5   I can't resist inappropriately applying the words from Psalm 23:5, 'You prepare a table before me in the presence of my enemies.'
6   See Martin Jones, *Feast: Why Humans Share Food*, Oxford University Press, 2007, pp. 1–2; the whole book is quite fascinating.
7   See Michael Palin, *Michael Palin's New Europe*, BBC DVD, 2007.
8   Acts 17:6.
9   See Desmond Tutu, *No Future Without Forgiveness*, Rider Books, 1999, pp. 34–36 and *God Is Not a Christian: Speaking Truth in Time of Crisis*, Rider Books, 2011, pp. 21–24; also <en.wikipedia.org/wiki/Ubuntu_(philosophy)>. The worldview expressed in the word *ubuntu* is found across the languages of southern Africa; *botho* in the Tswana language of Botswana, *uMunthu* in the Chewe of Malawi, *obuntu* in the Kitara of Uganda and Tansania and *unhu* in the Shona of Zimbabwe, to name a few.
10 See 1Cor 11:24, 29 and 12:12 amng many other texts.
11 I am grateful to Revd Phil Barnard, now a friend, for these reflections. On a later occasion he invited me to lead an Easter Sunday service where three congregations from different churches came together to celebrate a Peacemeal with a focus on the risen Jesus in the context of a full meal which included an abundance of bread and wine; it was a very special occasion.
12 See Mt 14:20; 15:37; Mk 6:42; 8:8; Lk 9:17; Jn 6:12.
13 See Joachim Jeremias, *New Testament Theology*, SCM, 1971, pp. 114–116; and Norman Perrin, *Rediscovering the Teaching of Jesus*, Harper & Row, 1967, pp. 104–107.
14 Lk 7:34.
15 Mk 2:15-16; Lk 5:29-32.
16 See Marcus Borg, *Conflict, Holiness and Politics in the Teaching of Jesus*, Trinity Press, 1984, pp. 5–6, 39, 93–134.
17 Geza Vermes, *Jesus the Jew*, Collins, 1973, p. 224.
18 See Mt 26:17–30; Mk 14:12–25; Lk 22:7–23; Jn 13:1—18:1 (also 6:22–59). I am fully aware of the arguments that suggest this was not a Passover meal but rather a *Shabbat/ Kiddush* meal, or a *Chaburah* meal where like-minded people ate together for a purpose (see W Barclay, *The Lord's Supper*, SCM Press, 1967, pp. 20–34 for a simple statement of the different views), but I am unconvinced.
19 See Chaim Raphael, *A Feast of History: The Drama of Passover through the Ages*, Weidenfeld & Nicolson, 1972 – for an excellent presentation of the history, structure and meaning of the Passover meal.
20 Lk 24:13–35.
21 Jn 21:1–14.
22 See Acts 20:7.
23 *Shavuoth* celebrates God's gift of the *torah*; its name in Hebrew simply means 'weeks' following the instruction that it is to take place for seven weeks from the

time of the barley harvest at *Pesach* at the beginning of the wheat harvest – see Exod 34:22; Deut 16:10; 2Chron 8:13.

24 *Pentecost* is the Greek name for *Shavuoth* and means 'fiftieth'; it is the fiftieth day after *Pesach* – see Lev 23:16.

25 Acts 2:44–47 (adapted).

26 See Lk 14:12; Jn 12:2 for *deipnon* as 'supper' (KJV), 1Cor 11:20 – 'Lord's supper'; 1Cor 10:21 – 'Lord's table'.

27 See Isa 25:6; Mt 8:11; Lk 14:15; 22:30; Rev 19:9. It also seems likely that the 'common meals' shared by the Essenes of the Qumran community were celebrated as an anticipation of the coming Messianic feast; see Geza Vermes, *The Dead Sea Scrolls in English*, Penguin Books, 1968, p. 47.

28 See J Behm, 'Klao', in G Kittle (ed.) *Theological Dictionary of the New Testament*, vol. 3, 1965, pp. 728–729.

29 See Jude v. 12.

30 1Cor 11:17–22, 27–34.

31 I recognise that this is a strong statement, but I believe it to be true. Initially it is a meal that makes sure that the poor within the community are fed and then reaching out beyond that to wider society (more below). While there will of course be more intimate occasions of sharing, this fundamental truth must never be lost.

32 See Clement of Alexandria, *Paedagogus* 2.1.10.

33 See W Barclay, *The Lord's Supper*, SCM Press, 1967, p. 60. The *agape* was debated, fasting rather than feasting was encouraged; in 692 CE the Council of Trullan forbade the holding of an *agape* altogether.

34 If the Peacemeal were genuinely seen to be the centrepiece of being a Jesus-community the whole way in which it expresses itself would have to change. To their credit the Orthodox and Roman Catholics place the Eucharist centrally but sadly as an exclusive ritual, not an inclusive meal.

35 It originally had the sense of 'something set apart', then a 'pledge', or 'oath', then a 'promise', eventually a 'sign'. It was linked by early Christian thinkers to the idea of 'mystery'.

36 This is the view held by the Orthodox, Roman Catholic and high Anglican churches.

37 This is the view held by most Protestant churches (in one form or another) with the exception of the Quaker and Salvation Army communities who, seeing it reduced to a mere ritual, do not share the Eucharist but seek to experience its truth spiritually.

38 See CEB Cranfield, 'Thank', in A Richardson (ed.), *A Theological Word Book of the Bible*, SCM Press, 1957, p. 256; and J Behm, 'Klao', in G Kittle (ed.) *Theological Dictionary of the New Testament*, vol. 3, 1965, p. 736. Whatever secondary meanings we may find in the images of the bread and wine this is the primary one, especially when taken back to Jesus' original Aramaic words.

39 Jn 6:53.

40 In cannibalistic societies the main purpose of eating the other human being was to imbibe their qualities of strength and courage, for them to become part of you.

41 The 'Society of Friends' was the original name for the Quakers. For more on 'the kiss of peace' as a sign of wholeness or reconciliation in relationships, see 1Cor 16:20; 2Cor 13:12 and Mt 5:23–24, also Eleanor Kreider, 'Let the Faithful Greet Each Other: The Kiss of Peace', *Conrad Grebel Review 5*, 1987, p. 44. Interestingly, in Scandinavia mistletoe was believed to be a plant of peace; to kiss under it on entering a home was a sign that all relationships were right, and soldiers walking under mistletoe growing in the wild were to drop their weapons and remain unarmed for a day; see Tess Ward, *The Celtic Wheel of*

the Year: Celtic and Christian Seasonal Prayers, O Books, 2007, pp. 251–252 and <http://www.goddessgift.com/Pandora's_Box/mistletoe.htm>.

42 For details of the Abraham story see Gen 18:1–15; also Heb 13:2.

43 We discussed *epektasis* when reflecting on being a '*Radical Mystic*', based on Phil 3:13–14. Gregory of Nyssa said that the essence of perfection is never becoming perfect because there is always deeper and higher perfection to reach out towards, becoming more and more like God, along with God.

44 1Cor 11:26.

45 Mt 6:11; Lk 11:3.

46 The only other place the word *epiousion* has been found was on a first-century CE papyrus shopping list discovered on an Egyptian rubbish dump by archaeologists. The list was 'the food for tomorrow'; it is thought that early Christians may have used it with both a present sense of today and an eschatological sense about 'the age to come'.

47 The history of this table – 'breaking-bread', the 'Eucharist' – in most Christian denominations, is one of exclusion rather than inclusion. All the high-sounding theological reasoning that attempts to justify this only illustrates how Jesus' teaching and example is either fundamentally misunderstood or simply disregarded.

48 Prov 9:5; see also Isa 55:1.

49 Lk 14:17.

50 Mk 10:14.

51 The arguments that children cannot participate because of original sin and not yet having been baptised simply miss the point completely and is totally at odds with the attitude and example of Jesus.

52 Quoted on 29 July 2011 on the 'Food Pantry' blog – <http//thefoodpantry.org>.

53 Lk 14:21, 23; see also Mk 16:15.

54 See <www.speak.org.uk>.

55 Thanks to Rob Telford for this reflection.

56 See <http://www.somewhere-else.org.uk>.

57 See Barbara Glasson, *Mixed-up Blessing: A New Encounter with Being Church*, Inspire, 2006 and *I Am Somewhere Else*, Darton, Longman & Todd, 2006.

12 Faith Friend
– sharing the circle of belief

There were just six of us: three Muslims and three Christians, sitting together at a local cultural centre. We met as a group of spiritual people affirming one another as individuals with a deep personal faith commitment, holding each other in respect as we sat together in a circle of belief.

Our starting point was to acknowledge how much our own spiritual journeys had in common, including prayer, study of scripture, nurturing good character, ethical decision-making – to name just a few – and of course our collective experience of living as people of faith in a secular culture. We reflected on how our society presented each of us with the same challenges and opportunities. Muslims face prejudice, Christians encounter indifference, 'god-talk' is scornfully tolerated, as is our behaviour when it deviates from the norm; nevertheless we each appreciated the freedom to express our faith. Our differences weren't important; the most joyful aspect of our time together was focusing on the common ground we each shared.

How do we react when we meet someone from another faith?
Do we stress our differences or our similarities?
Do we assume superiority and steer the conversation to prove them wrong?

When we learn someone is a Baha'i, or Sikh or Pagan, do we stereotype them with our assumptions about their faith, pre-judging them rather than taking the time to talk and find out exactly what they – a unique individual – actually believe?

Respect is due; we share spirituality, but where do spirituality and faith begin?

Quietly, almost unknowingly they start at birth, maybe even before.[1] In its own awareness a newborn baby is the universe, and centre of all that exists; every other presence merely serves their needs. Gradually this perception is shattered as the child slowly discovers they are but a fragment in a vast and complex cosmos. Belief develops through coming to terms with this reality. It is a steady spiritual, mental and emotional maturing.

So it is not *religion* but our experience as a *person* that stimulates the beginning of faith and belief. It is a consequence of our thinking, questioning, investigating and behaving; and discovering a sense of the spiritual however that may be perceived.

Deep within each one of us is the profound sensation of our own existence. From this fragile base we look out into a world using our senses, and are provoked to ask searching questions:[2]

- 'What is reality?'
- 'What is human?'
- 'What is truth?'
- 'What is good?'
- 'What is society?'
- 'What is time?
- 'What is death?'

They are all relevant to every living person; we cannot function as a mature human being without finding an answer to each one. We rarely encounter them in a formal way – they seem to creep up on us quietly – but our response to them creates the framework within which we interpret our existence and find meaning for our lives.

Every person who has ever lived has grappled with these questions. This process of forming a worldview is something subtle yet more fundamental than any philosophy or theology. A worldview is a way of thinking:[3]

- *A foundation* of assumptions on which we build our understanding about the world and what we perceive to be reality;
- *A universe* fashioned by words and concepts which work together to make a more-or-less coherent frame of reference for all our thoughts and actions;
- *A perspective* structuring our thoughts with instinctive ideas fairly consistent with each other, rarely mentioned or questioned, helping us make sense of experience.

Everyone has a worldview, even though some might struggle to express it in words. Without it we could not think or reason; it is as unconscious as it is conscious and as emotional as it is intellectual. It is part of the very fabric of our personhood. We take it for granted and rarely think about it unless it is challenged. This is exactly what happens when we meet people of other faiths – and the experience can be very disturbing.

When it comes to making sense of the world we all recognise that something exists, that there is something rather than nothing.

But what is this something?

The clamour of voices answering this question is overwhelming; we group them together and call them philosophies and religions.

It is very much easier to identify people and ideas in terms of broad cultural groups and religious faiths – we may even think of ourselves in this way – but it is not the whole truth.[4] The reality is that under each umbrella of people-group or creed there are multitudes of individuals, each with their own unique way of viewing the world and making sense of it. It is like a kaleidoscope of worlds within worlds – each person with their own particular perspective as personal as their fingerprint or DNA code.

When it comes to faith and belief, I always try to remember that they are first and foremost personal, and that there are as many worldviews as there are people who view the world.[5]

✻ ✻ ✻ ✻ ✻

We got talking in a café; the young woman opposite asked me what I did. When I said I taught on a Christian learning programme her immediate response was, 'Oh, well, I am not religious but I am spiritual.' How often people have told me this; it is almost a mantra in the media; it is a significant summary of our times and important to reflect on.

'Religion' is a slippery word; I don't like it. I use it as little as possible, but cannot avoid it. I prefer to speak of 'faith' and 'belief'. The word 'religion' is given great significance by most people but used indiscriminately. It comes from the Latin: *religio*, which has obscure origins, possibly meaning 'obligation' or 'ritual', perhaps 'to bind' or 'connect'.[6] For some people it becomes a clumsy alternative to 'spirituality'; for others religion implies an organised and authoritative system of belief, usually involving God, with rituals, doctrines and ethics that must be accepted. However, in Asia philosophy and faith are so fused together the word 'religion' becomes confusing as it is not a separate aspect of life that is opted in or out of. In indigenous communities spirituality is so integrated into daily life that the idea of religion is virtually meaningless.[7] I would argue this should also be true for those who choose to live from a Jesus perspective.

- Katie's profound spiritual experience does not fit any religious or belief system; she fears they would contaminate something so special or threaten what is deeply significant to her, so she distances herself from all religion out of integrity.
- Sam has come to a place of faith and spiritual experience as a result of encountering Hinduism; he is very comfortable staying and growing within that environment and feels liberated in finding his place as part of this religion.
- Rebecca is an atheist, yet her Jewish culture is so shaped by religion she joins in all the major festivals as a social activity; they are part of her identity as a member of that community, but she no longer accepts the basis on which the religion is founded.
- Jamal was brought up as a Muslim and Jenny comes from a Christian family; both feel inhibited by their backgrounds
- and are searching for something more; neither can remain in a religion that is no longer true to their beliefs and experience.
- Ruth is a Humanist who rejects the word 'religion' because it implies a belief in God, the unquestioning acceptance of ideas that have no rational basis in science and requires a belief in doctrines for which she sees no reason or purpose.

Religion is culture from a faith–belief perspective.[8] We find it at the point where spirituality and culture come together. While this definition is so broad that people will continue to give religion whatever meaning they wish, it is nevertheless a reminder that spirituality and faith are always clothed in culture whenever you express them personally or meet them in others on the street.

The word 'religion' also helps me not to forget there is a long history of spiritual journeying. I am not alone, and there remains a vast amount to learn from people in the past as well as my faith friends in the present.[9]

About twelve children between the ages of five and ten years old sat around an extended kitchen table; this was 'Children's Table-Talk' organised by Phoebe and her friends. Her family are at the heart of 'PeaceChurch' in Birmingham, UK, where 'Table-Talks' are a commonplace event. They are gatherings where theological and ethical discussions take place over a meal, sometimes lasting three to four hours. Phoebe told me, 'I didn't think it was fair, I could never join in so decided to do a kids' "Table-Talk" without adults joining in. They take over and it becomes only what adults think. It is important for us kids to grow to be totally independent in our thinking.'

I have actually been a silent observer at two of Phoebe's 'Table-Talks'; the first had the theme of 'God' and the second was about 'Faith'. They were amazing. Before each of the three courses – everyone bringing food contributions from home – one of the children would introduce their thoughts on a question like, 'Who is God? What is God like? How do you believe in God?' or 'What is faith? How do we use faith? How do you have faith?' The quality of the conversation was remarkable with an innocent maturity and razor-sharp honesty. Each child listened respectfully and spoke insightfully.

On both occasions a highlight for me was the contribution from Avani, a Hindu friend. Phoebe had talked about believing in one God who was good and everywhere. Avani replied, 'As a Hindu I believe in one God too, but for us in Hinduism different aspects of life are shown through different gods and goddesses. As a girl the female goddesses show me how to be strong and to have faith in my heart.'[10] And so the conversations unfolded and continued.

Listening to the children, who are quite literally 'Faith Friends', was a reminder how much every faith has in common with all other faiths. Yet at the same time it is quite obvious all faiths are not the same; the reality is much more complex and respectful than that. So the question is, 'Why do there seem to be such close similarities but also clear differences between faiths?'

Imagine a large circular banqueting table around which are seated a member of each of the world's faiths and beliefs. You are a guest at the dinner. Each person is sitting on a large high-backed wooden chair, on the front of which is carved images and symbols representing their particular beliefs and worldview. Spread out before them is the food for the feast.

world-views

world-views

The food on the table is what each guest at the banquet will share with everyone else and represents the life-giving values we all hold in common – love, compassion, peace, justice, truth and so many more – which we have discussed previously (in the *Values Master* chapter). These shared values are what every person sees in the actions and aspirations of different faiths and beliefs, leading many to conclude all religions are the same. This is something to celebrate; it identifies the common ground between us, a place where we can connect, communicate and share, learning from one another and working together. In truth, we have a great deal more in common than most of us are prepared to recognise.

Each person around the table is not only a representative of their faith, but also a unique individual bringing their personal understanding and experience of life and belief to the conversation. We must not let anything shaped by culture and religion mask our ability to see each other's humanity or connect with their ideas, hopes and fears.

The large high-backed wooden chairs carved with images and symbols representing our particular beliefs and worldviews illustrate the most obvious points of contrast between us as guests. What we perceive as religious differences are often cultural ones; the way we dress for example, or our attitude to family life. Nevertheless, there is significant divergence between the worldviews of different faiths. For example, belief in reincarnation and resurrection do not hold together, nor does the idea of *nirvana* and a renewed creation.[11] All religions are not the same; to suggest otherwise displays ignorance and disrespect.

Some people are startled when I say that, properly understood, the teaching of Jesus has more in common with Buddhism than Judaism or Islam. Jesus' focus on values and behaviour, his lack of interest in ritual, the simplicity of his thinking and teaching and the way his ideas can easily communicate across global culture are just a few initial examples. Yet there is a primary difference between the teaching of Gautama and Jesus; they have completely contrasting worldviews, where Islam and Judaism share a much closer one with Jesus.[12]

Interestingly, a man who had recently converted from Christianity to Judaism said to me, 'Noel, I hope you won't find this offensive, but since becoming a Jew I have realised how very alike Judaism and Islam are; they appear to be almost a different type of religion to Christianity.'

What do you make of this man's observation?
Why do people say, 'All religions are the same'?
How significant are differences between faiths?
How would you describe the uniqueness of Jesus?

✳ ✳ ✳ ✳ ✳

It is twilight. Imagine a clearing at the heart of a rainforest; in the fading light with the air filling with sounds of the night an indigenous community sit encircling a large fire, talking, singing, eating and storytelling. From among the dark trees a figure walks slowly into the open space and sits quietly among the group; it is Jesus.

How do you think he would introduce himself?
What might he say or do?
Where would he begin, to make connections with their culture?

How can this imagined encounter help us reflect on his character and message?

Jesus quite naturally takes his place among the world's great spiritual leaders, like Zoroaster, Lao Tzu, Mahavira, the Buddha, Muhammad or Guru Nanak to name but a few. He is widely recognised as a godly teacher or *guru* and in Islam he is honoured as *rasul* or prophet. There are Hindus who see him as a possible *avatar* of Vishnu[13] while some Buddhists view him as a *bodhisatva*.[14] He also fits all the criteria of a *shaman* in indigenous cultures.[15] Most people across the world, when presented with an account of Jesus, see him as a 'good man' and a 'holy person' worthy of respect.

However, as we have already seen, Jesus' style is also deliberately provocative: 'Blessed is anyone who takes no offence at me.'[16] You cannot just place Jesus among other global faiths and spiritual leaders and hope he will blend in; he doesn't cooperate; he stands out making disturbing statements:

> I am the way, the truth and the life.
> No one comes to the father (*Abba*) except through me.[17]

In these words Jesus declares that he is the road to God. What he is saying is that only a person who follows him can know God with the intimacy of *Abba* and the quality of personal spiritual experience this enables. But he is not claiming there is no truth or life without him, or that God cannot be known apart from him.

Jesus is a remarkable teacher, prophet and person, who different people will see quite differently. For me he is one in whom the life of the Spirit is complete, someone 'in whom the whole fullness of deity dwells bodily'.[18] Thomas Merton described Jesus as God's self-vision or self-imagination.[19] I have often found it helpful to say Jesus is like the surface of the sea – 'the perfect expression of all the depth that lies beneath'.[20]

Other faith leaders ask disciples to follow their teachings. Jesus calls them to follow *him*;[21] even allowing people to worship him,[22] something the Buddha and Muhammad would have recoiled from in horror had their devotees attempted it.

Caught up in the age-old religious debate between Jews and Samaritans, Jesus surprises:

The hour is coming when you will worship God
neither on this mountain nor in Jerusalem …
God is spirit and those who worship must worship in spirit and truth.[23]

He is making it clear that what God wants for all people is for them
to live truthfully and spiritually, open to God, and that this will most
certainly happen in the future. Like the Hebrew prophets before
him, he also makes it clear that the trappings of religion are of no
concern to God.

I also believe words like these show that Jesus had *no* intention of
beginning a new religion; instead he was calling for a completely
different way of expressing faith within and across the cultures of
the world.[24]

Jesus' rejection of formal religion with its powerful social and
political implications led to his execution. However, he saw his
crucifixion not only breaking the stranglehold of evil and death
through his resurrection but also enabling total all-embracing
salvation for every person who has ever lived:

And I, when I am lifted up from the earth,
will draw all people to myself.[25]

The early Jesus-community affirmed this understanding by
weaving a statement about him into a declaration made by the
Hebrew prophet Isaiah:

At the name of Jesus every knee will bend
in heaven and on earth and under the earth,
and every tongue confess that Jesus Christ is Lord.[26]

Sadly, generations of Christians have used these words to claim
their faith will triumph over all other faiths; even suggesting the
'confession' would be coerced if necessary. This hideous
interpretation perverts the uninhibited joy expressed in these
words. This is not Jesus proving other faiths wrong. Quite the
opposite; it is God in Jesus bringing the totality of global and
historical spiritual experience to a *shalom*-filled completeness,
embracing its richness and affirming all its goodness through the
process of *mishpat*-judgement. As Jesus said, 'People will come
from east and west, from north and south, and will eat in the
kingdom of God.'[27] The Hebrew scriptures make powerful inclusive
promises about the future:

> The treasure of all nations shall come
> and I will fill this house with splendour ...
> in this place I will give *shalom*.[28]

> Foreigners ... I will bring to my holy mountain,
> and make them joyful in my house of prayer;
> their offerings and sacrifices will be accepted on my altar;
> for my house will be called a house of prayer for all peoples.[29]

As we have seen previously, these words find clear fulfilment within the book of Revelation:

> A great multitude that no one could count, from every nation,
> from all tribes and peoples and languages ...[30]

This is not some vague pluralism but the certainty of robust and rigorous universalism.

With this awesome vision and climax as our backdrop, it is important to focus on the present and recognise God deliberately created humanity not only to have wide cultural difference, but spiritual diversity as well. The commissioning words from the first creation story set the scene:

> So God created humankind ...
> God blessed them and said to them,
> 'Be fruitful and multiply and fill the earth.'[31]

However, it is the voices of the early Christian community that are the most provocative. While they are certain God is doing something unique through the person of Jesus, they also believe:

> God allowed all the nations to follow their own ways;
> yet they have not been left without a witness in doing good –
> giving you rains from heaven and fruitful seasons,
> and filling you with food and your hearts with joy.[32]
> God made all nations to inhabit the whole earth
> – subject to the seasons and places that are habitable –
> they were created so they would search for God,
> feeling after and finding the divine,
> though God is not far from each one of us.
> For in God we live and move and have our being.[33]

[God is] the true light that enlightens everyone coming
into the world.[34]

Ever since the creation of the world God's eternal power …
[has been] seen through the things God has made.[35]

God deliberately scattered humanity across the earth to become
diverse cultures, and to develop a living relationship with the
spiritual and divine by drawing on both revelation and wisdom.

God is mysteriously at work among every faith across all nations to
fulfil the divine purpose. What God looks for in every belief is purity
in heart, justice in character, godliness in spirit and a hunger for
truth. Wherever this is found true worship is present:

From the rising of the sun to its setting my name is great among
the nations,
and in every place incense is offered to my name, a pure offering;
… for I am the great king and my name is revered among
the nations.[36]

The biblical story tells of God communicating directly with
individuals who worship other gods by 'stirring their spirit', or giving
them dreams, visions and verbal messages;[37] also having
significant relationships with people of other nations:

- *Abram:* from a Mesopotamian idol-worshipping family, his
  encounter with God was direct and personal; he exampled the
  faith and obedience that God desires;[38]
- *Melchizedek:* a priest–king from early non-Jewish Palestine,
  was called 'king of righteousness', priest of the 'God Most
  High', a godly figure who blessed Abraham;[39]
- *Job:* a sheik from Trans-Jordan, 'blameless and upright', was
  wise, righteous and faithful to God in spite of total personal
  devastation, God called him 'my servant';[40]
- *Jethro:* an indigenous desert priest who brought practical
  wisdom to Moses and the Israelites; made sacrifices to God'
  and then returned to his own country;[41]
- *Naaman:* a foreign warrior healed of a skin disease by Elisha,
  chose to worship *Yahweh* but was permitted to continue
  worshipping his national gods at their temple.[42]

Jesus appears to meet very few people who are not Jews. Those
he does – a Roman centurion, a Greek woman from Phoenicia, a

man from Trans-Jordan and several despised Samaritans –
each were *very un-*Jewish but *all* are presented as having
remarkable faith, in marked contrast to the majority of Palestinian
Jews.[43]

Peter, a close companion of Jesus, had a deep prejudice against
anyone who was not a Jew – until he met the Roman centurion
Cornelius, 'a devout person who feared God with his whole
household; gave alms generously to the people and prayed
constantly to God'; his 'prayers and alms ascended as a memorial
before God'.[44] Peter's response to the godliness of Cornelius is
striking:

> I truly understand that God shows no partiality,
> but in every nation anyone who fears God
> and does what is right is acceptable to God.[45]

Biblical writers also speak of:

> The wise [who] shall shine like the brightness of the sky[46]
> and
> The spirits of just-righteous people made perfect.[47]

In both cases they are drawn from across the nations and belief-
groups of the world. The Hebrew philosopher Qoheleth reflects:

> God has also put eternity into the human heart,
> yet we cannot comprehend what God has done from
> beginning to end.[48]

This deep God-given spiritual-intellectual desire for meaning is
insatiable and has led people to understand the world in terms of
everything from animism to atheism.[49] Where these views are
held with integrity there is much to learn from them – as I know
from my own experience of being enriched by my conversations
and friendship with people across the spectrum of beliefs. We
should embrace the opportunity to walk together and in doing so
leave behind us footprints of peace. This is part of the wealth that
will make up the final climax of humanity's spiritual journey into
God.

Sadly, when Christians have tried to share their understanding of
faith with people of other cultures they have almost always failed to
listen and learn from the spiritual experience of those to whom

they have gone and have remained impoverished as a result. Other faiths hold up a mirror to our own faith and demand we examine it more deeply. Christians need the wisdom and insights of other faiths and beliefs to grow spiritually and deepen their understanding of Jesus, just as much as other faiths need Jesus and the challenges he brings.

However, there is another reality recognised by all people – the mystery of moral evil and wickedness. This spiritual, social, structural and personal evil causes suffering and twists, perverts and distorts aspects of all cultures and faiths. That is why what God has done in Jesus is pivotal and why living by life-giving values in the power of the Spirit is vital.

This being so, across every faith – including Christianity – we see:

- Behaviour that is honourable, inspiring and challenging; a spirituality deep and sensitive pointing towards the mystery of God's revelation and the work of the Spirit;
- Much that is the result of the genuine human struggle to resolve the mysteries of life and unravel the physical and spiritual paradoxes of being;
- Examples of clear spiritual deception, deviant practice and evil influence manifesting horror and fear.

Sadly in every faith there are:

- Those who go through the rituals without them seeming to have any spiritual meaning for them – just something cultural – though they may be important personally;
- Leaders who are manipulative and controlling, for whom their power is more important than truth and integrity;
- Superstitions and traditions that corrupt and pervert, which we need the courage both to challenge and to change on the basis of values, not cultural prejudice.

Christians are particularly guilty of comparing what they see as the best of Christianity with the worst of other faiths, which is fundamentally dishonest. They would do well to remember: 'If Christianity is unique it is only because Christ is. If it ceases to witness to him, it ceases to have any value for the human race.'[50]

Previously I have said that the biblical vision for the ultimate future of all cultures, faiths and beliefs is breathtaking. It is a vision that promises a coming day when our different worldviews and understandings will be fully resolved in a way that is marked with dignity, respect and honour, not humiliation or arrogance. This will be the result of *mishpat*-justice 'putting everything right', demonstrating that true spirituality is about grace and gift, not merit or credit.

One thing seems quite clear, however certain any of us are about what we believe: the final outcome will be filled with more surprise and astonishment than any of us can ever anticipate.

All this will lead many Christians to ask, 'If this is so then what about mission and evangelism?' My reply is simple. We have already seen our mission is to establish God's *shalom* upon the earth – often working alongside those of other faiths and beliefs. We share the good things we are discovering as we live from a Jesus perspective, while at the same time listening to what people on other faith journeys have to share with us. If as a result of our lifeways or words people are drawn to join us in following Jesus they are to be welcomed. If they do not they are to be honoured in their difference.

* * * * * *

I regularly convene multi-faith groups of Baha'is, Buddhists, Jews, Muslims, Pagans and others, as a learning experience for my students, so they can listen to a range of stories from other spiritual travellers with the opportunity to ask their own questions and deepen their understanding.

The faces of my faith friends stimulate a '*Namaste*' response in me, 'honouring the image and likeness of God in them'. I am also reminded they are: 'like all others, like some others, like no other'.[51] They share humanity with me; they share a worldview and beliefs with many others, yet they are each completely unique individuals.

In order for communication and learning to take place there must be trust, truthfulness, empathy and vulnerability between us, creating the possibility for really positive encounters where we ask questions of our own faith and learn from them. It is only when we open ourselves up to genuinely being persuaded by the ideas and beliefs of other faiths that we can continually rediscover the truth of what we ourselves believe.

Endnotes

1 There are those who would argue it begins some time before birth, during foetal development in the womb. There may be some biblical support for this idea; see Ps 139:15–16; Jer 1:5.

2 The first six questions were suggested by David Burnett, *Clash of Worlds*, MARC/ Monarch 1990, p. 34. The seventh question, 'What is death?', is so fundamental that I added it myself.

3 The literature on worldviews is immense; two very accessible sources are JW Sire, *The Universe Next Door: A Guide Book to World Views*, Inter-Varsity Press, 2010; and David Burnett, *Clash of Worlds*, MARC/ Monarch, 1990.

4 I recognise that people who are grouped together as part of a particular culture or religion appear to have a lot in common and this is a powerful force in developing human identity, but this is not the whole truth. The convenience of this approach too often masks the importance of the uniqueness of the individual in terms of worldview, belief and faith.

5 It is also helpful to remember that this being so spiritually I may find that I have more in common with someone of another faith than many people in my own faith or belief – I am grateful to my friend Steve Bonner for this thought.

6 See the very helpful discussion on <http://www.religioustolerance.org/ rel_defn1/2/3.htm>, which looks at a range of dictionary definitions and concludes there is a real problem in finding any satisfactory or agreed meaning.

7 For a brief, readable and very positive exploration of the idea of religion, see Symon Hill, *The No-Nonsense Guide to Religion*, New Internationalist Publications, 2010, a detailed and inspiring book.

8 This is a definition I have coined, in the light of the wide range of unsatisfactory definitions available; see <http://www.religioustolerance.org/rel_defn1/2/3.htm>. Its simplicity and the thinking behind it reveal both the complexity of the word and how it should be viewed. I recognise that not all cultural forms of belief are necessarily religion. Clearly a secular education system is shaped by many beliefs but it is not a religion, yet most forms of organised (usually atheistic) Communism do bear the hallmarks of religion. I am grateful to my friend Amy Hailwood for her conversation around this point.

9 See Symon Hill's excellent, *The No-Nonsense Guide to Religion*, mentioned in endnote 7 above.

10 Two of the goddesses that Avani knows about are *Lakshmi*, who is the goddess of spiritual and material wealth, light, beauty, wisdom, fertility, generosity and courage (all the wives in the stories of *Vishnu* and *Shiva* are forms of *Lakshmi*); and *Kali*, the goddess associated with eternal energy, time and change, who many see as the mother goddess.

11 However, that is not to say that there is not some extremely fruitful and faithful work that has examined the crossover between Christian and Buddhist eschatology. See for example, Masao Abe, 'Beyond Buddhism and Christianity: "Dazzling Darkness"', in Stephen Heine (ed.), *Buddhism and Interfaith Dialogue*, Macmillan, 1995, pp. 127–150; and Thomas JJ Altizer, 'Nirvana and Kingdom of God', *Journal of Religion*, vol. XLIII, April, 1963, pp. 105–117.

12 One popular voice for the harmony between Jesus and the Buddha is the *Zen* Buddhist master, Thich Nhat Hanh, particularly *Going Home: Bringing Christ and the Buddha together in Daily Life*, Rider Books, 1999 and *Living Buddha, Living Christ*, Riverhead Books/ Penguin USA, 2007. I find his writing stimulating, but my primary criticism is his refusal to mention the worldview difference, always interpreting Jesus solely from a Buddhist perspective; Jesus was not a Buddhist though he and Gautama shared a huge amount of common ground.

13 From the Sanskrit, an *avatar* is 'one who descends'; the sanctity of their lives
    mediate wisdom, grace and truth. Some are manifestations of the divine come
    to overthrow evil. G Parrinder, in *Avatars and Incarnation*, Barnes & Noble,
    New York, 1970, shows twelve characteristics which all *avatars* share:
    - *Avatars* are real not mythological;
    - *Avatars* that are human have a worldly birth;
    - *Avatars* mingle both the human and divine in their lives;
    - *Avatars* finally die;
    - *Avatars* may in some cases have been historical;
    - *Avatars* are repeated;
    - *Avatars* are important in their example and character;
    - *Avatars* come with work to do;
    - *Avatars* show some reality in the world;
    - *Avatars* are a guarantee of divine revelation;
    - *Avatars* reveal a personal god;
    - *Avatars* reveal a god of grace.

    They all match biblical teaching on the incarnation with the exception that
    Jesus' work is not repeated.

14 The *bodhisattva* ideal is found in Mahayana Buddhism; the term means 'one
    whose essence has become enlightened'. Historically it meant one who
    dedicated their life to the welfare of humanity, delaying their entry into *nirvana*,
    their personal rewards for enlightenment – see C Humphreys, *Buddhism*,
    Penguin Books, 1951, pp. 55, 155–165.

15 The word *shaman* comes from the Machu-Tangu language of Siberian Asia,
    originating from the word *xaman* – 'to know', implying 'one who is wise'.

16 Mt 11:6; see also 10:34.

17 John 14:6. Similar themes are struck by Jesus elsewhere; cf. Jn 1:12; Mt 11:27.
    The title *Abba* was the Hebrew–Aramaic word for 'Daddy'. It is not always used
    directly, as in Mk 14:36, but is implied whenever Jesus refers to God as 'father'.
    This in no way implies male gender to God, though in Jesus' day that would
    have been a popular assumption in revered terms, so Jesus is being both
    deliberately scandalous and warmly parental both at the same time. In referring
    to these texts I am very aware of those people who find the notion of God as
    'father' both disturbing and painful due to destructive experiences at the hands
    of their own fathers and patriarchal attitudes in churches. This is a very real
    issue, concerning which Jesus is pointing towards the complete opposite and
    showing what true parenting should be.

18 Col 2:9; this is the translation from Peter T O'Brien, *Colossians, Philemon:
    Word Biblical Commentary*, Word Publishing, 1982, p. 102.

19 He says, 'The Son is the Father's idea of himself.' See Thomas Merton, *The
    Seven Storey Mountain*, SPCK, 1990, p. 395. He was a Trappist monk whose
    writings and teaching have had a huge influence on spiritual searchers and
    many in the peace movement; he also had sustained dialogue with people of
    other faiths for whom he had enormous respect.

20 In my late teens I remember looking at a record album cover for a recording of
    Debussy's *La Mer* where the copywriter quoted someone as saying, 'The
    surface of the sea is the perfect expression of all the depth that lies beneath.' I
    have always remembered the quotation but do not recall the name of its author.

21 On more than twenty occasions in the Gospels, Jesus calls people to follow
    him.

22 Cf. Jn 20:28.

23 Jn 4:21–24.

24 I recognise that this is a very controversial statement, but I believe it to be true.
    I recognise the complexity surrounding the Jewish identity of Jesus. His

teachings and actions radicalised the Jewish faith of his day (that is why they crucified him). Following Jesus' death–resurrection the perspectives of the *rabbi* Saul/ Paul of Tarsus brought a universalist and multi-cultural perspective to Jesus' teaching that was absolutely correct but it was only just beginning to be understood when it was halted by the development of Christendom by the fourth century CE. This is a complex topic we cannot develop here (for a very accessible discussion of the whole topic see Stuart Murray, *Post-Christendom: Church and Mission in a Strange New World*, Paternoster, 2004). However, the popular idea that Jesus came to found a religion called 'Christianity' to stand alongside other world religions I believe to be mistaken. Rather Jesus taught a spirituality to radicalise every person's spiritual understanding and journey across all cultures and beliefs.

25 Jn 12:32; see also vv. 33–34; 3:14. The Greek word *pantas* implies 'all people' and of course includes 'all things', as we have discussed before.

26 See Phil 2:10–11; Isa 45:23.

27 Lk 13:29–30.

28 Hag 2:7, 9. These words were originally spoken in the context of building the second temple after the return from exile; originally suggesting material wealth from the nations (which was never fulfilled even with Herod the Great's extravagant rebuilding of the temple site). They only find meaning and fulfilment eschatologically as the spiritual and cultural richness as we are suggesting.

29 Isa 56:6–7.

30 Rev 7:9.

31 Gen 1:27–28.

32 Acts 14:16–17.

33 Acts 17:26–28. My paraphrase is based on the suggestions of FF Bruce, *The Book of Acts: The New London Commentary on the New Testament*, Marshall, Morgan & Scott, 1965, pp. 357–359; also the translation by William Barclay, *The Acts of the Apostles: The Daily Study Bible*, St Andrew Press, 1955, p. 139.

34 Jn 1:9 – the NRSV alternative translation. William Temple, in *Readings in John's Gospel*, Macmillan, 1938, p. 9, says, 'There is only one divine light and everyone by their own measure is enlightened by it.' The early Christians spoke of this as the *logos* – the divine word of reason that held the universe together – and identified it with Jesus, a universal 'Christ conciousness'. However, for the purposes of our discussion here I choose simply to speak of God.

35 Rom 1:20; see also 2: 6–8, 14–16.

36 Mal 1:11; see the detailed discussion in Ralph L Smith, *Micah–Malachi: Word Biblical Commentary*, Word Publishing, 1984, pp. 312–316.

37 Note Cyrus (Ezra 1:1); Abimelech (Gen 20:3); Nebuchadnezzar (Dan 2:1, 45); Belshazzar (Dan 5:5); and Balaam (Num 22:9).

38 Gen 12; Josh 24:2.

39 Gen 14:17–20.

40 Job 1:1–12.

41 Exod 18:1–27.

42 2Kgs 5:1–19.

43 See Mk 5:1–20; 7:24–30; Lk 7:1–10; 10:29–37; 17:11–19; Jn 4:1–30.

44 Acts 10:2, 4.

45 Acts 10:34–35.

46 Dan 12:3.

47 Heb 12:23.

48 Eccl 3:11.

49 I am well aware of the debate over the use of the word 'animism' and its colonial associations, so I use it here cautiously; see D Chidester, 'Animism', in

Bron Taylor (ed.) *Encyclopedia of Religion and Nature*, vol. 1, Continuum, 2005, pp. 78–81; also G Harvey, *Animism: Respecting the Living World*, Hurst & Co., 2005. I shall discuss atheism and faith further in our next chapter, *Childlike Inquisitor.*

50 Christopher Lamb, *Lion Handbook of World Religions*, Lion, 1982, p. 363.
51 C Kluckhohn and H Murray, *Personality in Nature, Society and Culture*, AA Knopf, 1948, p. 49.

13 Childlike Inquisitor
– questioning and struggling with truth

Children are searingly truthful. We have all heard them loudly voicing the unspeakable, 'Mummy, why does this man smell?' in a public place. In the story of 'The Emperor's New Clothes', Hans Christian Andersen uses this skilfully when in the end it is only the child in the crowd who has the honesty to declare, ' … but he's naked!'

'What are you painting?' a primary-school teacher asked a young girl who was slapping bright colours onto a big sheet of white paper. 'I'm painting a picture of God,' came the confident reply. 'But Sarah, we don't know what God looks like, do we?' the teacher said gently. 'Well, you will do in a minute!'

Razor-sharp truth and generous innocence blend to form childlikeness. Along with the fun, joy and playfulness – full of delight, hope, confidence and trust – there is their awe and wonder at the world and their insatiable curiosity, plus that unerring ability to constantly ask frank questions with honesty and shrewdness.

Yes, those questions …

A recent BBC poll revealed four out of five parents are either too embarrassed or else intellectually incompetent to engage with the questions their children ask them.[1] You will remember the seven key questions I posed in the previous chapter:

- 'What is reality?'
- 'What is human?'
- 'What is truth?'
- 'What is good?'
- 'What is society?'
- 'What is time?
- 'What is death?'

When I ask groups who are the people most likely to ask questions like these, the answer is always the same, philosophers and children. They are of course right. It is significant these two are mentioned together.

Jesus' words and actions in relation to children and his instructions about how we respond to them are both astonishing and disturbing:

> And he took a child, and put it in the midst of them;
> and taking it in his arms, he said to them,
> 'Whoever receives one such child in my name receives me;
> and whoever receives me, receives not me but the one
> who sent me.'[2]

> Unless you change and become like children,
> you will never enter the kingdom of heaven.[3]

Most Christians do not believe these words. Western culture is incapable of engaging with them because attitudes marginalising children are so ingrained. Our society provides for them physically, it parents and educates them anxiously, exploits them economically, but believes the sooner a child reaches adulthood the better.[4] There is no real interest in children as they are; their value lies in their future potential, not their immediate presence. The church reflects this attitude; in fact it has been a major influence in shaping it. So these words of Jesus are ignored or sentimentalised; childlikeness is reduced to childishness, and to embrace either would be considered ridiculous.[5]

Most societies demand adults display a sophistication that is not truthful. We wear our so-called maturity like a mask; playing out roles and social stereotypes that rarely reflect who we really are and certainly not what we should be. We recognise this when using the phrase 'loss of innocence'. To 'become like children' requires us to 'turn', 'change', in fact 'think differently' (*metanoia*) and be re-formed.

Take the time to just watch children – listen, observe and learn. Reflect on what you *see* and *hear* in the way Jesus asks us to and apply it to your own life.

We should reflect on Jesus' principle that you encounter him, and in fact God, most directly in children.[6] This truth once led the most talented children's worker I have ever met to comment, 'Next time you are in a Sunday service and all the adults are standing up with their hands in the air, praising God – look around. Somewhere in the congregation you are likely to see a little child sitting hunched up on their chair, bored out of their brains, just wanting it all to be over. Ask yourself, is it possible this is exactly how Jesus might be feeling at this precise moment too?'

✳ ✳ ✳ ✳ ✳

Following Jesus' birth-stories there is only one account of his childhood.[7] As a 12-year-old his parents took him on a pre-*bar mitzvah* visit to Jerusalem.[8] At one point they thought they had lost him, but we are told:

> After three days they found him in the temple,
> sitting among the teachers,
> listening to them and asking them questions.
> And all who heard him were amazed
> at his understanding and his answers.[9]

This statement is striking. It says the young Jesus was listening and asking questions, but the onlookers remembered his insight and answers – even as a child he was communicating through questions. Nothing changes. Years later, as a mendicant *rabbi* one of the marks of Jesus' teaching style was his constant questions.

Questioning is at the heart of wisdom.

We see that Jesus, like the Greek philosopher Socrates before him, demonstrated how questions are an unthreatening yet scalpel-like way to open up a subject while at the same time provoking people to think for themselves. Questions show how much someone already knows without realising it; they reveal hidden attitudes and make clear how much more remains to be learned.

How are questions able to be so versatile?
Is there a question that has changed your life?

Searching questions are at the heart of all true childlikeness. Children are as eager to prod the world with their questions, as they are to poke a toad or dog-dirt with a stick. They are scientist–philosophers to the core.

In choosing to be a 'Childlike Inquisitor', they are my example.

The Hebrew word *olam*, used by biblical writers to describe 'the eternal experience of time', is fascinating. The philosopher Qoheleth, who we quoted previously, says:

> God has also put eternity (*olam*) into the human heart,
> yet we cannot comprehend what God has done from
> beginning to end.[10]

The *rabbis* use *olam* to speak about 'the world', in fact 'the universe'. Added to this, *olam* is formed from the verb-root *alam*, which means 'to hide'. All this implies that the truth about the world – in fact about the universe itself – is hidden, wrapped in a mystery and waiting to be explored and discovered:

> It is the glory of God to conceal things,
> but the glory of kings is to search things out.[11]

We are required to question, search for answers, engaging in discussion, argument and debate. We need to experiment; truth like wisdom is robust, needing to be tested intellectually and practically. We are to be an inquisitor – relentlessly searching and enquiring, persistently and painstakingly questioning and struggling with truth.

God is not playing games with us; rather calling us to join in the divine adventure of exploring the vast complexity of truth and knowledge. It is true that the more we know the more there is to know. Imagine shining torchlight onto a dark wall; the circle of light represents what we know and the surrounding darkness what we do not. As our knowledge increases so does the circumference of the circle of light, by the same token the area of contact with the darkness also increases, and therefore the extent of our ignorance.[12] Our response should be joyfully childlike inspiration, not cynical adult frustration.

Are you an inquisitor?
Does the vastness of what is unknown excite you or disturb you?

'Faith' is an important word to mention here. Daily I test my faith in the harsh reality of the laboratory of life and so far believe it to be true and trustworthy, but I am always open to it being falsified. I would love my Humanist friends to join in using the word 'faith' without compromising their convictions, but sadly few Humanists are comfortable with this word; most feel it implies some mindless acceptance of ideas beyond physical testing. I believe the reverse is true. Like faith, science holds many ideas it cannot practically demonstrate; yet scientists act on the basis of them being true, always open to being proved wrong.[13]

Nevertheless, there are circumstances that test our faith and questioning to the core. Elie Wiesel was a devout orthodox Jewish child, a Romanian who suffered in the ghetto and then several Nazi concentration camps, experiencing what no child should ever have to endure. As a 15-year-old boy amid the horrors of Auschwitz, he watched his Jewish inmates celebrate *Yom Kippur* and reflected:

> This day I ceased to plead. I was no longer capable of lamentation. On the contrary I felt strong. I was the accuser, God the accused. My eyes were open and I was alone – terribly alone in a world without God and without man. Without love or mercy. I had ceased to be anything but ashes, yet I felt myself to be stronger than the Almighty, to whom my life had been tied so long. I stood amid that praying congregation observing it like a stranger.[14]

The child is the inquisitor and God the accused; the evidence is incontrovertible. How can a powerful loving God permit such moral evil to happen?[15] Faced with questions like this atheism is very attractive; yet, after a lifetime of interrogating the divine, Ellie Wiesel still believes in God.

A friend of mine, confronted with unspeakable stories from post-Holocaust literature and numerous other global atrocities, asked the searching question: 'Can a human being atone for the sins of God?'[16] A childlike question if ever I heard one. Yet people are offended by it; arguing that God cannot sin and that people's actions are responsible for moral evil in the world. They fail to realise that God takes full responsibility for creating the *possibility* for moral evil:

> I am the Lord, and there is no other.
> I form light and create darkness,
> I shape peace and create woe,
> I am the Lord who does all these things.[17]

The answer to my friend's question is 'Yes'. God chose to create the possibility of pain, suffering and evil and is culpable. In becoming a human being God, in Jesus, personally experiences and endures the full weight and consequences of that choice – during life and through the violence of crucifixion. In resurrection the roots of this evil are torn out, the full implications of which are still to be seen.

I am not suggesting these brief reflections are more than a tentative response to just one of a myriad of intellectual, spiritual and moral challenges we face, but I hope they confirm how important it is to question and to embrace doubt. We talk about God being light but forget we are also told the divine is enveloped in 'clouds' and 'deep darkness'; the mystery of everything we cannot comprehend.[18] It also affirms that God is to be found in those areas that are disturbing and unsettling.

We are told it was in the darkness before dawn that Jacob wrestled with God on a riverbank, demanding to know the divine name – that is to know God's character. At sunrise we see him walking away limping, he has a wounded thigh but he is blessed. The wrestling-place became known as *Peniel* – 'the one who strives with God'. This is an essential prerequisite for mature spirituality.[19]

In an inquisition into God's behaviour would you be accuser or defender?
What is your experience of wrestling with God in darkness?

Doubt is universal, a global human experience inseparable from reason. Across the cultures of the world it is associated with the word 'two', such as 'to be in two minds'.[20] It is not doubt that is the opposite of faith – it is unbelief. Traditionally religion has no place for doubt, demanding unquestioning belief, ostracising those who cannot give it, binding them in guilt and fear. This attitude continues, even among churches that most vehemently deny it.

The relationship between doubt and faith is like the link between courage and fear. Steeplejacks tell us it is their fear of heights that keeps them safe – fearlessness leads to carelessness. Doubt is the same; it keeps faith safe and strong. Doubt is the dynamic that holds faith and knowledge together; we work with doubt to deepen both. We see this in the prayer of a father of a sick boy who brings him to Jesus for healing, saying, 'I believe, help my unbelief.'[21]

Of course doubt can calcify into unbelief, 'the pliable heart becoming a heart of stone',[22] but there are usually reasons other than doubt when this happens. Living faith is strong and uses doubt to mature. God, of course, has no problem with atheists and agnostics for whom any other position would be a lie. Their atheism does not disprove God; they live with integrity and dignity. I believe a day will come when our difference in understanding will be resolved with respect and honour. And if in the end there is no God then they will have been right all the time. It is intolerant atheism and bigoted religion that are the real signs of deep malaise.

The philosopher Mark Vernon suggests that one of the reasons for the decline in mental health in the west is an intolerance of doubt and our lust for certainty. He believes resistance to every form of fundamentalism must be healthy. All the evidence suggests both mental health and spiritual well-being require a skilful toleration of darkness and doubt.[23]

* * * * *

It is with some embarrassment I recall my childhood enthusiasm singing, 'Jesus loves me, this I know, for the Bible tells me so.'[24] Harmless enough perhaps, but a powerful illustration of the naive and unquestioning authority most Christians give to the biblical text, instilled into church culture from an early age with songs and statements exactly like this. The Hebrew–Christian scriptures are another area where many people experience a great deal of struggle and doubt. The mindset of 'God says it, I believe it, that settles it' is everywhere; I wish it was funny but it isn't.

What is your attitude to the biblical writings?
What are the issues that they raise for you?

At the outset one thing needs to be made clear, the Bible is *not* the 'Word of God'. This title belongs uniquely and exclusively to the person of Jesus;[25] it cannot be transferred to a book however much people may believe it speaks God's truth or communicates God's words. We may refer to this book as scripture in recognition of its spiritual value and worth, but to call it the 'Word of God' is quite simply wrong and indeed offensive.

By now you will have realised I love the biblical text – considering how often I have quoted It – but working with it is like being a member of a bomb disposal unit. There is the constant threat of shock and explosion; it is never obvious where the detonator is, and you have to be constantly alert.

JB Phillips described the task of translating the Greek New Testament into modern English like rewiring a house with the mains still left on.[26] There are constant sparks, arcs of light, painful burns – moments that are electrifying and inspiring along with others that are simply shocking.

Scripture is fiendishly annoying at so many levels. It always assumes you know exactly what it is talking about, when this is often far from clear. Added to this the critics are quite right when they say it is full of contradictions and it can be made to say anything the reader wishes.

Time and again I turn to the text in an attempt to hear a clear voice only to find myself engaged in a threatening struggle, trying desperately to fend off confusion or disentangle myself from conflicting ideas. As if that wasn't enough; like a street fight, a crowd quickly gathers in the form of scholars and teachers whose raucous shouts confuse the struggle even further.

As Walter Wink declares,

> I listen intently to the book. But I do not acquiesce in it. I rail at it. I make accusations. I censure it for endorsing patriarchalism, violence, anti-Judaism, homophobia, and slavery. It rails back at me, accusing me of greed, presumption, narcissism and cowardice. We wrestle. We roll on the ground, neither of us capitulating, until it wounds my thigh with 'new-ancient' words. And the Holy Spirit is there the whole time, strengthening us both.[27]

The truth is the biblical writings are simply not what people want them to be. The unambiguous divine statement most people crave is rarely there. In its place is something far more exciting: the story of the relationship between God and creation, the voices of storytellers speaking from the heart. Very occasionally God speaks directly, but more usually it is through human experience.

Why do people prefer a 'closed book' of certainty to an 'open book' of discovery?

What do you think about the idea of 'wrestling with scripture'?

The genius of scripture is the way the words of an individual or community are taken and shaped into a meticulous memory by biblical editors to meet particular needs. Different sources are cut, spliced, threaded and woven into a single tradition; layered and intertwined like a rare oriental carpet. The result is a masterpiece.

The text, which we now have as scripture, was shaped, edited and given its final form within the environment of past communities. In the same way, today, these documents need to be interpreted within spiritually sensitive communities and then experimented with in life to see if they are true. There is an exciting symmetry here.

The Hebrew scriptures tell of the Jewish struggle to make sense of God and the world; they also subvert the popular religious and social ideas of their time. In the writings of the early Jesus-community we see the attempts to come to terms with the scandalous implications of this rogue *rabbi*, who further subverts the ideas of the Hebrew scriptures.

Today both texts serve us well as we continue to engage with some of the same issues, and many new ones, and also seek to subvert our own society. These texts are an unfolding revelation in terms of relationship and values, and open-ended in terms of detail.

I want to take scripture seriously; these texts are a primary source for the radical values we have discussed at length already. Properly understood they are words of life, so reject anyone who would try to force the texts upon you legalistically. Look instead for those who would offer you the skills to handle them affectively and appropriately.[28]

Which biblical text has proved most subversive in your experience?
What skills does handling scripture require?

Watch an archaeologist examining an artefact; listen as an insignificant object is interpreted as a momentous find. It may be only a shard of pottery, a coin, or an iron axe-head, but it becomes a key in the puzzle of reconstructing a historical moment, a living voice in a story from the past. You feel the excitement as the expert enthuses and eulogises about this ancient object. Biblical

interpretation needs the same care and wisdom, the same
sensitivity to see and to hear, the same raw enthusiasm, the same
mature childlikeness.

* * * * *

A south London Buddhist network facilitator phoned me. He had
kindly emailed their extensive contacts asking if any ex-Christians
would be willing to take part in the inter-faith conversations I
organise. 'Noel, I'm shocked. I had a huge response to your
request but everyone was negative, accompanied by levels of
anger and abuse toward the church I would be embarrassed for
you to read.' Other faith groups have given me similar feedback. I
estimate across the UK alone thousands of ex-Christians who are
now part of other faiths, and many who are not, carry rage about
the church. Why?

Every story will be different. Of course there are those who just slip
away silently from church because it no longer meets their
personal needs or relates to their everyday life. For others the
worship style and teaching no longer connect with them. The
community does not hold them or it quietly excludes them;
circumstances change so time and money are needed elsewhere,
or they feel there is simply no room to grow spiritually.[29]

However, in my experience the anger comes from those who have
been damaged by the leadership, structure and ethos:

- Like the person whose theological questions were dismissed as
  irrelevant and who was advised to keep quiet about them;
- Like the young woman who was told her father died of cancer
  only because she did not have enough faith;
- Like the social justice activist who was informed their concerns
  had nothing whatever to do with the Christian gospel;
- Like the young man who came out as gay, and was dismissed
  from youth leadership and instructed to get healing;
- Like the many whose church experience has made them more
  aware of guilt and sin than forgiveness and freedom;
- Like those who describe their encounter with church as
  'spiritual rape'.[30]

Sadly I could continue with many other examples.[31] This is
disturbing, painful but far from marginal. Those for whom spiritual
commitment is deeply personal are likely to struggle forward but

without any further reference to local church, while those for whom church was essential to their faith will often find their beliefs destroyed completely. Of course there are many truly inspiring expressions of Jesus-community to be found, but all too often the word 'church' and the name 'Christian' are now dismissed as by-words for legalism, narrow-mindedness, hierarchy, patriarchy, intolerance, abuse of power, authoritarian and much more besides, and not without reason.

To rephrase a quotation we used in the previous chapter, '... if the *church* is unique it is only because Christ is. If it ceases to witness to him, it ceases to have any value for the human race.'[32] Where this is the case it must be challenged and marked by a fingerprint of fire, while those who have been abused must be *listened to* and supported.

Why does toxic-church happen?
Why are so many Christians leaving church but not their faith? [33]

I have already stressed Jesus had no intention of founding a new religion or institution, but rather to touch the lives of individuals and enable communities to flourish and thrive.

So true spirituality is *both* plural *and* personal.

The English word 'church' translates the Greek word *ekklesia*, which is just one of some 96-plus images used by the early Jesus-community to describe themselves.[34] Jesus is clear, there is only *one* church, which is both cosmic and local both at the same time.[35] One of the reasons the word *ekklesia* was used was because it had nothing whatever to do with religion; it referred to a political gathering. This underlines the subversive agenda of the early Christian community to work for the transfiguration of the existing order, which should be ours as well.

Breathing together as they shared the 'Peacemeal' was conspiracy indeed.

Authentic church is simply being community in a way that lives out Jesus' good news. So the foundational question has to be, 'What *is* this gospel?' The answer, we have seen, is the single word *shalom*.

True church is peace-church or it is nothing.[36]

Most so-called innovative thinking about church today sadly focuses on structure.[37] Apart from the centrality of the 'Peacemeal' this is secondary. The single most important thing about 'peace-church' is to think differently (*metanoia*) and the ethos that this brings: a community shaped by a *shalom* understanding of values.

Every expression of Jesus-community should be unique, shaping itself locally with the greatest possible diversity. Its focus is the person of Jesus and the centrepiece is always the 'Peacemeal'. In practice, what it means to be peace-church in any particular locality is for each group to decide, depending on the character and cultures of the people involved – there can never be a fixed pattern.

My personal test when meeting a local church for the first time is two-fold. First I look for surprise – does it make me say, 'Wow, so this is how you do it here!'? It should be unpredictable. Second, I look for a sense of welcome and spiritual connection that transcends language or culture.

How do you respond to the phrase 'peace-church'?
What is the most exciting Jesus-community you have been to, and why?

The main purpose of a Jesus-community is to nurture mature spirituality, individually and collectively in the fullest sense of that term, to share physical resources and be a base for *shalom* activism, with every member empowered to take initiatives, develop and share their gifts, each playing their part as servant–enablers to the whole, without hint of hierarchy or control;[38] a place where mavericks are as important as conciliators.

Peace-church should be a place of celebration and reflection that is both safe and dangerous, secure and risk-taking. It should be characterised by mature wisdom; but childlike in its ethos. In fact children and those most recently come to faith should be like a bubbling spring at the centre of the community bringing freshness and joyful playfulness. Their questioning, arguments and challenges – even rage – should promote thinking and debate will that enable everyone to engage effectively with the intellectual and moral challenges of the times, and lead to a way of living that is both provocative and attractive. Those more mature may support and nurture the whole group.

Tradition is only of value if it is truly life-giving and liberating.

This energy of spontaneity and freedom must also be marked by compassion and love for those in need. A Jesus-community should be a place of sanctuary with space for reflection and healing. It should be fearless in challenging injustice, while gentle in all their relationships among people and within wild nature, creatively engaged with contemporary society at every level, working to meet the many needs of their particular locality and to enrich all aspects of its multi-faceted cultures. It should proclaim the joyful good news of *shalom*, inspired by a living hope, which looks for substantial change in the present through the power of the Spirit as a sign of transfiguration for the future.

✳ ✳ ✳ ✳ ✳

'Loss of innocence' is a phrase often used to describe damaged childhood or the transition to adulthood; it implies something that can never be restored. Jesus challenges this. Not only can it be recovered; it is essential that we do so as we engage with a hostile world:

See, I am sending you out like sheep into the midst of wolves; so be wise as serpents and innocent as doves.[39]

Jesus' use of the word 'innocent' (Greek: *akeraios*) is rooted in three Hebrew words: *naqi* (clean), *tam* (perfect) and *zadik* (righteous). The Greek is subtle and almost untranslatable; it suggests 'still being in its original state', intact (not unlike virginity), gentle (not harming with violence or deceit) and beyond reproach (without blame or guilt). Innocence is *not* ignorance; it is the character qualities of purity and integrity.[40]

The early Christian community picked up on Jesus' words:

Be wise in what is good and innocent in what is evil.[41]

Be blameless and innocent children of God
without blemish in the midst of a crooked and perverse generation,
in which you shine like stars in the world.[42]

Childlike, we are to stand tall and strong within a dark and evil world, with wisdom and maturity providing the muscle and sinew to our athletic frame. Like serpents we are to be mysterious and

211

disturbing, creatively cunning, yet bringers of healing and symbols of life. Like doves we are to be attractive but elusive, gentle and pure, yet bringers of *shalom* and the power of the Spirit.[43]

It is unlikely we will ever fully fathom Jesus' call to 'become like children'. Its haunting simplicity is profound, something to be continually rediscovered.

Jesus says we are to be 'reborn', a process as much as a crisis.[44] We need to be constantly rediscovering the astonishing depths of 'childlikeness' and our task as a ruthless inquisitor.

Endnotes

1 See <http://news.bbc.co.uk/1/hi/8200022.stm>.
2 Mk 9:36–37.
3 Mt 18:3.
4 Added to this there is the development of the 'teenager' and more recently the 'kidult', which have completely skewed the concept of childhood and push their influence on to younger and younger children.
5 I am fully aware of the remarkable work that individual Christians and small groups have done for the welfare and support of children; caring for orphans, bringing in legislation to protect children from cruelty at home and harm in the workplace, educating them in 'ragged schools' and Sunday schools. Even today there are some very creative programmes and dedicated people working with children, but none of this has changed the basic 'marginalising' attitude towards children in either church or society
6 See Mk 9:36–37.
7 This is in terms of the Synoptic Gospels; I am fully aware there are other stories about Jesus' childhood and youth found in the Gospel of Thomas, an Arabic infancy Gospel and elsewhere, which centre on miraculous events, a few of which are malevolent, quite different in tone from the Luke story below and difficult to reconcile with the statement in Jn 2:11 that the miracle at Cana in Galilee was 'the first of his signs'.
8 The term *bar mitzvah* means 'son of the commandment'; it is the ceremony marking a boy's thirteenth birthday, when he takes religious responsibility for his own conduct, begins to pray as an adult and to count as a member of the quorum for worship. More recently Reform and Conservative Jewish congregations hold similar *bat mitzvah* ('daughter of the commandment') ceremonies for 12-year-old girls; Judaism has always recognised that girls mature earlier than boys.
9 Lk 2:41–52.
10 Eccl 3:11.
11 Prov 25:2.
12 This illustration is used by CEM Joad in *Teach Yourself Books: Philosophy*, English Universities Press, 1944, p. 8. All illustrations have their limitations but I have always found this one a helpful way to picture a very abstract concept.
13 The word 'faith' in its most basic sense is very practical and could equally be translated as 'trust'; it does not imply a belief or involvement of God. The biblical understanding that sees everything rooted in the divine makes this a

logical development but it is not there in the initial concept.

14 Elie Wiesel, *Night*, Penguin Books, 1981, p. 79.

15 The end of the book of Job is seen as very provocative by some scholars. Their reading of the text sees Job model a biblical character who condemns God and expresses a rejection and a despair of the divine role in the face of injustice. See for example: <http://faculty.gordon.edu/hu/bi/ted_hildebrandt/OTeSources/18-Job/Text/Articles/Newell-JobRep-WTJ.pdf> – which challenges the usual translation of Job 42. The most extreme is JB Curtis who sees Job as 'totally disenchanted with this god', and whose translation of 42:6 reads: 'Therefore I feel loathing contempt and revulsion (toward you, O God); and I am sorry for frail man.' Job thus totally and finally rejects this unjust, unfeeling and irrelevant deity. I am grateful to my friend Drew Worthley for drawing my attention to this reading.

16 This question was framed by mky friend Mark Ostrowicz as a possible subject for a degree dissertation.

17 Isa 45:6–7. The phrase 'I form light and create darkness' clearly refers to the Zoroastrian belief in *Ahura Mazda*, 'the god of light (goodness)', and *Ahriman/Angra Mainyu*, 'the god of darkness (evil and destruction)'. Here Yahweh is making it clear that there are not different deities, but only one supreme being within whom all understanding of good and evil has to be understood and reconciled.

18 See 1Jn 1:5 for light; see Ps 18:11; 97:2; 1Kgs 8:12; 2Ch 6:1 also Deut 4:11; 5:22 for darkness.

19 Gen 32:24–31.

20 See the interesting background in Os Guinness, *Doubt*, Lion Publishing, 1987, pp. 16–19.

21 Mk 9:24.

22 See Ezk 36:26.

23 See <www.ekklesia.co.uk/node/14262>.

24 This the first time in this book I have used the phrase 'the Bible' (because it is part of the words of the song). I use it as little as possible because the phrase means 'the Book' with the deliberate implication that not only is it superior to all other books but especially those that make an equal claim to be scripture like the *Quran* (Islam), the *Guru Granth Sahib* (Sikhism), the *Bhagavad Gita* (Hinduism), the *Trapitika* (Buddhism) and many others. However much I love the Hebrew–Christian scriptures I try to avoid using a term that is not biblical and quite deliberately has the intention of disparaging texts sacred to other faiths. I recognise my use of the word 'biblical' is an unsatisfactory compromise but it is an attempt to step away from an inappropriate term.

25 See Rev 19:13 and Jn 1:1, 14; the phrase 'the word of God' is used in other places to refer to the good news and the 'testimony of Jesus'. These are spoken living words (cf. Rev 1:2, 9; 6:9; 20:4); see also 1Jn1:1–4. Nowhere is it used in a way that could be imagined as a title for a book. See William Barclay, *Jesus as They Saw Him*, SCM Press, 1962, pp. 421–429 for a simple clear background to the title being used for Jesus; and DE Aune, *Word Biblical Commentary: Revelation 17–22*, Thomas Nelson Publishers, 1998, pp. 1057–1058 for comment on the use of the title in Rev 19:13.

26 He wrote this in his introduction to JB Phillips, *Letters to Young Churches*, G Bles Publishing, 1947, p. xii.

27 Walter Wink, *The Human Being*, Fortress Press, 2002, p. 16.

28 To take many of these issues much further see Lloyd Pietersen, *Reading the Bible After Christendom*, Paternoster, 2011.

29 Two of a number of books that engage with this topic are P Richter and LJ Francis, *Gone but Not Forgotten: Church Leaving and Returning*, Darton,

Longman & Todd, 1998; and A Jamieson, *A Churchless Faith: Faith Journeys beyond the Churches*, SPCK, 2002.

30 This phrase was given to me by my friend Gillie Jenkinson, who is an experienced psychotherapist who specialises in helping people who have been abused by churches and spiritual cults.

31 On the theme of abusive church see Stephen Parsons, *Ungodly Fear: Fundamentalist Christianity and the Abuse of Power*, Lion Publishing, 2000; also Harold Enroth, *Churches that Abuse*, Zondervan, 1993; and D Johnson and J van Vonderen, *The Subtle Power of Spiritual Abuse: Recognizing and Escaping Spiritual Manipulation and False Spiritual Authority within the Church*, Bethany House/ Baker Publishing, 2005.

32 The original quotation, which referred to *Christianity*, came from Christopher Lamb, *Lion Handbook of World Religions*, Lion, 1982, pp. 363.

33 In P Richter and LJ Francis, *Gone but Not Forgotten: Church Leaving and Returning*, Darton, Longman & Todd, 1998, the authors suggest that 1,500 people a week are leaving UK churches (see p. xii), but that only 18% of these are leaving because they have lost their faith (see p. 137). I am grateful to my friend Stuart Murray Williams for pointing out the significance of these statistics. Some believe that anecdotal evidence suggests this is the fastest-growing group of Christians in the UK.

34 See Paul Minear, *Images of the Church in the New Testament*, James Clarke & Co, 1960.

35 See Mt 16:18 and Heb 12:22–24.

36 To read a more extended reflection on PeaceChurch thinking, see my contribution to JR Krabill and S Murray (eds), *Forming Christian Habits in Post Christendom: The Legacy of Alan and Eleanor Kreider*, Herald Press, 2011, pp. 131–138.

37 For example, café-church, liquid-church, house-church, pub-church, deep-church, organic-church, fresh-expressions and very many more.

38 The question of leadership is too complex to develop here other than to say the example of Jesus shows it to be an attitude of exampling mutual service that is devoid of any form of hierarchy, with every person offering their gifts and experience to others and these being recognised and honoured by the community. Authentic authority is a presence and demeanour that inspires confidence that something is true, but is also always open to question and challenge. Hierarchy has the double curse of creating the opportunity for individuals to wield self-interested power awhile encouraging the majority to be passive and conform – neither has any place in peace-church.

39 Mt 10:16.

40 See EC Blackman, 'Innocent', in A Richardson (ed.). *A Theological Wordbook of the Bible*, SCM Press, 1957, p. 114; and G Kittel, '*akeraios*', in G Kittel (ed.) *Theological Dictionary of the New Testament*, vol. 1, 1964, pp. 209–210.

41 Rom 16:19; see also 1Cor 14:20.

42 Phil 2:15.

43 See Gen3:1–19; Num 21:6–9; Jn 3:14–15 for serpents and Gen 8:8–12; Lk 3:22 *et al* for doves. The cultural and religious symbolism surrounding both the idea of the 'serpent' and the 'dove' is extensive; see W Foerster, O Grethere and J Fichtner, '*ophis*' in G Friedrich (ed), *Theological Dictionary of the New Testament*, vol. 5, Eerdmans, 1967, pp. 566–582; and H Greeven, '*periostera*' in G Kittel and G Friedrich (eds), *Theological Dictionary of the New Testament*, vol. 6, 1967, pp. 63–72.

44 See Jn 3:3–7 and Mt 18:3.

14 Footprints of Peace
– walking with destiny

My footprint is the mark I leave behind me as I move across the earth. It shows where I have been and suggests where I am going; it may also remain long after I have gone. It is as unique and personal as my fingerprint, and it can be 'read'. Skilled trackers can tell a great deal about a person just from their footprints. We are also able to follow them.

It is my feet that connect me to this world, giving me poise and balance whether I am standing or moving. They enable me to run, jump, climb, dance, but most of all to walk. In many cultures walking is a symbol of character and integrity so I choose to stand tall and walk upright. Walking should always be life-giving.

* * * * *

The Japanese anime film, *Princess Mononoke*, tells the story of a fight to save the wilderness from relentless urban-industrialisation, and it has a beautiful scene in which the 'Spirit of the Forest' walks among the trees. Every stride leaves a footprint, and from each footprint bursts a profusion of wild flowers.[1] Whenever I reflect on this image I think of the words of the psalm: 'Justice unfolds like a path and God's footsteps bring *shalom*.[2]

Shalom has been our focus throughout this book, both as a treasure in our hands and a vision that fills the sky. Its presence and meaning is able to inspire us and overwhelm us in equal measure. Within these pages I have been able only to lift up one small corner of the fabric that cloaks its mystery; nevertheless I hope it has excited you.

We began with the question, 'Who am I?' and quickly discovered the most important question was, 'What kind of person do I want to be?' However eagerly I embrace the vision of *shalom* and its call to activism, my response will always be shaped by the quality of my character.

Are integrity and meekness my personal hallmarks?
Am I *zadik* – just and righteous in my actions?
Do creativity and wisdom set the rhythm I live by?
What footprints do I leave behind me?

These are delicate questions. They personally touch the very
essence of my identity and who I am at my most insecure and
vulnerable and so easily raise a shadow of guilt and inadequacy.
Truth will always be a challenge, but its purpose is to inspire and
set us free, not to accuse or condemn. We are invited to follow
Jesus, with the promise of the energising strength of the Spirit and
the support of others journeying with us.

Nurturing spirituality should be deep, gentle and joyful. By its very
nature it takes time, moving us forward from whatever place we
find ourselves at this moment. It flows through our lifeways, our
choices and our activism, both strengthening them and being
strengthened by them.

As a first step forward from this point, ask yourself which *one*
thought, idea or action are you taking with you from this book?
Reflect on why this is your choice and how you would like to make
it personally important in the future.

★ ★ ★ ★ ★

In 1967, studying in my college library, I chanced upon the concept
of *shalom* for the very first time. That moment changed my life. My
personal faith was turned upside down. The more I studied and
explored, the more certain I became that I had stumbled on the
secret of the universe.[3]

Here in front of me, distilled into a single word, was a concept that
enabled the total integration of absolutely everything without
exception centred on the person and peace of Jesus. It broke like
a wave over my understanding of spirituality, discipleship, justice,
community, evangelism, nonviolence, ecology, human destiny and
so very much more. Everything changed.

I was swept into uncharted territory. In the following decades the
momentum has only increased. My vision and experience of
shalom has been tested at every level and never failed or been
found wanting, only deepening my longing to understand it even
better and example it more powerfully.[4]

I warned at the outset this would be a passionate book filled with conviction. I hope you understand why. I also hope, amid my eagerness to share, you have found it gentle and considerate, open to questions with space to think, doubt and disagree. I hope it has also inspired you – that is my prayer.

Have you ever experienced a situation where you have been given a piece of information that completely changes a relationship? This is what it was like when I encountered *shalom* for the first time; it was emotionally, spiritually and intellectually disturbing. All my usual points of reference either looked quite different or simply evaporated.

If you come from a more traditional Christian background you may have found ideas in this book at odds with those you are familiar with and have been taught. This can be disturbing and unsettling, as though someone has ripped up the map you have been following, or a once-secure handhold is now crumbling in your grasp. Please take the time to ask, 'Is it true?' Think prayerfully and question everything thoroughly. Discuss it with others. However, in the end only you can decide whether you believe what I have written has the ring of truth.

How are the new ideas different from what you are familiar with?
Do the themes do justice to the person of Jesus?
In what ways would these ideas change you?

Have you ever taken a familiar picture to be reframed – giving it a new style, with fresh colour-card around the edges, and finally hung it on a differently textured wall? You step back and look – it can seem like another picture entirely. Your overall relationship with the picture changes; certain details become clearer, some tones are sharper and even more of its beauty is revealed.

If you come from the wider community of faith and belief I trust that reading this book may have been something of a 'reframing' of your ideas about a Jesus perspective. I hope you have found a view of the Christian faith that is inclusive and welcoming, with ideas and approaches that bring you a different understanding and reveal more common ground than you thought was there before, creating a place where we can learn from each other and work more closely together. Whatever you think of Jesus I trust some of the ideas have been provocative and bring a different tone and colour to how you viewed things previously.[5]

Does the Christian faith feel more open towards you?
Have you seen more common ground between yourself and
Christians?
What ideas have you found most interesting?

There is a legend that tells how Rome was in flames at the height
of Emperor Nero's persecution of Christians, leading Peter, the
disciple of Jesus, to flee the city for his life. On the road he meets
Jesus travelling in the opposite direction. Speaking in Latin Peter
asks, '*Quo vadis*?' (Where are you going?). Jesus replies, 'To
Rome, to be crucified again.'[6]

This question, '*Quo vadis*?' hangs in the air. Where are you going?

The challenges are huge. These issues tower before us: global
politics, ecological catastrophe, financial instability, wars, world
hunger and so much more – all too familiar to each of us. The
temptation to close our mind and turn our back on it all is
understandably strong.

But Jesus walks directly towards these challenges saying, 'Follow
me.'

As a '*Shalom* Activist' that is where my commitment lies. That is
where I am going. That is the choice I want to make. But we have
also heard Jesus say: 'I am sending you out like sheep into the
midst of wolves.'[7]

This seemingly absurd situation focuses on one clear issue –
power: that ability to act in order to make something happen and
bring about change.[8]

Power exists – you cannot abolish it, you can only choose how you
use it. From a Jesus perspective, God is the source of all power:

> Yours, O Lord, are the greatness, the power ...
> In your hand are power and might.[9]

In truth, the stark reality seems to be that today power rests in the
hands of those presiding over the very systems that have created
and maintain the huge challenges that we face – either
manipulating them or being manipulated by them. In contrast we
appear to be quite powerless.

Then, to our amazement, we hear God saying something astonishing: 'Power is made perfect in weakness.'[10]

This remarkable statement set me on a quest to explore a biblical understanding of power, which finally led me to the conclusion that *at the centre of all power there is weakness and at the centre of all weakness there is power.*

At the centre of all power there is weakness: weakness is not a contrast to power but is found at its very heart. Throughout history tyrants and rulers, arrogant in their strength, have often been ultimately exposed by their impotence, which has always proved their downfall.[11] We see, in the case of God, that absolute power alone is incapable of accomplishing divine will. It is only through embracing the weakness of incarnation and death that God could vanquish the power of evil: 'For Jesus was crucified in weakness, but lives by the power of God.'[12] Also, God's desire for a living and loving reciprocal relationship with *all things* can be fulfilled only by the weakness and powerlessness of love, never coerced by power or force.

At the centre of all weakness there is power: weakness properly understood has enormous power.[13] A paradox with possibilities hidden from most eyes, but when activated provokes astonishment, incredulity and shock. Some everyday examples of the power of apparent weakness are:

- Fragile snowflakes in a blizzard making snow drifts that create a stand-still;
- Yeast kneaded into flour disappears only to enable the bread to rise;
- A tiny seedling germinating under a heavy slab can break the concrete.

Historically, seemingly insignificant individuals and small groups have been catalysts for huge social, political and spiritual change – overthrowing despots, obtaining civil rights, preventing ecological destruction and inspiring freedom. They have done so fearlessly, creatively and without the use of violence.

As I said previously, radical political engagement involves devising plans that confront those concentrations of power in societies that stifle spirituality and humanity; strategies, which are creatively imagined, fearlessly executed and beautiful in their outcome.[14]

This fusion of power with weakness is a profound and exciting conundrum. It can seem counter-intuitive, but it is true. It flows up from the grassroots, inspiring people that *shalom* is possible. It is liminal; seeping through the cracks and trickling from the edges, contaminating the mainstream with life until it becomes a flood.

I have mentioned before the fascinating link across the biblical text between *shalom* and feet,[15] and how this affirms that our message of peace to the earth is about *a spiritual destiny that will be fully expressed as a physical reality within this creation*. This being so, the peace–feet image stresses the importance of integrity and activism to bring this about.

So I choose to stand boldly and declare, 'I am Noel, why do I have to be anything else?' I hope you feel able to say something similar about yourself, working each day to incarnate the essence and the energy of all the themes we have shared together.

As we stand together confident in our growing sense of identity we can look outward towards others, touching both people and wild nature with our fingerprints of fire and walking among them, leaving footprints of peace in our path.

Jesus promises that we will be 'clothed with power from on high'.[16] So I wrap that cloak around me and feel its strength. I remind myself I am a unique individual, 'a person of peace'.[17] I am also part of the broader community of *shalom* who are choosing to live from a Jesus perspective, enlarged by those from the wider spirituality also inspired by this vision and excited by the question, 'How do you change the world?'

You change it one step at a time.

Endnotes

1 See Hayao Miyazaki, *Princess Mononoke*, Studio Ghibli, Toho/ Miramax, 1997.
2 Ps 85:13 – my paraphrase draws on the Jerusalem Bible reading of this text.
3 For a more detailed account of these events, what led up to them and some of the consequences, see A Kreider and S Murray (eds), *Coming Home: Stories of Anabaptists in Britain and Ireland*, Pandora Press/ Herald Press, 2000, pp. 102–104.
4 I once led a 'Table-Talk' that had as its sole aim to find faults and weaknesses in *shalom* as both a broad vision and a practical basis by which to live. After more than three hours of rigorous argument and debate we failed to come up with a single negative feature – even I was astonished!

5   One of the many things I love about *shalom* is that agnostics and atheists can engage with it without any difficulty, connecting with its basic principles of physical well-being, justice in relationships (with a *mishpat* understanding) and integrity of character. This is exciting common ground.

6   The legend is found in 'The Acts of Peter' (Vercelli Acts XXXV). The phrase is also found in the Latin Vulgate version of Jn 13:36, where again Peter asks this question of Jesus in different circumstances. The phrase became popular from the title of the 1896 historical novel by the Polish author, Henryk Sicnkiewicz, *Quo Vadis: A Narrative of the Time of Nero*, Hippocrene Books, 1997; and the 1951 Metro-Goldwyn-Myer film of the same name directed by Mervyn LeRoy.

7   Mt 10:16.

8   I am fully aware of the complexity of the subject of power, whether from a sociological, psychological or spiritual perspective (to name just a few). I hope you will forgive the simplicity with which I deal with the subject here to make the point I wish to raise.

9   1Chron 29:11–13; see also Rom 13:1.

10 2Cor 12:9.

11 This may often be demonstrated in their lifetime, or in the collapse of the power-structures they created in the years after their death.

12 2Cor 13:4; see also Isa 40:28–29; 1Th 5:14–15; 1Cor 9:22–23; 2Cor 11:30.

13 Cf. for instance Mt 20:25–28, Lk 22:24–27, Jn 13:3–5, 12–15 and 2Cor 12:9–10.

14 For strategies and stories see G Sharp, *The Politics of Nonviolent Action*, Boston: Porter Sargent, 1974 and *Waging Nonviolent Struggle: 20th Century Practice and 21st Century Potential*, Boston: Porter Sargent, 2005; also P Ackerman and J Duvall, *A Force More Powerful: A Century of Nonviolent Conflict*, Palgrave/ Macmillan, 2000.

15 See for instance:
    • 'How beautiful upon the mountains are the feet of the one … heralding *shalom*' (Isa 52:7, cf. Nahum 1:15);
    • 'Justice makes a path before him, his footsteps bring *shalom*' (Ps 85:13; Jerusalem Bible);
    • 'The God of peace will soon crush Satan under your feet.' (Rom 16:20);
    • 'To guide our feet into the way of peace' (Lk 1:79);
    • 'Having shod your feet with the equipment of the gospel of peace' (Eph 6:15).

16 Lk 24:49.

17 See Lk 10:6.

Glossary

Note: words with (q.v.) after them means they can be found elsewhere within this glossary.

Abba (Hebrew) – literally 'Daddy'; the most intimate affectionate term for a male parent, considered scandalous when applied to God by Jesus. In later eastern Christian monasticism it was used as a title of respect for an older ascetic – 'Father'.

Adam (Hebrew) – 'human being'; also refers to 'a person' or 'humankind'; one shaped from red clay – *adamah* (q.v.). It is the masculine form of *adamah*

adamah (Hebrew) – a feminine word, which means 'ground' or 'earth'; related to the root *adm* (red, fair, handsome), *adomi* (ruddy) and *dam* (blood).

agape (Greek) – 'unconditional love'; first used by the *rabbis* (q.v.) to translate *chesed* (q.v.), and then by the early Christians, who also used it as a name for their shared meal to celebrate the death and resurrection of Jesus.

aheb (Hebrew) – the most widely used Hebrew word for love, as in family, friendship and sexual relationships. The other important Hebrew word for love is *chesed* (q.v.).

ahimsa (Sanskrit) – 'to renounce the desire to kill or harm'; often popularly translated as 'nonviolence'. It is 'the abstention from harming others' that also leads to living in reciprocal harmony with wild nature.

Ahriman (Avestan) – Zoroastrian understanding of the personification of evil, also known as *Angra Mainyu*; there is a firm conviction that ultimately *Ahura Mazda* (q.v.), God as goodness and light, will overthrow *Ahriman.*

Ahura Mazda (Avestan) – Zoroastrian understanding of God as goodness, represented as a fire of uncreated light; also associated with wisdom, truth, righteousness and purity, who will ultimately be victorious over *Ahriman* (q.v.), the manifestation of evil.

akeraios (Greek) – 'innocent'; it is a subtle and almost untranslatable word, which suggests 'still being in its original state', intact (not unlike virginity), gentle (not harming with violence or deceit) and beyond reproach (without blame or guilt). Early Christian use rooted it in three Hebrew words: *naqi/* clean, *tam/* perfect and *zadik/* righteous (q.v.).

akolouthein (Greek) – 'to follow'; it implies a close relationship between the person being followed and the person following, as with a disciple and their teacher.

amon (Hebrew) – 'nurseling' (a breastfeeding child), the natural sense and the one emphasised by the *Kabbalah* (q.v.). This is a rare word, which later Judaism used in the sense of 'workman' or 'builder'. It is significant in terms of translating the difficult meaning of Prov. 8:30.

anarchos (Greek) – 'without a ruler' with the sense of 'to be set free from powers'; the term from which the word 'anarchist' is formed.

anaw (Hebrew) – 'meekness'; paralleled with the Greek word *praus* (q.v.).

angeloi (Greek) – 'messengers', 'angels' or 'powers', they may be either human or divine.

archai (Greek) – 'ruler', 'principalities', 'authorities' and 'first principles'.

ashray (Aramaic) – 'to set yourself up on the right way for the right goal; to turn around, repent; to become straight or righteous'; from the verb *yashar*, translated by the Greek word *makarios* (q.v.) in Jesus' 'Beatitudes'.

avatar (Sanskrit) – 'one who descends'; a being who is often the manifestation of the Hindu god *Vishnu* (q.v.). The sanctity of their life mediates wisdom, grace and truth. They are manifestations of the divine, they come to the world at times of distress to overthrow evil and restore harmony.

bedouin (French) – it is a transliteration of the Arabic *badawi* 'those who live in the desert'; they live across the middle eastern wilderness in strong kinship and tribal groups guided by powerful honour codes.

Bar mitzvah (Hebrew) – 'son of the commandment'; a ceremony where a Jewish boy is recognised as an adult in terms of his moral and spiritual responsibility before God at the age of thirteen. Jewish girls at the age of twelve become *bat mitzvah.*

bar nasha (Aramaic) – 'son of man'; it literally means 'a human being'.

berith (Hebrew) – 'binding covenant' that establishes a relationship between two or more parties.

betach (Hebrew) – 'hope'; biblically speaks of confidence in God whose goodness and mercy are to be relied on and whose promises cannot fail – as in the Greek *elpis* (q.v.).

bhakti (Sanskrit) – 'devotion', from *bhaj* 'to share' or 'belong to'; it describes the intense love and relationship leading to union with the divine.

bina (Hebrew) – 'understanding'; an important aspect of the creative wisdom of *hokma* (q.v.). It is like a child joining up dots to reveal a picture.

Bodhisattva (Sanskrit) – 'one whose essence has become enlightened'; a person who has dedicated their life to the welfare of humanity and leading others to enlightenment, delaying their entry into *nirvana* (q.v.), their personal reward for enlightenment.

centrifugal (Latin) – 'to seek or to be drawn towards the centre'.

centripetal (Latin) – 'to flee or to be dispersed from the centre'.

chaburah (Hebrew) – friend'; the name given to a meal where like-minded people ate together for a purpose; it is suggested by some that the 'Last Supper' was a *Chaburah* meal, rather than being a *Pesach* (q.v.) or 'Passover' meal as is traditionally believed.

chadash (Hebrew) – 'new', which can express the ideas of both something completely new or something already existing that has been 'renewed'.

chesed (Hebrew) – 'covenant love', 'steadfast love', 'loving kindness', 'mercy', faithfulness'; the essence of a relationship which is based on commitment rooted in love, translated by *agape* (q.v.) into the Greek of the New Testament. The most widely used Hebrew word for love is *aheb* (q.v.).

deipnon (Greek) – 'supper', the main meal of the day eaten in the evening.

diaiosune (Greek) – 'righteousness/ justice'; closely linked to *zadik* (q.v.) and *mishpat* (q.v.).

discipulus (Latin) – 'one who learns'; a student, an apprentice, the word from which the English word 'disciple' is formed.

diyafa (Arabic) – 'hospitality'; it is the covenant of the desert Bedouin, where no traveller, even a sworn enemy, is ever turned away but is given food, shelter and protection and then is able to leave in peace.

dunamis (Greek) – 'power', from which we get the English word 'dynamite'; used to speak of Jesus' miracles as a demonstration of the age to come in the immediate present.

eirene (Greek) – 'peace'; used by New Testament writers with the sense of *shalom* (q.v.), in contrast to the secular understanding of a 'truce', which would inevitably collapse back into violence – perceived to be the natural state of existence – once more.

ekklesia (Greek) – 'called out ones'. Popularly translated with the English word 'church', originally it had nothing whatever to do with religion; it referred to a political gathering. It is just one of some ninety-six plus images used by the early Jesus-community to describe themselves.

eleuchos (Greek) – 'firm evidence'; strong enough to bring a conviction in court, used in relation to faith.

elpis (Greek) – 'hope'; biblically speaks of confidence in God whose goodness and mercy are to be relied on and whose promises cannot fail – as in the Hebrew *betach* (q.v.).

Enuma Elish (Akkadian) – the Babylonian creation myth, where *Marduk* the god forms the cosmos from the dismembered cadaver of his mother *Tiamat*, the symbol of chaos.

epektasis (Greek) – 'reaching forward'; the essence of perfection is never actually becoming perfect because there is always deeper and higher perfection to reach out towards.

Ephphatha (Aramaic) – 'be opened'; a command used by Jesus in Mark 7:34.

epiousion (Greek) – translated 'daily', it is an intriguing word, with a possible double meaning: not only 'sufficient for today' but also 'in anticipation of tomorrow', as in the prayer, 'Give us today our daily bread' in Matthew 6:11.

erga (Greek) – 'works'; used to speak of Jesus' miracles as a demonstration of God continuing to work through the *Messiah* (q.v.).

ethikos (Greek) – literally 'moral character within culture'; it is the word from which we get the English word 'ethics'.

euanggelion (Greek) – 'good news'; the message carried by an 'evangelist' who ran from the battlefield with news of victory and peace, or told of the long-awaited birth of a child. *Euanggelion* could only ever be good news, never bad news.

eucharisteo (Greek) – 'I give thanks'; early Christians used it as a name for their shared meal to celebrate the death and resurrection of Jesus; transliterated as 'Eucharist'.

eusebeia (Greek) – 'godliness'; it is an attitude of mind, which honours God, holds all others in high esteem, and has strong self-respect.

exodus (Latin) – 'going out', it is a transliteration of the Greek *ex* (out) *hodos* (way). The word is used to refer to the ancient Israelites leaving slavery in Egypt for the promise of freedom in a new land. It also gave its name to the second book of the Hebrew scriptures which tells this story.

exousia (Greek) – 'rulers', 'powers', 'authority', both physical and spiritual; also used to speak of Jesus' miracles as acts that demonstrate God's rule and authority being immediately present.

Gadol hashalom (Hebrew) – a rabbinic phrase meaning '*shalom* is the highest of values'.

Ge hinnom (Hebrew) – literally 'the valley of the sons of Hinnom' on the west side of Jerusalem; the rubbish tip where everything foul was destroyed, including pagan idols during the reforms of Hezekiah and Josiah. Often referred to by the Latin *gehenna*. Some believe the word 'hell' was formed from it. For an alternative view see the Nordic word *Hel* (q.v.).

Grundnorm (German) – 'ground rule' or 'highest basic norm'; an assumed initial principle not deducted from anything else, the basis of Hans Klesen's pure theory of law.

guru (Sanskrit) – 'teacher'; formed from two Sanskrit words: *gu* meaning 'darkness' and *ru* meaning 'to push away forcibly' or 'to scatter'; someone whose presence and teaching 'pushes away darkness' and by implication radiates light – *prakasha* (q.v.).

Hades (Greek) – a place of darkness where the dead are, whether righteous or unrighteous, named after the god of the underworld; often unhelpfully translated in English bibles by the word 'hell'. It has similarities to the Hebrew word *Sheol* (q.v.).

Hadith (Arabic) – 'traditions' from the life of Muhammad, compiled from the memory of the Muslim community after his death to help provide guidance on how to live an appropriate life; along with the *Quran* and philosophical reflection they help form the *Sharia* (q.v.).

hatha (Sanskrit) – literally 'force'; formed from *ha* (sun) and *tha* (moon), the bringing together of opposites in the physical exercise and postures of *yoga* (q.v.).

Hel (Nordic) – name of the unlovely goddess of the sunless region where souls unworthy of Valhalla were relegated; probably giving us the English word 'hell'; for an alternative view see the Hebrew word *Gehenna* (q.v.).

hokma (Hebrew) – 'wisdom', which is always personal, pastoral, practical and philosophical; the main biblical term for creativity. Three words closely linked to *hokma* are *tbumal* insight (q.v.), *binal* understanding (q.v.) and *yadal* knowledge (q.v.). It finds parallels with the Greek *sophia* (q.v.).

Homo sapiens (Latin) – 'wise person' or 'knowing person'; this is the scientific classification of modern humans.

humus (Latin) – 'soil'; from which we get the English word 'humility'.

hupomone (Greek) – 'hope as tenacity'; used to describe the inhabitants of a city under siege refusing to leave any stone unturned in their single-minded resistance against their oppressors.

hypostasis (Greek) – 'substantial reality'; used in relationship to faith.

ichthus (Greek) – 'fish'; this is a very early Christian symbol, each letter representing a word in the declaration 'Jesus Christ Son of God Saviour' (*Iesous Christos theou uios soter*).

Interahamwe (Kinyarwanda) – 'those who stand, work, fight and attack together'; this is a title given in this Rwandan language to the Hutu paramilitary organisation carrying out the massacre of Tutsis in 1994.

jihad (Arabic) – 'struggle', doing one's utmost to reach a goal, in personal spiritual development, to improve society and to protect the truth; it does not mean 'holy war'.

jnana (Sanskrit) – 'knowledge'; in *yoga* (q.v.) it is achieving understanding that leads to enlightenment and release from the cycle of rebirth/ reincarnation.

kabash (Hebrew) – usually translated 'subdue'; has the sense of 'to stamp on something'; taken from the language of ancient kingship. It must be understood in terms of humans being called to 'image God' within wild nature, in harmony with the character and values of God's kingship, which are love, mercy and compassion.

Kabbalah (Hebrew) – 'tradition'; it is the name given to Jewish mysticism developed from the eleventh century CE.

kainos (Greek) – 'new', something completely renewed, the old made new again'; in contrast to *neos* (q.v.).

Kali (Sanskrit) – means 'the black one', she is the Hindu associated with eternal energy, time and change, and death - in the sense 'that time has come'. Many modern Hindus see her as the benevolent mother goddess. She is consort to the god *Shiva* (q.v.).

karma (Sanskrit) – 'action' or 'deed'; from *kri* 'to do'. In *yoga* (q.v.) it is achieving perfection in action; more generally good or bad behaviour determines the nature of your rebirth/ reincarnation – 'you reap what you sow'.

kashrut (Hebrew) – the word literally means 'fit' and it implies that something (usually food) is 'ritually clean and appropriate'; the Ashkenazi Jewish pronunciation gives us the more widely known word *kosher*.

Kethubim (Hebrew) – 'writings', which make up the last of the three sections that comprise the Hebrew scriptures – the *tenakh*. The first section is the *torah*/ instruction–teaching (q.v.) and the second is the *nebim*/ prophets (q.v.).

koan (Japanese) – a disturbing statement, verbal puzzle or paradoxical story given by a *Zen* (q.v.) Buddhist master to a student to be a focus for meditation and a means of provoking spiritual awakening and enabling enlightenment.

koinonia (Greek) – 'shared equality'; generosity based on close relationship, friendship and commitment.

Lakshmi (Sanskrit) – derived from the word *laksya* meaning 'aim', 'goal' or 'objective', it is the name of the Hindu goddess of spiritual and material wealth, light, beauty, wisdom, fertility, generosity and courage. All the wives in the stories of *Vishnu* (q.v.) are forms of *Lakshmi*.

Lamed Vav Zadikim (Hebrew) – 'thirty-six righteous ones'; from the legend that in every generation they share the pain of the world with God, without whom the world would not continue and God's heart would be broken. Also known as the *Zadikim Nistarim* or 'concealed ones'.

makarios (Greek) – 'blessed'; better 'to be congratulated', 'to be envied', or 'Oh, the joy …' It translates the Aramaic word *ashray* (q.v.).

manna (Hebrew) – this is a Greek transliteration of the Hebrew *man hu* meaning, 'What is it?' In context it refers to a bread-like substance (origins uncertain) that miraculously sustained Israelites when wandering in the wilderness after the exodus from Egypt.

Maranatha (Aramaic) – 'Our Lord, come!' – this is an exclamation conveying all the yearning of a lover's cry.

Matador (Spanish) – 'one who kills'; the title given to a bullfighter, whose role emphasises the rift between humans and nature.

matzos (Hebrew) – 'unleavened bread'; eaten during the Jewish spring festival of *Pesach*/ Passover (q.v.).

memesis (Greek) – 'to copy, imitate or mimic', which French philosopher and anthropologist René Girard saw as the basis of human violence.

Messiah (Hebrew) – 'anointed one'; a person marked out for leadership and service, often by God – *Christos* (Christ) is the Greek equivalent.

metanoia (Greek) – 'to change your mind, choosing to think and act differently'; this word is central in referring to a Jesus-focused transformation in mind and behaviour.

mishpat (Hebrew) – both 'justice' and judgement'; in each case 'the process of putting absolutely everything right', establishing *shalom* (q.v.).

missio (Latin) – 'sending'; this is the word from which we get the English word 'mission'.

Mitakuye Oyasin (Lakota Sioux) – a phrase which means 'all my relatives', or 'we are all related'; a prayer for oneness and harmony with all forms of life: other people, animals, birds, insects, trees and plants, and even rocks, rivers, mountains and valleys.

Namaste (Sanskrit) – 'I honour the divine in you', a greeting formed from two Sanskrit words: *namas* – 'to bow' and 'to honour', and *te* – 'to you'.

Nebim (Hebrew) – 'prophets'; which make up the second of the three sections that comprise the Hebrew scriptures – the *tenakh*. The first section is the *torah*/ instruction–teaching (q.v.) and the third is *kethubim*/ writings (q.v.).

neos (Greek) – 'new', which refers to something completely new, never having existed before, in contrast to *kainos* (q.v.).

nephesh (Hebrew) – 'a living being' or 'a person physically alive as a body'; often mistranslated as 'soul', but at death *nephesh* is no longer a reality.

nihil (Latin) – 'nothing'; this is the word from which the term 'nihilism' is formed.

Nirvana (Sanskrit) – literally 'to extinguish', like 'blowing out' a candle flame; the ultimate goal of Buddhism (also Hinduism and Jainism), a state of transcendence/ bliss, free from rebirth/ reincarnation, it is not annihilation.

olam (Hebrew) – this word is used by biblical writers to describe 'the eternal experience of time'. The *rabbis* (q.v.) use *olam* to speak about 'the world', in fact 'the universe'. Added to this, *olam* is formed from the verb-root *alam*, which means 'to hide'. All this implies that the truth about the world/ universe is hidden and waiting to be explored and discovered. See also *Tikkun Olam* (q.v.).

paras lechem (Hebrew) – 'breaking bread', which refers to the Palestinian custom of breaking a loaf of bread with the hands at the beginning of a meal along with words of thanksgiving, and then tearing and sharing the bread together while eating the meal (never cutting it with a knife).

palingenesia (Greek) – 'renewal' and 'restoration'; used in the New Testament with reference to the 'new heaven and earth'.

panentheism (Greek) – 'God *in* everything'; as opposed to 'pantheism', which understands God *to be* everything.

panta (Greek) – 'all things', 'the totality of absolutely everything without exception'.

peirasmos (Greek) – 'temptation'; it has a double meaning, both 'to entice' towards wrongdoing and 'to test' the quality of human character.

Peniel (Hebrew) – 'the one who strives with God'; the name of the place where the biblical figure Jacob wrestles with God and demands to know the divine name.

Pesach (Hebrew) – 'Passover'; the name for the Jewish spring festival that celebrates the events of the ancient Israelite exodus from slavery in Egypt.

philosophos (Greek) – 'friend of wisdom'; formed from the words *philos/* friend and *sophia/* wisdom (q.v.), from which we get the transliterated English word 'philosopher'.

pneuma (Greek) – this word can be translated as 'breath', 'wind' or 'spirit'.

prakasha (Sanskrit) – inner light or clarity.

praus (Greek) – 'meekness'; it holds together in perfect balance anger, control and gentleness. It is paralleled with the Hebrew word *anaw* (q.v.).

qadosh (Hebrew) – 'unique'; usually translated 'holy'. It has a double meaning, 'belonging to' and 'separate from'.

qana (Hebrew) –'create' or 'to get/ possess/ aquire'. It is significant in terms of wisdom in translating the difficult meaning of Prov. 8:22, which some have seen as a pre-Christian link to the logos/ Christ reference in Jn 1:1. Was wisdom/ logos/ Christ created or eternally co-existent with God?

Quo vadis? (Latin) – 'Where are you going?'

rabbi (Hebrew) – popularly translated 'teacher', but from *rav* meaning 'strong', 'important', 'honoured', 'revered', 'great', so better 'my master'. The Hebrew for 'teacher' is *moreh* (m) and *morah* (f).

radah (Hebrew) – usually translated 'dominion'; has the sense of 'to rule over' or to trample like a winepress'. Taken from the language of ancient kingship, must be understood in terms of humans being called to 'image God' within wild nature, in harmony with the character and values of God's kingship, which are love, mercy and compassion.

radix (Latin) – a root (as with a plant) or a point of origin, this is the source from which the word 'radical' is derived.

raja (Sanskrit) – king, ruler, royal; with reference to *yoga* (q.v.) it refers to the way of meditation.

rasul (Arabic) – 'prophet'.

religio (Latin) – it has obscure origins, possibly meaning 'obligation' or 'ritual', perhaps 'to bind' or 'connect'; it is the basis for the English word 'religion'.

ruach (Hebrew) – 'breath', 'wind', 'spirit', similar to the Latin *spiritus* (q.v.).

sacramentum (Latin) – 'something set apart', then it was understood as 'an oath' or 'pledge'; today it has come to mean 'making invisible truth physically tangible'.

salamu (Akkadian) – 'to be faultless, healthy, complete'; close to the Amorite word *salimum* with the sense of 'reconciliation' and 'agreement'; both roots to *shalom* (q.v.).

Samhain (Gaelic) – 'summers end'; the Celtic autumn festival of shadows and darkness that honours the dead, when the threshold between the material and spiritual worlds dissolves; also called 'Halloween' ('All Hallows' Eve').

samsara (Sanskrit) – 'continuous flow'; referring to the unending cycle of birth, suffering, decay, death and rebirth/ reincarnation – the world as we experience it – as understood by Buddhists, Hindus and Jains.

savaka (Pali) – 'one who listens' or 'hearer'; a general term for a disciple.

semeion (Greek) – 'signs'; used to speak of Jesus' miracles as signs of the presence, power and character of God's kingdom.

Shabbat (Hebrew) – 'ceasing' or 'stopping'; the Jewish weekly day of rest begins with the Friday evening Sabbath meal; it celebrates the gifts of creation and *berith*/ covenant (q.v.).

shalom (Hebrew) – popularly translated 'peace', more accurately 'wholeness', 'intactness', 'integratedness', 'harmony', it is 'everything fitting perfectly together'; only present to the extent there is physical and material well-being, justice in relationships and integrity in character.

Shalom Aleichem (Hebrew) – 'peace be unto you'; some scholars believe it was originally a question, 'Is everything well with you?' 'Do you have everything you need?'

shaman (Machu-Tangu) – 'to know'; implying 'one who is wise'. In this language of Siberian Asia it originates from the word *xaman.*

shanti (Sanskrit) – 'peace'; a person who is fully integrated within themselves, an internal spiritual wholeness of character and personality; similar to the internal dimensions of *shalom* (q.v.).

sharia (Arabic) – 'the path' or 'the way that leads to the source of water'; law and instructions about practical daily living based on statements in the *Quran*, examples from the *Hadith* (q.v.) traditions from the life of Muhammad, and philosophical reflection used in the Muslim community.

Shavuoth (Hebrew) – 'Feast of Weeks'/ Pentecost, the Jewish feast that takes place seven weeks after *Pesach* (q.v.); it celebrates God giving the gift of the *torah* (q.v.).

shekinah (Hebrew) – 'the unique and full expression of the presence of the Spirit of God'; it is formed from *shakan* 'to inhabit', 'to settle', 'to dwell'; strongly feminine.

Sheol (Hebrew) – 'grave', 'pit', 'abyss', 'a place of darkness where the dead go: both righteous and unrighteous'; often unhelpfully translated in English bibles by the word 'hell'. It has similarities to the Greek word *Hades* (q.v.).

shishya (Sanskrit) – 'one who learns'; it is used to describe the disciple of a *guru* (q.v.).

Shiva (Sanskrit) – 'the auspicious one', he is one of the three supreme God's in Hinduism along with *Brama* the creator and *Vishnu* (q.v.) the protector and preserver. *Shiva* is said to do important works in creating, preserving, destroying, transforming, concealing and revealing blessings.

shophar (Hebrew) – 'ram's horn trumpet'; sounded at times of proclamation including the beginning of the year of Jubilee when slaves, debtors and the landless were set free.

sophia (Greek) – 'wisdom'; from which we get the word *philosophus* (q.v.) meaning 'friend of wisdom', transliterated into

English as 'philosopher'.

spiritus (Latin) – 'breath', 'wind', 'spirit'; similar to the Hebrew *ruach* (q.v.).

Staretz (Russian) – 'elder' and venerated advisor and teacher within the Russian Orthodox church; someone who is looked up to as an inspiration to others.

stoicheia (Greek) – the physical and spiritual elements of the universe.

Sufi (Arabic) – the name given to someone in the mystical tradition of Islam. The name comes from either *safa* meaning 'purity' with reference to their spirituality, or *suf* meaning 'wool' describing their usual clothing.

talmidim (Hebrew) – 'disciples' (*talmid* singular), from the Hebrew *limmud* (instructed); someone who leaves home to study and follow the ways of their teacher.

taonga (Maori) – 'a treasure' or 'something precious'; an object of good or value, used in terms of moral values as well.

tbuma (Hebrew) – 'insight', an important aspect of the creative wisdom of *hokma* (q.v.); it is the ability to see and act in a way others are unable to.

tekton (Greek) – 'carpenter–builder', implies someone who works with hard materials such as wood, metal, stone or iron; used to describe Jesus' occupation.

teleios (Greek) – 'mature', 'perfect', 'complete' or 'whole'; and as such a *shalom* (q.v.) word.

Tetragrammaton (Greek) – literally 'the four letters'; it is a technical theological word that refers to the Hebrew consonants YHWH, usually pronounced *Yahweh* (q.v.), used in place of naming God in the Hebrew scriptures.

thaumasios (Greek) – 'wonder'; used to speak of Jesus' miracles as events that fill people with a sense of awe.

Tikkun Olam (Hebrew) – 'repairing the world'; from the root of *tikkun* 'to arrange' or 'put in order' and *olam* (q.v.) 'the world' in rabbinical understanding; phrase rooted in the mysticism of the Jewish *Kabbalah* (q.v.), used by social activists since the 1950s.

torah (Hebrew) – 'instruction' or 'teaching'; primarily refers to the first five books which make up the first of the three sections that comprise the Hebrew scriptures – the *tenakh*. The other two sections are the *nebim*/ prophets (q.v.) and the *kethubim*/ writings (q.v.). *Torah* can also refer to the whole bible, and in fact all authentic teaching.

Tsaar baalei hayyim (Hebrew) – this is a rabbinic phrase, which means 'not to cause pain to living creatures'.

ubuntu (Xhosa) – an approach to life that can be translated as, 'a person is a person only through other people', or 'I am because we are'.

Utopia (Greek) – literally means 'no place'; similar in sounding to '*eutopia*' meaning 'good place'; this almost double-meaning was played on by Thomas More as the name for his fictional Atlantic island with what he believed to be a perfect social–political–legal system.

Vishnu (Sanskrit) – 'the all pervading one', he is one of the three supreme God's in Hinduism along with *Brama* the creator and *Shiva* (q.v.) the destroyer and transformer. *Vishnu* is the preserver and protector of the universe. He comes to earth in the form of an *avatar* (q.v.) at times of crisis and distress to rescue the world and overthrow evil.

v'yirdu (Hebrew) – usually translated 'to have dominion'; this phrase also has the sense of 'to descend'. Either a warning that wrongful dominion will lead us to 'descend' into ecological crisis or a call to 'descend' from arrogance and wander within wild nature as an equal with it.

whakapapa (Maori) – which is usually translated 'genealogy'; it suggests a flat foundation, forming a base with layer on layer laid upon it, linking individuals to their kinship group but ultimately connecting the whole creation together as a single cosmic family.

yada (Hebrew) – 'knowledge'; an important aspect of the creative wisdom of *hokma* (q.v.); it is the experience of life, not just information about it.

Yahweh (Hebrew) – the most likely vocalisation of the four consonants YHWH given as the name of God; a form of the verb 'to be', most likely translations are 'I am who I am', 'the One who is' or 'God is who God is'.

yoga (Sanskrit) – 'yoke'; from the root *yuj* meaning 'to join', 'unite', 'attach'. Refers to physical, mental and spiritual discipline, involving meditation, action, knowledge, devotion and physical exercise.

Yom Kippur (Hebrew) – 'day of expiation'; the name for the autumn celebration of the 'Day of Atonement', the most solemn day in the Jewish calendar with a twenty-five-hour fast which focuses on the themes of atonement and repentance in preparing for another year.

zadik (Hebrew) – 'righteous one' or 'just person' (sometimes spelt *tzadik*); in Jewish tradition it is also closely linked with the *Lamed Vav Zadikim* (q.v.).

zen (Japanese) – it is the Japanese pronunciation of the Chinese word *chan*, which in turn is derived from the Sanskrit *dhyana* meaning 'absorption' or 'meditative state'; it stresses self-realisation and enlightenment through actions and meditation rather than intellectual reasoning and the study of scripture.

Acknowledgements

I have always loved the African proverb, 'It takes a village to raise a child.' I now believe, 'It takes a community to write a book.' The love, energy and support that have embraced me at every stage of the process have been astonishing. The words 'Thank you' just don't begin to get close.

Since 1983 thousands of students have attended the 'Workshop' study programme – the furnace in which many of the ideas of this book have been forged. If you have ever been part of 'Workshop' then you have contributed to these pages, for which I am grateful. This is also true of the participants of 'Peace School' founded by Jonathan Dorset. Thanks to all of you; it has been a joy to learn from you.

On Thursday 22 May 2008, as a guest of the Franconia Mennonite Conference in Philadelphia, USA, I was invited to speak to a group of church leaders at a lunchtime gathering and a company of young activists later the same evening. On both occasions I worked with some of the phrases that now make up our current chapter titles. Each time I was asked if I had written anything on these themes. It was the enthusiasm of Steve Kriss, Gay Brunt Miller and Jessica Walter that particularly inspired my decision to write this book. Thank you.

A remarkable group of people chose to give me practical support by reading and editing my text as it was being written. Foremost among them have been Fran Tattersall and Amy Hailwood, whose attention to detail and incisive critique of every paragraph has been astonishing – their time, effort and kindness humbles me, my gratitude is boundless. Drew Worthley brought me friendship, enthusiasm, scholarly spirituality and cultural astuteness; each has been vital to the outcome. Liz Ray's belief in me and in this book was a sustaining encouragement through the darkest times of writing, plus her knowledge of contemporary spiritualities and unique wisdom and experience have enriched every part of this book. Lynsey Anna Jones' joyful enthusiasm and razor-sharp eye have cut through the text like a scythe, keeping it focused while always encouraging it to breathe life; your passion and skills are a gift. To each one of you, thank you.

Aglaia Barraclough, Claire Barraclough, Jonathan Bartley, Charletta Erb, Stuart Masters, Tim Nafziger and Martie Newton have all read the whole manuscript from beginning to end, offering encouragement and suggestions as to how it could be improved. Thank you.

Elizabeth Allison, Joe Baker, Peter Barraclough, Matthew Barton, Rebecca Cole, Nigel Couper, Catherine Dale, Shila Desai, Jo Frew, Don Gwillim, Kathryn Gunstone, Allan Hayes, Gillie Jenkinson, Deborah Jones, Keith Judson, Jill Mann, Marilyn Mason, Olivia Merriman, Tony Neesham, Richard Norman, Mark Ostrowicz, Lloyd Pietersen, Tom Skinner, Lora Steiner, Rosemary Taylorson and Hannah Wallace have all read parts of the manuscript, advised on particular chapters or made helpful suggestions at key points. Thank you.

Thanks to Sara Miles who personally gave her permission allowing me to quote from her book, *Take This Bread*, at the beginning of the *Subversive Celebrant* chapter.

Thanks also to Phil Barnard and Rob Telford for sharing their reflections in the *Subversive Celebrant* chapter.

A big thank you is due to Phoebe Baker and Avani Williams for helping me to tell the story of the 'Children's Table-Talk' in the *Faith Friend* chapter.

Thanks to Trisha Dale and Hilary Soper who have used their skills and expertise to carry out the professional and technical editing and typesetting on the manuscript, preparing it for final publication. It has been a joy working with you both.

Without all this input the book would be very much poorer, but decisions and choices have to be made and for these I take full and final responsibility.

Special thanks to Fran Stockley, Rosemary Nuamah Williams and Steve Bonner for quite different reasons, but you each know why. Also to Andrea Stevens, whose regular encouragement, 'This book has got to be written', has been a greater inspiration than you will ever realise.

Deep gratitude and thanks to Andy Stonehouse and s2design for producing such powerful graphics for the book cover – I love it, it says it all.

Thanks to Jonathan Ferreira Powell for drawing the diagrams that are used in the chapters *Radical Mystic* and *Subversive Celebrant*.

Thanks to Sarah and Tim Belton for the use of your home in Northumberland, UK, as a silent retreat for some of the writing of this book.

From the very beginning the trustees of Anvil Trust, under their then chairperson Simon Browning, could not have been more supportive of 'the project'; this has continued right to the end. I am so grateful.

Thanks to John Hunt and Trevor Greenfield from John Hunt Publishing for being willing to publish this new author and for your patience and care with my questions and queries as I found my feet as a published writer. I hope you feel your time and trust have been well invested.

Finally, and above all others, my deepest thanks go to Rowena, my wife, who has journeyed with me each step of the way encouraging and supporting me. I treasure your love, wisdom and insight and it is to you I dedicate this book.

Circle Books

Circle is a symbol of infinity and unity. It's part of a growing list of imprints, including o-books.net and zero-books.net.

Circle Books aims to publish books in Christian spirituality that are fresh, accessible, and stimulating.

Our books are available in all good English language bookstores worldwide. If you can't find the book on the shelves, then ask your bookstore to order it for you, quoting the ISBN and title. Or, you can order online—all major online retail sites carry our titles.

To see our list of titles, please view www.Circle-Books.com, growing by 80 titles per year.

Authors can learn more about our proposal process by going to our website and clicking on Your Company > Submissions.

We define Christian spirituality as the relationship between the self and its sense of the transcendent or sacred, which issues in literary and artistic expression, community, social activism, and practices. A wide range of disciplines within the field of religious studies can be called upon, including history, narrative studies, philosophy, theology, sociology, and psychology. Interfaith in approach, Circle Books fosters creative dialogue with non-Christian traditions.

And tune into MySpiritRadio.com for our book review radio show, hosted by June-Elleni Laine, where you can listen to authors discussing their books.

mySpiritRadio